SONIC BOOM

The World's Most Travelled Man

by
Fred Finn

Gift from David Scowsill

Copyright © Fred Finn 2024

The right of Fred Finn to be identified as author of this work has been asserted by the author in accordance with section 77 and 78 of the Copyright, Designs and Patents Act 1988.

All rights reserved. No part of this publication may be reproduced, stored in a retrieval system, or transmitted in any form or by any means, electronic, mechanical, photocopying, recording, or otherwise, without the prior permission of the publishers.

Any person who commits any unauthorised act in relation to this publication may be liable to criminal prosecution and civil claims for damages.

ISBN 978-1-3999-9009-7

www.fredfinn.uk

Finn Associates Limited
5 Fordham Place,
Ixworth,
Bury St Edmunds,
Suffolk,
IP31 2GJ

First Published 2024

Introduction

When you say goodbye to someone or something that has been dear to you, knowing that you'll probably never see them again, it's always an emotional moment. Part of your life has changed forever.

In many cases, time dims the memory and gradually the image, the character, the aura of that person, place or thing recedes from your mind until all that is left are yellowing photographs and maybe a tombstone.

With Concorde, the world's most outrageously beautiful, fast and characterful passenger aircraft, the opposite has happened. Despite the passage of 20 years since its last flight, everything to do with the plane seems to be crystal clear in the public's mind, even for those who weren't even born in 2003. Every year there seems to be more interest and obsession.

Out of 20 Concorde's built, 18 of them are kept in pristine condition, many in purpose-built facilities where hundreds of thousands of visitors come to be astonished once again by Concorde's extraordinary sleek frame, its supersonic engines, its unique, almost comical nose cone and its fascinating history. New generations marvel at the fact that, conceived more than 70 years ago – as old as their grandparents! – Concorde is still ahead of its time, with no realistic supersonic challengers about to replace it as Queen of the Skies.

With all this aviation history condensed into one aircraft, I have to pinch myself sometimes to be sure that I flew on Concorde 718 times. I've met so many people who never had the chance to fly even once on the aircraft. What an incredible privilege it was!

With each passing year since Concorde's flying days, the more incredible they seem. Only a handful of people have experienced 'space tourism', the most recent ones paying $55 million each for a brief trip on SpaceX. According to NASA's definitions, Concorde flew into space on virtually every voyage, something we passengers sometimes took for granted. We could see the darkening of indigo blue of space above us, the majestic curve of the Earth and hundreds of square miles of ocean and continents below. But we were simply travelling from A to B, treating this as normal when it was perhaps anything but.

That was the reality of Concorde, a reality which has passed into the history books, where it sits supremely. Unattainable, an impossible dream.

But nevertheless, an enormous part of my life and that of thousands of other passengers and crew who enjoyed its pleasures over those intensely special 27 years.

In this book I've tried to set down what made Concorde so special, my memories of those years, the stories I heard and the ones in which I played a part. People fondly reflect about Concorde's community of passengers, flight crew and cabin attendants as a family. That was indeed my experience. We realised how special the aircraft was, how unique the experience was and how the thrill of the ride bonded us together in a remarkable way. Many of us are still in contact with one another, all these years later, still awestruck at how extraordinarily real it was.

Besides telling the story of my life on Concorde, I've written about a few of the other things I've been lucky enough to experience, like flying more than 15 million miles on many of the world's airlines, where I am recognised still today by the Guinness Book of Records as the World's Most Travelled Passenger by air. And being fortuitously good enough at cricket to play alongside many of the greats in the game, at home and overseas, over many years. Or meeting dozens of fascinating and entertaining people, from rock stars to royalty. It's been a wonderful life and I'm grateful for every minute of it.

Enjoy the journey!

Foreword by Sir Geoffrey Boycott Kt OBE

I first met Fred Finn at the end of the Summer in 1968.

A team of famous cricketers called the International Cavaliers toured Cornwall and Devon playing against various local cricket teams.

Fred and I guested for the club teams with Gary Sobers and Lance Gibbs. The opposition had the great fast bowler Fred Trueman, my boyhood hero Tom Graveney and Basil D'Oliviera fresh from his marvellous 158 against Australia in the last Ashes Test at the Oval.

Fred was a cheerful presence in the team, always enthusiastic and uplifting with a positive word, clearly thrilled to be rubbing shoulders with some of the best cricketers in the World.

We were all there to enjoy ourselves, play some good cricket, entertain the crowds who rarely got to see top class cricketers and most importantly raise a bit of money for some local charities.

We struck up a friendship and met from time to time at my home in Yorkshire and in London when he was passing through.

Fred was never lost for a word, always full of laughter and a delightful friend and companion.

Fred has had a lifetime of travel and adventure interspersed with an occasional game of cricket.

He has met so many interesting people, so it is about time he put down his memories of a lifetime for us all to enjoy.

Sir Geoffrey Boycott Kt OBE

My story would be incomplete without making some extra special mentions and so I dedicate,

to my wife, Alla - a beautiful wife and friend

to my nephew, Richard - for his dedicated commitment to our family

and finally, to Ben - without your selfless input, this book would never have left the departure lounge!

CONTENTS

Introduction		*i*
Foreword by Sir Geoffrey Boycott		*iii*
1	My Life on Concorde	1
2	A Beautiful Bird	24
3	My Childhood	72
4	Starting Work	87
5	The New World	96
6	Licencing to the World	111
7	Narrow Escapes	119
8	Airlines - the Good the Bad and the Ugly	143
9	World's Most Travelled Man	186
10	A Passion for Cricket	196
11	Giving Back	207
Conclusion		217
Acknowledgements		*iv*
Index		*vii*

Chapter 1
My Life on Concorde

It was love at first flight. The moment I saw this sleek, beautiful, gorgeous plane, I was smitten. It just looked out of this world. It was the most amazing and most beautiful aeroplane that was ever built, and it still is.

My first impression was of how long and slim it was. Of course, it had to be, to fly that fast, faster than the speed of a rifle bullet, 23 miles per minute, at a cruising altitude of 60,000 feet.

My first trip was from Dulles Airport in Washington DC to London. In fact it was Concorde's maiden flight on that route, on 25 May 1976. At the time, I was living in the States and flying across the Atlantic very regularly. I'd bought a British Airways ticket from Nashville to London via Dulles, expecting the main flight to be on a Boeing 747 Jumbo Jet.

John D'arcy Meredith, President USA at British Airways got in touch and invited me to fly on Concorde, so I accepted, not really understanding how much of an impact it would have. In America at that time, there wasn't a great deal of coverage. Even so, I remember being excited about the prospect of flying supersonic.

The sense that something special was about to happen began even before you reached the plane. You arrived at a dedicated check in area, went through fast-track security and into the Concorde lounge where the best champagnes, liquors, whisky selection and snacks were spread out for you. Telephones were available so you could call anywhere in the world. All passengers were in the same class, it was Concorde, better even than First Class, and everyone was treated the same, i.e. like a film star. Your coat was taken by one of the lounge hosts and hung on a railing in the lounge, then wheeled on board.

At Dulles, Concorde didn't come to a boarding gate – they didn't have gates. Instead, you went into a mobile boarding lounge, which descended, then drove out to the plane and came up again. Straight away, it had this 'Wow' factor. Despite being slim, it was incredibly long, barely shorter than a 747. Inside, I could stand up to my full six feet two inches height with no problem at all. And even though the seats were a tiny bit narrower than traditional First Class seats, they had plenty of legroom, around 40 inches, so you didn't feel cramped or claustrophobic at all.

Since there were only 100 seats, configured in two sets of two either side of an aisle, Concorde carried far fewer people than the average long-haul passenger plane, so that's another big difference. You realised how unique it was to get this opportunity, compared with most other kinds of air travel. It was like flying in a private jet – a large private jet for 100 guests. Shortly after settling into my seat, pre-flight drinks were served.

On my first flight, the Captain Brian Calvert explained how we were about to experience supersonic flight. Once again, this was completely different to anything I'd heard on a plane before. He sounded almost as excited as we were, his voice brimming with pride in the astonishing technological leap that the aircraft's designers and engineers had achieved. It was like a little piece of space travel. He warned us that taking off on Concorde was unlike regular fights: it would be louder, faster and the G-force would pin us back into our seats.

We started to taxi out onto the Dulles runway, smoothly navigating the taxiways, probably watched with envious admiration by all the other pilots and passengers around. A slight whiff of aviation fuel wafted through the cabin, as if there wasn't enough high octane excitement already.

The next thing I noticed was that take-off was much quicker than for subsonic planes. You're travelling at around 250 miles per hour, compared with around 160 miles per hour for regular passenger planes. So, before you've even left the ground, you're already aware that things are very different. The captain would put on the engine reheats - where fuel is added to the engines to boost their speed – as we rocketed down the runway. That feeling you get, as you speed along before take-off, thinking "This is much sportier than other aircraft I'd flown on previously".

Instead of the Bentley-style take-off in a 747, where you can sense the underlying force of the engines, and the whole experience is one of comfortable power, Concorde's take-off was more like a McLaren F1 racing car. It was exhilarating, exciting, unforgettable. You felt the power of the four Rolls Royce Olympus engines through the cabin. The front of the aircraft flexed as we took off at a very steep angle of attack, climbing at an amazing rate.

Then, as the captain turned off the reheats about 90 seconds after take-off, there was a strange sensation as the aircraft fell considerably quiet. Once again, this was unlike anything I'd experienced before. Quintessentially unimaginable!

There were no TV screens on Concorde, no in-flight movies, just a display panel showing you our altitude, the outside temperature and how fast we were travelling. This was unique to Concorde because of course no other passenger plane could travel anywhere near as fast.

I can remember the excitement on my first flight as this display showed the speed and altitude rising as we headed out across the Atlantic. Later, on my regular flights out of JFK to London, we would leave Manhattan and cruise out to the end of Long Island, almost to Boston, then as we flew over the sea the pilot would put the reheats back on two at a time and we'd go supersonic – creating the sonic boom.

The reheats would stay on as we accelerated, faster and faster, until we reached Mach 1.71. Even after they were switched off, we'd continue accelerating until we reached Mach 2, climbing to 60,000 feet (12 miles) above sea level, on the edge of space. In fact NASA's definition of space travel is anything over 53,000 feet, so I guess you could say I've been an astronaut 718 times over. At this point, the cabin crew offered glasses of Dom Pérignon champagne along with gourmet starters for lunch or dinner, depending on the time of day.

What a difference from my first Atlantic crossing in 1959, which took 19 hours and four stops. The start and end points were pretty much identical to most of my Concorde flights – Heathrow and JFK (formerly known as Idlewild) – but the speed, comfort and cuisine could not have been more different.

The flight was so smooth that my glass of Dom Pérignon, served in an elegant fluted glass, would stay unspilled. Not a single drop would fall onto the starched napkin on the table. We might be offered lobster, foie gras, fillet steak, smoked salmon, sea bass, caviar… It was all of the highest quality, served on bone china tableware with silver cutlery. The whole experience was designed to make you feel like a film star – which of course was what some of the passengers were. Concorde even had its own wine cellar stocked exclusively for Concorde alone.

Dessert might be baked pear with prunes in Armagnac crème Anglaise or a selection of cheeses. When I first flew, smoking was allowed on board, and cigars were provided. I distinctly remember the wonderful Jamaican Macanudo cigars coming out, along with the finest cognac. Macanudo cigars were well liked by a certain captain and fleet director.

There were so many other differences from a normal cross-Atlantic flight. The windows were much smaller, and triple-glazed, to protect you from the kinetic heat of friction generated by the speed, which reached more than 100 degrees Centigrade on the outside. Looking out of them, you could clearly see the earth's curvature, while the sky was a very deep indigo, almost black. One of the Concorde captains, Brian Calvert, told me that from this altitude he could see 250,000 square miles of the Earth's surface.

Before I'd really had a chance to take it all in, we were over the Bristol Channel and decelerating to subsonic speed and dropping to 39,000 feet. Then as we came in to land at Heathrow, the famous nose cone was lowered, so that the pilots could see the runway. This was necessary because as Concorde approached landing, its body was slightly tilted upwards, in the way that large birds like swans and geese come in to land. Even so, our landing was faster than most aircraft, touching down at more than 180 miles an hour, before its carbon fibre brakes and reverse thrust slowed us down to taxiing speed. For me, landing showed the capabilities of Concorde more than anything else in the experience of Concorde's performance!

Concorde was the only passenger aircraft so far in history that could leave London on a cold winter's night, in the pitch dark, and take you into the light as you travelled west – flying faster than the earth rotated. You'd land in New York on the same day, an hour before you took off, in local time. Every so often, I'd spy a Boeing 747 a few miles below us, travelling at 550 miles per hour as we overtook it, making it look as though it were flying in reverse.

It wasn't just the three hours that we saved compared with subsonic flight, it was the lack of turbulence and jetlag, the ability to connect with ongoing flights the same day and being able to work on the same day without feeling tired. Plus, the added benefit of the express service available in the US at immigration and customs, and the complimentary limousine or helicopter transfer service. It was to become the signature Concorde experience.

As I gradually stacked up my Concorde flights, I came to know the various captains and their crews.

The other thing I worked out during my first flight was the best seat: 9a, because it was where the cabin service from the rear started, so I wouldn't need to wait, looking enviously while other passengers received their amazing food and drink. This became my signature seat, where every crew member knew my name and I'd find a chilled bottle of Dom Pérignon waiting under the seat in front of me ready for when I had boarded. All drinks on Concorde were complimentary.

Occasionally, when the plane was full, I give up my seat 9a so that we didn't leave that passenger behind, the captain would invite me to sit up on the flight deck, where I'd put on a pair of earphones so I could hear the conversations with air traffic control and other flights. I became familiar with the small white reheat switches immediately to the rear of the throttles. This was a real privilege, something that few other passengers got to experience. We were once contacted by an SR71 Blackbird jet flying nearby, they were all in space suits and we were in shirt sleeves drinking champagne. Its pilot couldn't believe how fast we were going.

Anyone who flew on Concorde can tell you how different it was from regular flights. Everyone was treated the same, rather than being in different seat classes. Everyone understood that the other passengers had somehow earned the right to be there, so everyone was equal. That gave you a great sense of community. Down on the ground, if I had tried to get a phone number for Paul McCartney or Bruce Springsteen, or to get into the office of Sir David Frost, it would have been almost impossible. But on Concorde, they'd be standing around in the departures lounge, or I'd be sitting next to them during the flight.

Many of the captains and cabin crew became friends. Over the years I've visited them all over the world – Singapore, the States, Europe – and even walked cabin attendant Gilly Mayes-Pratt's daughter down the aisle when she got married. This came out of the sense of family that Concorde created. There was a real friendship, a bonding that grew out of the aircraft. Being such a frequent flyer, sometimes I would help out the cabin crew by serving drinks. Gilly once told me she thought I would have made a good steward on Concorde except I was too tall! That's something you can't really imagine happening on any scheduled flights today. It would probably be illegal.

There's one thing I did on Concorde in the 1980s. I'd been staying with a captain called David Leney (RIP), who had piloted the Queen across the Atlantic on Concorde. He and I were good friends and I got on well with his family. So one winter evening, he said to me: "Fred, we have to go over to the airport." We drove off to Heathrow, with me having no idea what was going on. When we arrived at Hatton Cross, I saw Concorde parked outside. We left the car nearby and David said: "Come on Fred" and we headed up the stairs onto the aircraft and into the flight deck.

Inside, David turned to me and said: "There you go Fred, sit in the left-hand seat, we're going to do some brake tests." This meant being towed over to the airport, with Concorde being powered up. I strapped myself in and sat there with mounting anticipation. David spoke to air traffic control and got permission to use one of the runways, as it was late at night and there was barely any traffic. He opened the throttles and we accelerated down the runway. After a short while David applied the brakes and we came to a stop, then he taxied the aircraft back around for another run. Then came the real surprise and shock. On this run, David said: "She's all yours." I could hardly believe my luck as I pulled open the throttles with his hands on mine and we shot forward. David looked over to me with a grin and said: "She's quite responsive, isn't she?" All I could say, as I sat there tingling with excitement, was: "Wow, yes she is."

We concluded the tests and drove back to David's house, where I took some hours to come down from the elation of being probably the only non-crew member to have taken Concorde down a runway.

Even though we weren't airborne, I would put this experience right up there alongside flying with the Red Arrows and in the Phantom F4's last flight, or even doing an aeronautical display on Concorde for the press in Pittsburgh with pilot Norman Britton. Each of them made me feel ecstatic, but having your hand on the controls and feeling Concorde roar into action… that was something else.

One of the captains, Brian Calvert, was a keen cricketer like me and arranged a Concorde Team cricket match at The Bell Inn, Aldworth, near Reading. Another captain, Brian Walpole, was also in the team and looked a bit surprised to find me offering to play. "What do you know about cricket then?" he asked me. So, I fished out my Somerset county cricket sweater and that put a smile on his face. A lot of the female cabin crew members turned up to support and make sandwiches for tea. I remember they managed to smuggle some iceberg lettuces back from New York, because they were unavailable in England.

There's a time in many cricket matches when the sun starts casting long shadows across the ground, you've been playing for a few hours already and the game is coming towards a conclusion – can the last man hit the winning runs? Can the bowlers get the final wicket? – and it's like magic. Everything is bathed in a golden glow. Well in this case, the magic included the inbound Concorde flight coming in low over the cricket ground as it approached Heathrow. A perfect end to a glorious summer's day.

We all retired to the Bell Inn after the game, then I went back to the beautiful home of Brian Calvert and his wife Mary Danby, with its grand piano in the living room.

Brian was a fine example of the kind of person who became a Concorde pilot. Well before the aircraft came into service, he had already gained a terrific reputation as one of the best pilots of his generation. He was in the Fleet Air Arm, then flew Boeing Stratocruisers, Britannias, Comet IVs and VC-10s before joining the Concorde team. He was absolutely central to the aircraft's introduction, piloting it in trials and then negotiating with overseas governments over landing rights. Then he flew several of Concorde's inaugural flights on new routes.

He and his novelist wife Mary – who was Charles Dickens' great-great-granddaughter – were always so welcoming, friendly and relaxed. Such was his humility that you wouldn't guess that he was the President of the Royal Institute of Navigation.

Knowing the pilots well sometimes helped me to get out of a tight spot. When I was invited to go on a demonstration flight in Pittsburgh, British Airways asked whether I'd like to bring a senior business guest. So, I arranged for the president of my bank in New Jersey to come along, a guy called Bill Schott. To get across the Atlantic for the event, I turned up at Heathrow for that day's Concorde flight, only to discover that they'd changed the departure time and was told I was too late! "I'm never late for Concorde!" I protested, but they wouldn't budge – the plane was already taxiing towards the runway. I got them to call the captain John Cook (RIP), who I knew well, and tell him: "Fred Finn is a guest at a function arranged by British Airways at JFK to celebrate their association with American Airlines, then the press flight on Concorde in Pittsburgh, with the bank president."

When John heard about the problem he said: "Oh it's Fred, tell him to put his bags on the 747 for JFK and get out to the aircraft ASAP!" Another guy who was due to fly Concorde that day and had also fallen foul of the change of time, heard what was going on and asked if he could join me. I said: "Sure, if you can keep up." I was rushed through security and onto a waiting airside truck with an extendable ladder, which weaved through the various taxiways and out to where Concorde was waiting to depart. The engines were already running when we arrived and I had to climb this ladder all the way to the top, before jumping into the aircraft through the forward door, my ears ringing with the roar of the Rolls Royce Olympus jets where even today, my hearing remains impaired. For the entire flight my heart was racing and I couldn't hear a thing, but I was so relieved to make the flight. Thank you, John!

I had no idea what happened to the other guy: he'd disappeared as I bolted through the airport. I met with Bill Schott and we made our way to Pittsburgh where Norman Britton (aka 'the animal') was captaining Concorde for its demonstration flights, to show the assembled press what it was capable of on its first visit to the city. My reason for being there was to talk about my experiences with the aircraft. We did two flypasts with the wheels down and one with the wheels up, with the assembled press as passengers.

At first, I remember some of the journalists were a bit sceptical about Concorde's famous power and speed. But this soon changed when Norman raised the undercarriage, turned on the reheats and did some high-performance manoeuvres. We had lunch then flew back to JFK and I went back to collect my bags from the 747 which had just arrived from Heathrow. Who should I see coming off the flight but the guy who had earlier tried to follow me onto Concorde at Heathrow. "So, you didn't make the flight either then?" he said. "Actually, I did. I've been to Pittsburgh, done a demonstration flight on Concorde, had lunch, made a presentation and now I've come to get my bags." It just shows you how much you could fit into a day, when Concorde more than halves your trans-Atlantic flight time.

John Hutchinson was a Concorde pilot and later BA's Chief Pilot and was flying on the Heathrow-Singapore route when Roy Watts invited me to represent the airline on a press trip. He and I discussed the event and John asked if my wife and I would like to stay with him and his wife Susan in Singapore. We had a wonderful time together with John and his wife, shopping in the malls and exploring the island.

This was a time when Concorde was developing new routes and gaining a new international celebrity status – hence my appearance in the Far Eastern press. There was talk of the aircraft flying from Singapore to Hong Kong and Perth in Australia. Just around that time, a documentary film called Death of a Princess was shown on ITV in the UK, which ruffled a lot of feathers in Saudi Arabia. The then UK Prime Minister Margaret Thatcher told the Saudis that she couldn't interfere with independent television. In consequence, the Saudi authorities demanded that Concorde drop its flying altitude to 39,000 feet and fly subsonic over the desert. This helped to bring an end to the Singapore route. Concorde's first commercial flight on 21 January 1976 was to Bahrain which was how BA came to have the joint venture with Singapore Airlines to then continue on to Singapore.

John and I stayed in touch and have had many good times together. We went to a memorial for the Paris crash in 2019, invited by a French Concorde supporters' group - Olympus 593. We travelled by Eurostar, and on arrival were met by my friend and Concorde fanatic Frédéric Pinlet - the head of Olympus 593. Frédéric assisted by Jean Charles Dupré worked with Paul Evans and I to arrange a uniquely fitting commemoration of the Anglo-French excellence that brought us Concorde which included a reception at the residence of the British Ambassador whose former owner was Napoleon's Sister. Here is an account of the day, written by Katie John for Mach 2 magazine:

The British group included former British Airways Concorde pilot John Hutchinson and Concorde engineer Peter Ugle, as well as Fred Finn, who had put in a great deal of work to organise the events. Travelling by Eurostar, we arrived at Gare du Nord just after 11.15. Olympus had laid on taxis to take us to the residence of the British Ambassador, whose former owner was Napoleons sister. Our first view of the elegant building was impressive, with the courtyard adorned by vintage Rolls-Royces, Bentleys, a Triumph TR4, and other classic cars. The interior was just as stunning, with gilded walls, crystal chandeliers, and Aubusson carpets; amidst the splendour there were also items of Concorde memorabilia, including an attitude display indicator, on show.

Frédéric and Jean Charles met us there, together with former Air France

Concorde captain Jacky Ramon, Air France Concorde stewardess Nicole Menneveux, British Airways Concorde stewardess Laurence Keniston and her husband Kevin, and members of the car club Triel Auto Retro, who had loaned their vehicles for this occasion. Olympus had also brought a photographer, and a cameraman from Resonance Films, to record the day. We were welcomed by Matthew Lodge, Minister and Ambassador of Great Britain and Northern Ireland to UNESCO.

Mr Lodge gave a short speech commemorating the British and French pioneers who created Concorde. He explained that the British Embassy works with major companies in the aeronautical sector, including the Royal Air Force (currently conducting a joint operation with the French air force in North Africa) and Rolls-Royce. He said that events like this commemoration of the 50th anniversary of the first Concorde flight were very important for maintaining the relationship between our two countries.

Frédéric Pinlet gave a speech thanking the Embassy for receiving us and thanking the military personnel present: Air Commodore Tim Below, Defence Attaché; Group Captain Antony McCord, Air Attaché; and Group Captain Steve Kilvington, RAF Liaison Officers the French Air Force. He also thanked Concorde, saying that the gathering today made it seem as if Concorde was still alive, and hoping that this event would spark new ideas and new links between Britain and France. He paid tribute to all those who had built and operated the aircraft. Frédéric's sentiments about Concorde were echoed by Fred Finn. Fred observed that this event had taken the two of them a year to plan, and thanked Frédéric for all his efforts.

John Hutchinson also gave a speech to thank the Embassy. He said that he was a former Master of the Honourable Company of Air Pilots, who hold an annual event in the London Guildhall, and this year the Company's Brackley Memorial Trophy, for excellence in aviation, would be awarded to the members of the Concorde fleet.

Travelling in grand style Outside the Embassy, we admired the classic cars – which included a 1938 Packard and a 1938 Bugatti as well as the British vehicles – and met their drivers. To our astonishment, Frédéric then told us that these amazing cars would be taking us to the place where we were to have lunch. We proceeded in grand style through the boulevards of central Paris, while tourists and passers-by stopped to watch us and take photos of the cars, and swept along the motorway.

Lunch had been arranged at the Hotel Golf de Gonesse. We were joined by Geraldine of Olympus593, and Pascal Touzeau, a former ground engineer on Concorde. During the long and enjoyable lunch, Fred Finn presented Frédéric with a copy of the Concorde painting that he had been given to mark his 600th Concorde flight. Geraldine and Pascal presented us all with commemorative keyrings.

John Hutchinson gave a brief talk about his history in aviation and some of the outstanding moments he had experienced with Concorde. He had started his flight training in 1955, never dreaming that 22 years later he would be in command of a supersonic airliner. He mentioned one remarkable Concorde passenger – an old lady whose first memory of an aircraft was seeing the Wright brothers' aeroplane, and whose first ever flight was with Louis Blériot in 1911. The lady had stayed on the flight deck for the landing in Washington, then declared that she would never fly again.

Laurence Keniston said that she had been working on a Concorde flight in 2000 on which one of the passengers was an 89-year-old lady, who had said that this was her first ever flight in an aeroplane. Jacky Ramon recalled flying a Boeing 737 from the UK to Paris, and being joined on the flight deck by an elderly Canadian man. As they flew over the Normandy beaches, Captain Ramon made a remark about "no flak today" – at which point the passenger said he had flown over those same beaches in a Spitfire on D-day!

After lunch the day took a more sombre turn, as the cars conveyed us to the site of the Concorde crash in July 2000. The crash site where F-BTSC met its end has remained fenced off and untouched since the tragedy. The British and French Concorde Groups shared a silent tribute to the victims at the memorial to the 113 people who lost their lives on that day. Our French companions shared a quiet, emotional moment as they remembered their colleagues who died on the flight. John Hutchinson and Peter Ugle of British Airways and everyone there bowed their heads in respect.

The wonderful cars that carried us through Paris were very kindly supplied by the classic car club Triel Auto Retro, of Triel-sur-Seine. The 1938 Bugatti Coach Ventoux, the 2003 Bentley Arnage T, the 1988 Bentley Turbo 360

CV V8, the 1991 Rolls-Royce Silver Spur II, the 1938 Packard Eight Coupé Frenay, the 1965 Triumph TR4A and the 1936 Rolls-Royce Coupé.

*   *   *   *   *

There were a few of us passengers who flew very often. The TV presenter and journalist Sir David Frost was one of them – he flew the second greatest number of Concorde flights after me, around 300 compared with my 718. For some reason, David always liked to fly at the back of the plane, which was the noisiest part of the aircraft, so not as well-liked as the front. Maybe he wanted to see who else was on board, so he could network with them. He died on a Mediterranean cruise in August 2013 at the age of 74. Then there was my friend David Springbett, a great adventurer and businessman, who died in 2022, another very frequent flyer of more than 200 flights.

I felt that I knew the aircraft incredibly well after so long. How it would expand by up to 12 inches during flight and flex like a fishing rod. It had a personality to me, it was more than a collection of metal, electronics and plastic. It was something that you responded to emotionally. I've spent time with many Concorde pilots and read many of their books, so I've built up a picture of what the aircraft means to them and how it compares with the experience of being a passenger. We share a lot of the same feelings.

Mike Bannister managed British Airways' Concorde fleet for some years, having fallen in love with the aircraft the minute he saw it. "If you are lucky enough to have met your dream, which I have done, you are bound to be in love," he once said. "She is beautiful, stimulating and graceful – never infuriating or frustrating at all." Besides piloting Concorde in its regular scheduled flights, Bannister would take day trippers on a supersonic tour over the Bay of Biscay and back for just under two hours, where almost all of the passengers would be taking their first Concorde flight. "If you thought they were smiling when they got on, then you should see them when they get off – absolutely elated. People love it – it's the aviation equivalent of Disneyland – everyone going home with a smile," he said.

This sense of thrill and pleasure was something I enjoyed hundreds of times. Of course, it wasn't quite as intense as the first few times, but it was part of the justification for flying Concorde rather than subsonic. It was a business tool, enabling us commercial passengers to do things in two days that would otherwise take four. The cabin pressure was set at an altitude equivalent of 5,000 feet rather than the 8,000 feet you would get in a subsonic aircraft, which made a big difference to the experience and how tired you would feel afterwards. Then there's the sheer amount of time you spend in the air: normally just over three hours across the Atlantic instead of seven or eight, which also changes your recovery time. Three hours is just a long lunch, whereas eight is a whole day's work. Although I barely suffer from jetlag on any flights, for some people it can take a whole day or more to recover, which is costly if they need to be switched on at work. Around 80 per cent of Concorde passengers were business people like me, sitting alongside 10 per cent who were ultra-wealthy, 5 per cent famous entertainers or sportspeople and 5 per cent on a 'trip of a lifetime', for a birthday celebration for example.

As Mike Bannister points out, since Concorde was funded by British and French taxpayers, the citizens of those countries felt a sense of ownership and pride. For many people, Concorde was the European equivalent of the Apollo space programme, something that symbolised an extraordinary technical and scientific achievement, something that no other nation or collaboration had achieved (except for the short-lived Russian aircraft, the Tupolev Tu-144, which only made 55 commercial passenger flights).

Concorde's first test flight, on 2 March 1969 came just four months ahead of the first Apollo moon landing, in July 1969, when Neil Armstrong uttered the words: "One small step for man, one giant leap for mankind." The aircraft's first commercial flight from Heathrow, on 21 January 1976, came almost seven years later, but it made a similar impact.

"Norman Todd, Brian Calvert and John Lidiard were going to take civil aviation from a pedestrian 600 mph to 1,350 mph in one giant stride," said Brian Walpole, who was watching from the ground at Heathrow on that day and would go on to become general manager of the BA fleet. "I thought it was the biggest step-change in aircraft performance in the history of aviation." Whether he meant to or not, Brian Walpole was echoing those same feelings of achievement against the odds and pride in a sense of history that Americans felt with Apollo 11 in 1969. Michael Heseltine, who was Minister for Aerospace at the time, was equally ecstatic. It was "the biggest single leap forward in flying since the first flight of any aircraft," he said.

Concorde's first commercial flight became a major item of international news. The Queen described the event as "a magnificent achievement" and sent a message to the French President Giscard d'Estaing to say: "It is a source of pride that our countries have today inaugurated a new era in civil aviation." You might even say that Europeans felt there was a more useful side to this achievement than the moon landings. Concorde was something that we could all potentially experience for ourselves, rather than the more distant and specialised lunar landings.

Brian Walpole was one of an absolute throng of pilots who were determined to fly Concorde if they possibly could. Thousands of applications flooded in for each place on British Airways' Concorde pilot training course, something that took six months to complete and gave no guarantee of success: only 50-60 per cent of trainees passed the final tests. Over the 27 years of Concorde's active service, just 73 British Airways pilots qualified as captains on the aircraft, fewer than the number of US astronaut. And just one that flew more than most of the pilots and all the other passengers just yours truly.

John Tye was another young aspiring pilot in January 1976, clinging to the fence around Heathrow airport as the first commercial flight took off. It took him another 20 years to realise his dream, but finally in 1996 he sat in Concorde's cockpit in Seville, Spain, and started the engines. "To feel those four Rolls-Royce Olympus engines starting up and the airplane vibration for the very first time was just absolutely mind-blowing," he recalled. He and his co-pilot of a flight engineer prepared for take-off. "It's 'three, two, one – now,' and I pushed all four throttles fully forward in my left hand and I was just shoved back into my seat – an experience I could never describe, the acceleration as you shot off down the runway. That 20 minutes was the most incredible experience in my aviation career. It was just absolutely unbelievable."

It's always amazing to read accounts like this, reminding me of my own journeys, proving how mind-blowing it was to ride on Concorde, even for the most experienced pilots. It brings home the uniqueness of it and how much we've lost since the aircraft stopped flying.

The fascination with Concorde has stayed in the public imagination even though it's now 20 years since the final commercial flight, in October 2003. When I last visited the Runway Visitor Park at Manchester Airport, where one of the best-kept examples of the aircraft is housed in a beautiful hangar – well-lit with natural light, with plenty of space all around it, welcoming visitors on multiple guided tours every day, along with a screening room showing the aircraft's development and history – there were visitors who weren't even born in 2003, avidly learning about this phenomenon of aviation as if it were a thing of the future. And that's one of the amazing things: it still looks and feels futuristic, more than half a century after it first took to the skies.

Back in the late 1960s, when testing started, it was pilot Brian Trubshaw (RIP) who was called into action for the very first British flight. He was a decorated World War II pilot who joined the RAF in 1942, then flew Stirlings and Lancasters for Bomber Command in the war before joining the Kings Fleet in 1946, where he would pilot King George VI and the young princesses Elizabeth and Margaret, sometimes joining in with after-dinner games at their home in Balmoral, Northeast Scotland. In later years, the Queen would refer to him as "my Brian". (In fact, his fixation with aviation started as a child of 10 in South Wales, when he saw the Prince of Wales's light aircraft land on a beach at Pembrey in Carmarthenshire.)

In the 1950s he became a test pilot for Vickers, where he tested the delivery system for Britain's first atomic bomb, the 10,000 lb Blue Danube, from a Valiant V bomber. He also won a medal for 'outstanding test flying contributing to the advance of aviation' in 1965, after successfully landing a VC-10 bomber after an elevator section broke loose and the plane began to shake violently. You can tell a lot about Trubshaw's understated personality from his description of this life-threatening near-disaster: "One of my trickier moments," he said.

Trubshaw's flying history was momentous, and piloting the king was extremely high status, but nothing compared with what was to follow. Once he was selected to pilot Concorde's maiden flight, Trubshaw became a national hero. On April 9th 1969 he flew Concorde 002 from Filton near Bristol to RAF Fairford in nearby Gloucestershire, emerging from the cockpit to say: "It was wizard – a cool, calm and collected operation." For Trubshaw, these were emotional, even sensational words. Despite his years of extraordinary experiences, he was astonished by how advanced and precise the aircraft was to fly. "Many test pilots would have given almost anything to be in my shoes and I well appreciated how lucky I was," he said later. "The eyes of millions of people all over the world were focused on us."

Although he would tell interviewers that Concorde was the safest aircraft he'd ever flown, Trubshaw did have to deal with some technical challenges. On the initial flight, Concorde's altimeters failed to operate, meaning that he had to estimate his height for landing. In 1970 he had to land the plane on three engines after an instrument showed that the fourth was overheating and a similar issue happened in 1971, after a metal plate went through one of the engines. And he wasn't just a safe pair of hands: Trubshaw set a world record for an Atlantic crossing on Concorde of 2 hours 56 minutes, flying from Fairford to Bangor, Maine, in 1974. Trubshaw's place in aviation history and his amazing feats were recognised by an OBE, a CBE and becoming a Member of the Royal Victorian Order, an award that the Queen gave to people who served the royal family especially well.

When he died in March 2001, the world mourned the loss of a great pilot. HRH Prince Philip, Duke of Edinburgh said he was 'very sad' and British Airways said: "Everyone in BA who worked with him could not help but be inspired by his continued enthusiasm and joy for Concorde." I like to remember how he started his autobiography, Concorde: The Inside Story. "It is not unreasonable to look upon Concorde as a miracle."

Mike Bannister's book, simply titled Concorde, came out in 2022 and tells stories from the aircraft's history, many of which I experienced first-hand. After qualifying as a Concorde pilot at the age of 28 (BOAC's youngest) in 1977 he piloted the aircraft right through until its final flight on 24 October 2003, from JFK to Heathrow. He reckoned to have flown 9,600 hours on the aircraft, including almost 7,000 at supersonic speeds. These hours also included flying in formation with the Red Arrows, overflying the London Eye on Millennium Eve and flying as part of a 27-aircraft formation over Buckingham Palace for HM Queen Elizabeth II's Golden Jubilee celebrations in 2002. My main interest in Mike's book was because of his account of the crash in which he was part of the British Accident Team and we would finally get the truth.

I guess that Mike is the pilot equivalent of me, someone who has spent more of his life on Concorde than any other pilot, compared with me as the most frequent passenger. For him, part of the attraction was that he could do two Atlantic crossings in one day and get home to his family by supper time. For me, as for many business travellers, it was a similar story. It gave us more time, less hassle and an incredible experience just being in the aircraft. And I memorably once completed three transatlantic flights in a single day, hopping between London and New York in order to get a document signed by two sets of executives for an urgent deal.

For other pilots, flying Concorde had an impact on the wider aviation world and even on society in general. Barbara Harmer left school (like me) without qualifications at the age of 15 to become a hairdresser in Bognor Regis, West Sussex. Then through sheer determination and hard work she progressed through air traffic control training, studying for A levels, learning to fly and gaining a private pilot's licence. After accumulating flying hours she found work at Goodwood Flying School as an instructor, before deciding to qualify as a commercial pilot.

This route into the profession is very unusual, but Barbara was no ordinary pilot. It took more than 100 applications before she was hired by a tiny airline, Genair, based in Humberside. In the mid-1980s she joined British Caledonian, flying BAC One-Elevens, then long haul McDonnell Douglas DC-10s. Finally, when British Caledonian merged with British Airways in 1987, Harmer spotted an opportunity to fly Concorde. Out of 3,000 BA pilots at the time, only 60 were women, and none had ever piloted the aircraft. Undaunted, she passed the six-month conversion course in 1992 and became the first qualified female Concorde pilot in late 1993, flying to JFK. She continued piloting Concorde for ten years until it was withdrawn from service, when she switched to piloting BA's Boeing 777s. Not only was she a pioneer for women pilots, she was a leader among Concorde pilots, commanding the Concorde Crew in international yachting competitions. Following Barbara's lead, a Frenchwoman, Béatrice Vialle, qualified as a Concorde pilot in July 2000 and made 45 supersonic flights from Paris to New York. Sad to say, Barbara died at the age of 57 from ovarian cancer, in 2011.

A more common route to becoming a Concorde pilot, in contrast to hairdressing, was via the Royal Air Force. Several pilots besides Brian Trubshaw earned their stripes in the RAF, including Peter Duffey, who also flew de Havilland Comets and Boeing 707s. Duffey, like others before and after him, compared the experience of flying Concorde after conventional aircraft:

"It was like going from a bus to a Formula One sports car." As passengers, we definitely agreed with this assessment. There was a stripped-down feel to the cabin, despite the trappings of luxury, the gourmet food and the upmarket clientele. Just as Ferrari keeps the interiors of its sports cars relatively minimal, to save weight, Concorde had a similar feel. The aircraft was designed for speed above comfort.

Like us passengers, the pilots took special pleasure in the acceleration, take-off and climb phases, which had elements of the blast-off you'd experience on a space rocket, as opposed to the more sedate feeling of elevation you get on subsonic passenger planes. "Racing down the runway for the first time, accelerating to climb into the air was one of those experiences you never forget," Concorde pilot Richard Westray told a journalist recently. "The plane performed like no subsonic plane could perform."

Once airborne, the aircraft would be travelling at well over 220 miles per hour, quickly accelerating to 300 miles per hour and climbing at up to 4,000 feet a minute, far quicker than subsonic planes. Even though it would remain subsonic over land, Concorde would still be flying much faster than a typical 747 jet, until it reached the sea, at which point the pilots would give a brief warning to passengers that the aircraft was approaching the sound barrier. A tiny shockwave passing over external sensors would create a small blip on the aircraft's speed indicators, telling the pilots that they had gone supersonic. "Ladies and gentlemen, no bumps, no bangs. Concorde," was the official announcement created by Brian Walpole. After that, the pilot would announce to passengers: "Ladies and gentlemen, we've just reached the speed of sound, Mach 1. Welcome to the world of supersonic flight." Later, as Concorde climbed yet higher and its speed accelerated to 1,350 miles an hour, there would come a second announcement. "We're now up to twice the speed of sound and nearly 60,000 feet, on the edge of space," they would inform passengers.

For the pilots, as for the passengers, the sense of excitement and exhilaration never went away, no matter how often we flew on Concorde. One of the most experienced captains, Jock Lowe, reflected in 2019 about how a decision he took in 1969 to become a Concorde pilot changed his life. When he saw the aircraft take off from Filton, on 9 April 1969, "it looked beautiful, fast, built for the future." He flew Concorde for most of its career and had no regrets. "It's been a real privilege to be associated with this magnificent machine, a machine that turned into a dream for a whole generation of would-be passengers and spectators," he said. "And that is why it was built! The politicians of all parties for once agreed that Concorde would serve as an inspiration, an aspiration for the entire country."

As Lowe points out, when it was flying, Concorde tickets were first on the bucket list of things that lottery winners wanted to buy. It was an achievable dream for just about anyone, especially with the charter flights around the Bay of Biscay for a few hundred pounds. Jock Lowe described the atmosphere on board even the regular trans-Atlantic flights as 'fun', and I'd have to agree. "Everybody that worked on Concorde, from the hangar floor upwards, everybody had a great deal of pride in the aeroplane and getting it right," he said. I think even as passengers, we had a sense of contributing to this atmosphere, of representing the aircraft in various ways. Certainly, it became a big part of my life, through attending press events and new route launches.

Jock Lowe described how you get a quite extraordinary view when you're flying supersonic with Concorde. "By the time you're at 60,000 feet, you could see a quarter of a million square miles. So, you could actually see the things that you saw on maps," he said, like the outline of continents. Like those of us who flew frequently, Lowe had the pleasure of meeting people like Muhammad Ali, Richard Nixon, Mick Jagger and Paul McCartney. He also flew charter flights for VIPs such as the Queen and Prince Philip, including a trip back from Canada to the UK. "We had to slow down because the temperature in the upper atmosphere meant that we'd reached the limits," he said. The Queen notices and asked him what was going on. "I was able to explain a little bit – that we weren't slowing down much, we'd still arrive on time."

One of my favourite cabin attendants was Gilly Mayes-Pratt, who joined the Concorde fleet in the 1980s and remembers that on her first flight she was told: "Fred's with us today." Intrigued, she then met me and remembers thinking I must have been British Airways staff.

"No, he's not staff," she was told, "but he's a big part of the Concorde family." From here, she and I became great friends, to the point that I walked her daughter down the aisle when she got married. I would sometimes help her out in the galley and she would tell me how I'd missed my vocation – I should have been an airline steward. "You're a treasured member of the Concorde family," she told me recently. "Virtually everyone involved with the operation of the beautiful bird knew you and remembers you very fondly."

"During my ten years on the Fleet I met many famous people, including celebrities and Royalty but the main VIP had to be Fred. In 1985 The Mail did a full page spread about him (I still have a copy) as he had, even then, travelled the most times on Concorde. He went on to fly another eighteen years before she was prematurely retired. He is a true gentleman and has great sense of humour. I remember having dinner with him in a very swish restaurant when one of my false nails fell into my smoked salmon (it actually matched!) and Fred nearly wept with laughter.

The Concorde Family is a very special group of people. We worked hard, had a passion for the aircraft and share some wonderful memories. Fred is a treasured member of this group as virtually everyone involved with the operation of the beautiful bird knew him and remembers him very fondly. I have the privilege of being able to say he is a friend of mine."

My other favourite is Julie Reynolds. She was the youngest flight attendant to qualify to fly with BA so I knew Julie on Concorde and still know her as cabin director on 747s and 777s. We still stay in touch and when she is in my audience, she'll always ask me who is my favourite flight attendant. I always answer: "Do you tell your children which is your favourite?"

Concorde pilot John Tye remembered the sense of community, because he would see familiar faces on every trip, since the pool of crew members was relatively small. "It really was a day out with your mates every time you went to work," he said. Among the passengers, there would almost always be familiar faces too, like mine. The crew would remember our favourite drinks and welcome us back, as if it were a private club (which in a way, it was).

Tye recalled the in-flight service that would emerge on the flight deck. "They came in with three mugs of tea, one for each of us – the captain on the left, me and the flight engineer sitting behind. Then on the same tray were three mugs of some of the finest caviar in the world with a mother of pearl spoon each to eat it with."

Just as I do, pilots remember Concorde being like a "very big private jet" that was being shared by 100 people, with people like Elton John or Sting sitting in the front row or going onto the flight deck to chat with the captain.

Meeting Famous Passengers

The list of Concorde passengers would sometimes read like a celebrity fundraiser, it was so full of film stars, rock stars, entertainers and sportspeople. Here are some of my personal highlights:

Johnny Cash and I first met when we sat next to each other on a regular flight from Nashville to New York. We got on so well that we met up on several occasions for a prime rib in Manhattan, where he asked me about the singer Rob Lowe, who his daughter was dating. We stayed in touch for years and later I met his wife June Carter-Cash. "Do you mind if I come and sit by you?" she asked on one flight down to Nashville. "Would you mind writing a note for John to say when you'll be coming back to Hendersonville to see us all?" she asked me, so I wrote on a bottle of wine I'd taken from Concorde for her to give Johnny. Maybe not the best present for a recovering alcoholic!

Rod Stewart was a fellow Concorde passenger many times, as well as on subsonic flights across the Atlantic and one time on the QE2 liner, when I was giving a talk about kinetic friction to passengers coming back on the Concorde Afterwards, we sat around one of the pools, chatting about football and travel. He was really down to earth and good company.

In fact on one of those trips I was on the bridge of QEII with an earphone connected to Concorde in one ear, with David Leney as pilot I seem to remember and in the other Tim Miller piloting Red One for the Red Arrows whilst I was telling the passengers what was happening. This very nearly didn't happen because of inclement weather in the channel.

Meryl Streep came from Summit in New Jersey, home of my former parents-in-law. When we sat together on Concorde, I asked whether she remembered a teacher called Mrs Wilson. "I did indeed Fred, how did you know that?" "Because she's my former mother-in-law!" I replied and we chatted about what a great place New Jersey was. We flew together a few times after that.

Paul McCartney was a frequent Concorde passenger, along with his late wife Linda. He always seemed to be in a good mood and would draw happy faces on the Concorde stationery and menus, then pass them around the cabin. When you look at the price of Beatles memorabilia these days, you could probably earn a fortune from these. Fellow Beatle Ringo Starr was another passenger I'd see quite often.

Joan Rivers was the queen of the US comediennes. We sat together on Concorde and she started rummaging through her bag. "Have you lost something?" I asked her. "I'm looking for a photo to give you," she told me. She couldn't find one, but then, a few weeks later, we flew together again. "To Fred, how nice to be with you again, especially on Concorde, Love Joan xx" she wrote on her picture.

Buddy Rich was one of the greatest jazz drummers of all time. He and I met in the Concorde lounge in JFK before flying to London. He said: "It's my first Concorde flight, do you think they'll let me sit by you?" I arranged for him to sit in 9b and we chatted all the way to Heathrow. He was flying out again early the next day, so to save him a long journey out of central London, I offered him a room in my suite at the Excelsior, next to the airport. He left me a lovely note the next morning.

Dolly Parton and I sat together coming over from London to New York, then again down to Nashville, where we both lived. After seeing a photograph of her whilst on a trip in Rome, I told her what an impression she'd made on me and she said: "If you've got it Fred, flaunt it!" That was due to a photo published in the press a few days earlier of her getting off a plane in London. She was one of the funniest people I've ever met, as was her sister who was on the flight to Nashville.

Phil Collins used to fly Concorde quite often and I'd see him at charity events, or inaugural flights. He was friends with Sir Richard Branson. In 1985, when he completed his famous dash across the Atlantic to perform in both Live Aid concerts, I arranged the New York helicopter flight to get him to Philadelphia without which the performance couldn't have taken place.

Bruce Springsteen was involved in a copyright case in London and would fly over on Concorde, so I met him a few times in a short period. "How many flights has Fred done now?" he would ask the BA staff. On one of the flights, he was in a particularly good mood, since he'd won his case. "Let me buy you a drink," he offered, but of course all the drinks were free on Concorde. We chatted about him doing a concert with Johnny Cash – it could have been the start of my career as a rock promoter…

John Denver was flying back to New York on an Air France Concorde from Paris one Christmas Day, since BA didn't fly on that day at the time. When we boarded the flight, it was decked out in Christmas decorations and mistletoe – but there were only three of us on the flight! Once drinks were served, John took out his guitar and started playing songs, including *Take Me Home Country Roads*. Perhaps my favourite song. It was a sad day when I heard that he'd died when his plane crashed in 1997.

There were so many other well-known people: politicians like Mikhail Gorbachev and John Major, businessmen like Adnan Khashoggi, actors like John Mills and Jeremy Irons.

It seems like a strange dream now. Like being in heaven, where you think you might meet all the people you've heard about during your life. Except it really happened.

Chapter 2
A Beautiful Bird

Very often, I'm invited to give talks about my experiences on Concorde, about my life travelling the world, about aviation and hospitality. It's always a pleasure to be able to share these stories with other people.

With Concorde, so many people are fascinated by the aircraft and how it felt to travel at twice the speed of sound, partly because it's been virtually impossible to do this since the aircraft went out of service two decades ago. My friend Sir Iain Gray, professor of aerospace at Cranfield University, has invited me to speak to his students so that, as he puts it, they understand what makes a good experience in aviation. The passenger's point of view helps give them another dimension to their thinking, to see more about the value of tourism and business travel, about how to cater to passengers. I can also talk about how I saved my boss a lot of money through me travelling on Concorde with the business case I made that the expense was worth the time it saved. Iain loves hearing all my Concorde stories because there aren't too many other people who can tell them.

This is something that another friend, Ben Lord, feels passionately about. He was a teenager when Concorde came out of service and was devastated that he'd lost his chance to fly on it. Ever since being a boy of 12 he's been entranced with the aircraft and his devotion over the last twenty years has seen him run the Save Concorde Group, which originally campaigned to keep Concorde flying in a heritage capacity. When it became clear that this wouldn't happen, it has become an advocate to ensuring the remaining aircraft are preserved in good condition for future generations. He represents a massive community of people, hundreds of thousands strong, who post pictures and stories on the internet every day, keeping the spirit of Concorde alive. I'm honoured to be able to communicate with this community, to share my memories with them and encourage them.

Ben believes that, if social media had existed in 2003, Concorde would never have retired when it did, because the airlines would see what huge support and demand there was.

We can't turn the clock back, but we can celebrate the most beautiful bird ever to fly. So let me take you on a journey through Concorde's history, from its beginnings in dusty committee rooms in the 1950s, through years of development, to its glorious heyday and premature end.

From the drawing board to the skies

"She flies!" exclaimed Raymond Baxter (RIP) on the morning of 2nd March 1969, when Concorde 001's nose lifted off the runway at Toulouse, with test pilot Andre Turcat (RIP) at the controls, as millions of TV viewers around the world watched with bated breath.

This first, dramatic flight lasted just 40 minutes and proved that the previous 15 years' struggle since the director of the Royal Aircraft Establishment (RAE) set up a committee to study supersonic transport had been worth the effort. Thousands of people had contributed to this moment, commonly accepted as the most ambitious technological project ever conceived in European history, the equivalent of America's Apollo 11 moon landing.

For Britain, Concorde was an ambitious but logical extension of its existing role in aviation. During the Second World War and over the following years, it had developed aviation technologies that were years ahead of both Russia and the United States, particularly for military aircraft, while passenger transport was the province of the Americans. In 1949 the British-built de Havilland Comet became the world's first commercial jet airliner, but its unreliable performance, with two crashes in 1954, meant that it was overtaken by the Boeing 707 and the DC-8.

In the States, the Bell X-1 broke the sound barrier in 1947, but then the English Electric Lightning aircraft proved itself capable of flying at Mach 2 and could 'supercruise' at supersonic speeds without constantly using afterburners, something that was crucial to Concorde's development.

The RAE report decided that wing design was the first problem to solve. Too wide and there would be too much drag at high speeds. Too narrow and it would take too much power to lift off and need very long runways. Further RAE reports, this time from researchers Johanna Weber and Dietrich Küchemann, proposed a 'slender delta' wing design. They argued that a long, slim wing could help improve lift and performance at low speeds. The head of the RAE project, Morien Morgan, was convinced that this was the right solution. This was the moment that Concorde had lift off, as a feasible idea.

There followed years of back-and-forward debate over the number of passengers the aircraft should carry, its range in kilometres, the top speed it should reach and the likely cost. This last factor dogged Concorde all the way through to its launch and beyond. In the late 1950s the very lowest estimate - a supersonic jet with 100 passengers flying 'short range' - would cost £50 million to develop and would be ready to fly in 1968. This estimate was wrong by a factor of more than 20 and the schedule was out by eight years.

Cost overruns and delays are nothing new in major engineering projects, especially where so much of the technology is untested and pioneering. What is fascinating about what became the Concorde project is the combination of factors that kept everyone engaged, focused and even obsessed with completing it, when there were so many obstacles in the way. There was a constant tension between industry on one hand, which lacked the finance to underwrite the aircraft's development, and government on the other, which had the money but depended on the public's approval to spend it. Besides national pride, what other benefits would supersonic flight deliver for the man in the street? They might aspire to travel on such an aircraft one day, but it was a bit like buying a ticket for the lottery. You know your chances of winning are one in a million.

For the manufacturers and the project's proponents, the likely cost of Concorde was underplayed from the start. The German aerodynamicist Dietrich Küchemann who designed the wings and other parts of the aircraft admitted that the budget was drawn up "on the basis of, let me see, what will the politicians stand. In the whole STAC report, those estimates are the only thing that are rubbish. I have a very bad conscience about that."

In the late 1950s, with supersonic flight in its infancy, there were major doubts over whether the technology was suitable or even possible for passenger flights. Morien Morgan convinced the early sceptics by suggesting that the US had already started up a similar supersonic project. If Britain didn't press on with its own aircraft, it risked losing out on the international airliner market, which he believed would be dominated by supersonic jets in future. The project, he argued, would enable Britain "to look the Americans firmly in the eye again." A study contract was awarded to Hawker Siddeley and Bristol in 1959 to draw up preliminary designs, using the slender delta wing concept. Then the following year, the Bristol team began talks with Boeing, General Dynamics and Douglas Aircraft in the United States and Sud Aviation in France.

Over in France, the government had encouraged its aircraft companies to come up with similar plans, fearing that they too would be locked out of a supersonic future. After a design competition, Sud Aviation's plans were selected and the company's technical director Pierre Satre travelled over to Bristol to discuss a potential partnership.

According to Kenneth Owen in his book Concorde: Story of a Supersonic Pioneer, the Bristol team were surprised to discover that Sud's designs for a supersonic aircraft were almost identical to their own. Later, it turned out that RAE's Supersonic Transport Aircraft Committee (STAC) report, laying out all the plans, had been secretly passed to Sud Aviation, which had made some small changes then presented it as its own! There are suspicions that this was a piece of political manoeuvring by the British designers: if UK ministers threatened to cancel the project, they could say: "The French are going to go ahead anyway. Do we want to be left behind?"

In any case, the two teams found that they agreed on most issues and so could work together happily. They decided that Mach 2 should be the top speed, because it meant that the aircraft could be made of aluminium. Any faster and it would need to use stainless steel or titanium, which would have dramatically increased the cost and the development time. The other consideration was the likely difference in transatlantic times. At Mach 2.2, it would take around three and a half hours to travel from London to New York. At Mach 3, you'd only save an additional 20 minutes.

Today, we're still amazed that Concorde was able to fly so fast and how no other aircraft has superseded its achievements. At the time, many were convinced that the era of supersonic flight was just beginning and that Mach 3 would become routine within a few years. Concorde will be too slow, they said. An American rival will put it out of business.

By now the projected cost of the aircraft development had risen to £150 million, and the Treasury had deep concerns. An industry report published in 1962 decided that it was 'very unlikely' that there would be any financial return from the project. Even so, it recommended going ahead for the same reason as before: fear of missing out on future opportunities. In addition, the UK was trying to win membership of the European Economic Community, so the government hoped that signing a major agreement with France would help. The treaty was signed on 29 November 1962 and the French President Charles de Gaulle then vetoed the UK's entry into the EC on 25 January 1963. So much for Anglo-French relation!

It was in early 1963 that the name Concorde was first mentioned. Thought to have been the idea of the son of F.G. Clark, who was publicity manager at Filton in Bristol (and later wrote an excellent history of the aircraft), it soon caught on, with its dual French and English meanings of agreement, harmony or union. After a brief bit of resistance, the British agreed to the French spelling, with an 'e' on the end, with Minister of Technology Tony Benn (RIP) saying that it represented "Excellence, England, Europe and Entente Cordiale," which annoyed the Scots until they were told it also represented Ecosse, the French word for Scotland.

Meanwhile, the boffins at Bristol, in France and elsewhere set about designing the many features of Concorde that could not be transplanted from existing aircraft, which is to say almost all of it. The Olympus engine, a twinspool turbojet, had two independent compressors, each linked to its own turbine, reducing the amount of fuel needed to create thrust energy. Engineers refined the engine to boost its thrust from just over 9,000lb to more than 40,000lb in the Olympus 593 model, a huge increase.

The complexity of designing this engine for supersonic speeds was pretty astonishing. Dealing with the temperature range alone presented an enormous challenge: at Mach 2, air enters the intake at around minus-60 degrees centigrade. Once it reaches the engine it has risen to 130 degrees, but once it's left the high-pressure compressor, it is at 550 degrees. To cater for these extremes and to protect the engine from any ingested ice, birds or other objects, the designers used titanium, with nickel-based alloys in the high-pressure compressor, the combustion chamber and the turbine blades and reheat assembly. Before Concorde entered service, these parts underwent 46,000 hours of testing on the ground or in flight.

There were similar calculations required for the exterior of the aircraft. As it rose in altitude, the aircraft would cool, then as it sped up to supersonic speeds, it would heat up, reaching as much as 127 degrees centigrade, well above the boiling point of water. Passengers were always aware of this warmth when inside the cabin, but the aircraft's designers made sure there was no danger of them burning themselves on the walls or windows.

What the heat did cause was a gap between the flight engineer's console and the bulkhead of around 12 inches, as the fuselage heated up and expanded. To relieve the heat from the cabin, the designers used fuel as a 'sink' from the air conditioning, with the same method used to cool the hydraulics. And of course, it was well-known that Concorde's bright white paint was there to mitigate heating problems.

Next, the designers had to figure out a suitable air intake system for Concorde's engine. Put simply, they had to slow air down from 1,350 miles per hour to 550 miles per hour in the space of an 11-foot tube. And they had to ensure that the air intake remained stable at whatever speed the aircraft was flying. The solution was to build a variable intake 'throat', using ramps and flaps, with sensors providing continuous information to widen or narrow the intake. Air Intake Control Units, using digital processors for the first time in aviation history to provide full control of an essential passenger aircraft system, developed by genius designer Ted Talbot and his colleagues at the Electronics and Space Systems division of the British Aircraft Corporation.

To give extra thrust for take-off and when going through the sound barrier, Concorde developed a reheat system, where fuel was ignited in the jet pipe. This was something that had only ever been tried on military aircraft in the past.

This was just one of the issues that passenger aircraft designers had never had to deal with before. Another was Concorde's centre of gravity and its 'aerodynamic centre', which sound similar but are actually two different points. On subsonic aircraft, the aerodynamic centre moves relatively little and can be handled through moving the trim tabs on the wings or tail. When an aircraft accelerates to supersonic speeds, its aerodynamic centre shifts to the rear of the plane. If nothing is done about this, the aircraft would start tipping forward, nose towards the ground, adding drag and making it harder to control. Concorde's designers came up with a smart solution. Pumps shift fuel between the aircraft's forward and aft tanks, as necessary. This system was so successful that Concorde didn't need to have any slots and flaps, as you see on any subsonic aircraft. It also meant that the aircraft would flex as it accelerated and decelerated, as though it were arching its back. Passengers in the rear seats would get the best view of this, watching the front end curve downwards.

Concorde's droop nose, perhaps its most famous design feature and the one which made it look most like a giant bird, also distinguished the plane from its subsonic cousins. It was required because, in both landing and take-off, pilots needed to have a good view ahead of them. In landing especially, Concorde would come down (once again) looking like a giant bird, gliding at 90 degrees with its tail down and its body in the air before its landing gear touched the runway and the front of the plane followed. Subsonic aircraft land in a far more horizontal posture. Once airborne, the pilots raised the nose cone to streamline the aircraft and minimise air resistance, while a visor protected the flight deck windows against the heat and air pressure.

Not long after the treaty between Britain and France was signed in 1962, Concorde's sales teams set out to woo international airlines. It was a tough sell at first. A new generation of subsonic airliners was on the horizon, building on the success of the Boeing 707, which took to the skies in 1957. The 747 was still a few years away, but so was Concorde. Which would be the popular favourite? Some airlines argued that with 100 passengers, Concorde was too small to carry the numbers they needed. Concorde responded that, because it was twice as fast, it would carry twice as many passengers as a subsonic plane.

Despite their reservations, Pan Am took out an option for six Concordes in June 1963, followed by Continental Airlines with three, American Airlines with four and Trans World Airlines with another four in the following months. This was a big result, even if the true motive for Pan Am was to goad the US aircraft industry into developing its own supersonic aircraft. Sure enough, within days of the announcement, President Kennedy said that his government would help the US industry to develop and build a supersonic plane that would be bigger and better than Concorde. Many of the major airlines straight away signed up for options on this model, too. Kennedy, by the way, seems not to have known in advance about the Pan Am options on Concorde. He said that the deal "involves hundreds of millions of dollars in balance of payments, which is going to sabotage a program to put the United States up in the lead in the 70s."

For Concorde's designers, if not for the public back home, Boeing plans were no big deal. They knew that Mach 2.2 was the practical limit for a supersonic passenger plane and the American boast that they'd build one flying at Mach 3 left the British and French unimpressed. An aircraft of this size would have to weigh a million pounds and be at least 300 feet long, the length of a football field. Structurally, it was impractical, they decided.

More airlines soon joined the queue for Concordes, including Qantas and some Middle Eastern carriers, bringing the number of options to 43 in 1965. More than 100,000 technical drawings for the aircraft were sent to production companies to deliver the more than one million individual parts. And the twin teams on the British and French sides began collaborating more closely, as the entente cordiale went into a new phase.

Applying the same principles to Concorde as a carmaker like Ferrari did, its makers used every innovative opportunity to reduce the aircraft's weight. These included using 'sculpture milling', where a machine would carve out a part from a solid block of metal, both reducing its weight and making it stronger than an equivalent formed by welding or riveting. 'Concorde designers are more weight-conscious than the most ardent slimmer," wrote F.G. Clark in his history of the aircraft. At BAC Filton, where he worked, Clark could see the electron beam welding chamber, used to direct a beam with pinpoint accuracy at titanium parts, so that they retained their strength and integrity.

Technically, Concorde was making excellent progress in late 1964, when it came under threat from an unexpected angle. The Labour opposition party announced that if it won the October election it would withdraw Britain from the project. Labour won the election, bringing Harold Wilson to Downing Street, where he set up a review. The new aviation minister, Roy Jenkins, set off for Paris aiming to cancel the deal. The French pointed out that there was no termination clause in the 1962 treaty and that if Britain withdrew, they would take the case to the International Court of Justice in The Hague. The British attorney general calculated that the government would probably have to pay £200 million to the French to exit the deal. So even though Britain decided to press on with the project in the end, government indecision caused problems in terms of morale. It's a pity that the same reasoning and costs weren't put to Air France in 2003.

Labour's lack of enthusiasm for Concorde continued through the rest of its tenure in government. Some of its ministers kept pressing for withdrawal, while Tony Benn reminded them that 16,000 workers were busy building Concorde,

8,000 of them in Bristol alone (where he happened to be an MP). Benn was the original Save Concorde pioneer, making a case for the aircraft over many years. Indeed his family invited my friend Ben Lord (Chairman of Save Concorde Group) to his funeral in 2014, as a representative of the Concorde community in a gesture recognising his continued taking up the mantle of what Tony Benn had done fifty years earlier. Back in the mid-1960s, Benn warned that dropping out of the project could harm the rest of Britain's aircraft industry and possibly the wider economy. The 1967 devaluation crises put the government's budget under severe pressure, so it was keen to save money wherever possible. It was not really until the 1970 election, won by Ted Heath's Conservatives with a Eurocentric agenda, that Concorde was once again secure from political threat. Even then, there was plenty of concern about the cost of the project. "Concorde is a commercial disaster," wrote the Central Policy Review, while praising its usefulness in diplomacy and foreign relations.

Back in 1967, even more international airlines were jumping in and taking options on Concorde, including Japan Airlines, Sabena, Eastern Airlines, Braniff, Air Canada and Lufthansa, taking the total up to 74. All of them had also taken options on Boeing's 2707, however, along with others who hadn't taken out Concorde options. The competition between the two projects was hotting up. Even though Concorde was likely to enter service ahead of the Boeing jet, some feared that – like the earlier competition between Britain's Comet and Boeing's 707 – the Americans would swamp the market and blow Concorde out of the sky. Concorde's manufacturers were confident, however. At BAC, sales managers predicted that they would sell 225 models by 1975 "on the most pessimistic assumptions."

The first flight of Concorde in March 1969 added much-needed impetus to the whole project, convincing the sceptics that this long-awaited, endlessly-discussed and debated aircraft was real and could actually fly. As F.G. Clark wrote: "Concorde 001 carried the hopes and aspirations of thousands of people." TV viewers on five continents were glued to their screens, much as they would be four and a half months later, on 20 July 1969, for the Apollo moon landing. What an amazing time it was to be alive.

Forty minutes after it had taken off, Concorde returned and swooped in to land like a giant goose, the captain Andre Turcat activated the reverse thrusters and the tail parachute billowed out from behind. After taxiing to the airport building Turcat came down the steps, waved to his wife, as the crowd roared and cheered, then went to embrace the project leaders waiting for him. It was the same story at Filton, Bristol a month later, when Brian Trubshaw piloted Concorde 002 on its maiden flight, once again attended by the world's press and thousands of cheering spectators.

Over the next 18 months, Concorde first broke the sound barrier on 1 October 1969, reaching Mach 1.5 during a nine-minute supersonic burst. Then four airline captains were invited to fly Concorde 001, one from BOAC, another from Air France, a third from Pan American and a fourth from TWA. They wrote a joint report saying how pleasant and easy it was to fly and that they could see no problems training pilots and engineers to handle Concorde. Finally, in November 1970, both Concordes 001 and 002 sailed through Mach 2 for the first time within days of one another, using their newly installed Olympus 593 engines to fly long distances, something that no supersonic aircraft had previously achieved.

With all of these novel experiences, you might expect that there would be some major hitches to overcome. But such was the thoroughness of the preparation and testing, over so many years, involving so many thousands of experts, that this never really happened. Concorde was put through some extreme situations, to see how it reacted. Both engines on one side of the plane were shut down, but the pilots found that this did not affect their control of the aircraft. The worst that happened was in January 1971, when an engine surge caused a ramp in the intake to break free and fly into the engine, damaging it severely, but not affecting any other part of the plane. The pilots shut down the damaged engine and flew back to Toulouse safely.

The issue of the sonic boom was a constant factor. In 1970, the test crews were given permission to fly over the western coasts of Scotland and Wales, then over Cornwall, to see exactly what the effect of the boom would be on the ground. Residents of these areas were given plenty of warning and assured that there would be relatively few flights in total – maybe 50 spread over a period of years. Some threatened to stir up trouble, suggesting that the government was just trying to soften people up for a much more frequent service, but in general, the tests went off without incident.

The issue of noise had long obsessed Concorde's designers. In the earliest discussions, Rolls Royce presented a plan to produce an engine emitting only 100 Perceived Noise Decibels (PNdB), compared with the 112 PNdB limit imposed by Kennedy airport in New York. The Olympus SNECMA engine that was eventually selected had to undergo a series of revisions to reduce its noise, at the same time as raising its thrust power.

There were also a series of long-distance flights in 1971, with Concorde 001 jetting off to various destinations in South America, including Brazil and Argentina, entertaining almost 100 guests flying at Mach 2, with no ill effects. Concorde 002 made its own long-haul flights, spreading the aircraft's reputation and confirming its airworthiness. President Pompidou of France flew on the French prototype and Prince Philip on the British one. American aviation journalist Robert Holz reviewed the experience, noting that it was a pleasant trip and that he could walk around the cabin with ease. "Stewards will have no trouble serving martinis and meals. Passengers will find no difficulty consuming them," he wrote. "They will just have to drink a little faster – New York will be only a few hours away."

The worst thing to happen to Concorde in 1971 wasn't anything to do with the plane itself. It was the cancellation of the Boeing 2707 project, ditched by the American government on grounds of cost, technology and environment. Even though some were concerned that the US supersonic project could one day overwhelm Concorde, for most people engaged on the aircraft, competition was a positive thing. And major investment in supersonic technology was a vote of confidence in the sector.

Concorde 002 followed up its widening flight schedule in 1972 with a world tour, including a young government minister Michael Heseltine MP, taking in Athens, Tehran – where the Shah sat in the left-hand pilot's seat during a demonstration flight, Bahrain, Bombay, Bangkok, Singapore, Tokyo, Manila, Darwin, Sydney, where huge crowds greeted the plane, and Melbourne, before returning home more or less the way it came.

Concordski

From the British and French points of view, Boeing's efforts to build a supersonic aircraft were the main competition to Concorde. But there was another project that saw itself as the real contender for supersonic crown prince: the Russian Tupolev Tu-144. Tupolev was an aircraft maker which had already delivered competitive passenger aircraft for many years. Its Tu-104 came out in 1956, two years before Boeing's 707. Now its Tu-144 was vying with Concorde for primacy and making some headway. It went supersonic in June 1969, four months ahead of Concorde, and flew at Mach 2 in May 1970, another first.

In 1971, both jets appeared at the Paris Air Show at Le Bourget, demonstrating their capabilities but causing little fuss. Two years later, in 1973, competition between them had intensified, at least on the Russian side. After Concorde performed a fly-past including a sharp ascent in front of the crowd of 250,000 spectators, the Russian pilot Mikhail Koslov said: "Just wait until you see us fly. Then you'll see something."

As soon as the Tupolev Tu-144 took off, it was clear that Koslov meant business. He flipped the aircraft from side to side, came roaring towards the runway then performed an even steeper ascent than Concorde's. As it crested at around 2000 feet, the Tu-144 appeared to stall, pitch over and go into a steep dive towards the ground. Restarting the engines, Koslov engaged full power as he attempted to pull out of the dive, but as he did so, the left wing, then the tail both snapped off and the fuselage hit a nearby building before it smashed into a row of 15 houses and burst into flames, killing all six on board and eight on the ground.

Videos of the incident are still available online and it seems pretty clear that Koslov simply overestimated what the Tu-144 was capable of. Like Concorde, it was built to travel long distances in a straight line at very high speed. It was never meant to perform tricks and stunts. There would be no circumstances in any possible flight where the Tu-144 would need to do such crazy manoeuvres.

Nevertheless, conspiracy theories about the crash sprouted before the engine was cold. A Mirage jet was flying nearby trying to take spy pictures of the Tupolev and the pilot became distracted, or had to take evasive action. The French limited the Russian plane's flight time in order to favour Concorde. A journalist on board the plane was carrying a camera which flew into the controls and jammed them. And finally (my favourite), the British knew that the Russians were spying on them and trying to steal supersonic flight secrets, so they deliberately passed them some faulty plans. Crafty!

It was a massive set-back to the Russian supersonic plans and the Tu-

144 only lasted for another few years: its passenger service began in 1975 and ended in 1978. The crash was bad news for Concorde too. Just like the demise of the Boeing 2707, it put doubts into the minds of passengers and airlines about the viability of supersonic air travel. It showed that Concorde was safer than the Russian alternative, but that wasn't saying much.

Selecting pilots

Concorde had already proved itself an exceptionally safe and reliable aircraft, despite its incredible complexity and sophistication. It achieved this partly through a highly selective pilot recruitment system, taking only a tiny fraction of the applicants. Even when they were accepted into the training programme, only around half of the pilots made it through. In the post-War years of the 1950s and 1960s, pilots with years of experience had seniority in the profession. So when it came to Concorde, they naturally expected to be at the front of the queue. Yet piloting the aircraft meant getting to grips with technologies that had never been used before, such as the automatic intake system and the fuel-balancing and centre of gravity system. For several older pilots, these new issues were confusing and they struggled to cope. After a while, British Airways brought in a new rule that pilots had to be 49 years old or younger to be considered for Concorde. This was tough for some older pilots who were denied their chance.

There were a series of other health-related issues to consider. The higher an aircraft flies, the more risk there is of injury from cosmic radiation. At first, employee groups like trade unions were worried that crew members would be exposed to damaging radiation, so Concorde carried a miniature Geiger-Muller counter to measure it and found that the average dose was 0.92 millirem (one thousandth of a rem – the unit used to measure ionising radiation). Since this is such a tiny fraction of the radiation that could cause sickness, the British Medical Research Council and its French equivalent decided that Concorde was safe.

Concorde's cabin was pressurised to the equivalent of around 6,000 feet, a lower figure than the average for long distance airliners, which was closer to 8,000 feet. This was a positive for passengers and left them more refreshed at the end of their journeys, but the higher differential between internal and external pressure carried a higher risk. If the cabin de-pressurises when you're cruising at 60,000 feet, you only get around 10 seconds of 'useful consciousness' before you black out. Practically speaking, you'd not have time to put on an oxygen mask. These dangers meant that Concorde had smaller windows that regular airliners and the flight crew had a special reserve air system in case of emergencies.

To get Concorde not only airborne but full of passengers, the dozens of options put down by the world's airlines had to be converted into orders. And in July 1972, BOAC (the forerunner of British Airways) and Air France signed contracts for nine Concordes between them – five to BOAC and four to Air France - the first actual orders for the aircraft and a seminal moment in its history. There was no turning back now.

There followed a very tense six months, as BAC and the rest of the industry waited to see whether the American airline, led by Pan Am, would follow suit and sign full contracts. In the negotiations over their original options deal, the Americans agreed that they would make a decision one way or another within six months of BOAC and Air France deciding. If they chose to take up their options, it was likely that many other airlines around the world would do so too. With further options signed during 1972 with a Chinese airline for three Concordes, the stakes were extremely high. Potential revenue from these sales ran to many hundreds of millions of pounds.

Over in the United States, Pan Am was struggling. After ruling the skies for many years, it had suffered a series of poor years and was losing money. Since the introduction of the Boeing 747 in 1969, Pan Am had invested heavily, buying 25 of the wide-bodied jets and making it the corporate flagship: First Lady Pat Nixon christened the earliest Pan Am 747 in January 1970. The trouble was, Pan Am had grown too fast and by late 1972 had run into financial trouble. Its 747 fleet was under-subscribed and flying half-empty. TWA had similar problems and was running at a loss. Nobody doubted that Concorde could fly safely and speedily across the Atlantic or on any of its other prospective routes. They (Pan Am and TWA) just couldn't make the economics work. They didn't think that enough passengers would switch from business travel on regular flights to Concorde. On 31 January 1973, the final day of the six-month period, both Pan Am and TWA cancelled their Concorde options.

One by one, all the other airlines that had reacted so positively to Concorde's sales pitch – Continental, American, Qantas, Japan, Sabena, Eastern, Braniff and Lufthansa – fell by the wayside like so many dominoes. This was a terrible blow to the project. It was hard to see how so many airlines, which had reached the conclusion that Concorde was a great idea for them, technologically, economically and for the best interests of their passengers, could suddenly change their minds as soon as the two big American carriers pulled out.

As so often in aviation, there were suspicions of political interference. Decisions by BOAC and Air France to go ahead were widely seen as politically-motivated: both companies were government supported and could hardly have said no, after so many years and hundreds of millions of pounds of investment. The Americans may have wanted to protect Boeing's interests and the thousands of jobs that the company supported. They may have taken a nationalistic view and not wanted to cede leadership in global aviation to a European rival, as President Kennedy had warned back in 1963. Who knows?

The fact that Pan Am and TWA said that their decision was an economic one is at least believable. Airlines regularly go out of business because they cannot pay their bills, so in that sense you can't blame them. Instead of the $20 million per plane they'd signed up for, each Concorde would now cost $45 million. They took issue with Concorde's sales team saying they only needed to fill 37 seats per flight to make a profit. That figure was "extremely unconvincing and based on assumptions they thought highly optimistic, if not impossible," reported the US press. Pan Am's managers argued that Concorde's maintenance and fuel costs had been underestimated. This was debatable in 1972 and early 1973, but by the end of 1973 when the Yom Kippur War broke out and OPEC began its embargo of the West, they were dead right. Oil prices soared by 300 per cent between October 1973 and March 1974, adding hugely to the cost of flying anywhere. If the Americans hadn't cancelled their options by the end of 1973, they surely would have done in 1974.

It wasn't only the British and French who were left disappointed by the decision. One Pan Am captain, Paul Roitsch, explained how he and flight engineer John Anderson had spent time on Concorde simulators and on four actual test flights on Concorde 001, reaching a top speed of Mach 2.6 on one occasion, possibly reaching 72,000 feet flying with Frank Nutbeen (RIP). When the cancellation news came through, "John Anderson and I were tremendously disappointed," said Roitsch.

As the engineering and flight test teams soldiered on in the wake of the option cancellations, people who were actively involved remember it being "depressing in the extreme". Even though the project's leaders such as Sir George Edwards claimed that Concorde would still make a profit if it flew half full, everyone realised that any chance of recouping the hundreds of millions of pounds invested by the British and French had effectively disappeared. There were still thousands of people working on Concorde in both countries, in machine shops and assembly lines, in laboratories and on test rigs, computer centres and offices. It was, wrote F.G. Clark "a test of endurance, nerve and teamwork," as the deadline for passenger services to begin drew closer. Whereas in 1970 the STAC analysis reckoned that there would be a market for anywhere between 150 and 500 supersonic aircraft, just four years later, this number was looking more like a couple of dozen.

Meanwhile, testing and improvements continued. An updated Olympus 593 engine solved an earlier smoke problem during take-off. Test flights went off in search of icy conditions, extra hot conditions, and ways for Concorde to contribute to scientific knowledge. On 30 June 1973 Concorde 001 gave scientists a 74-minute view of a total eclipse of the sun. And a re-fitted Concorde 002, with chic French leather seating and décor, wowed VIP guests at the Paris Air Show.

In 1974, Concorde 002 took part in an unusual kind of race. It took off from Boston airport in the US at the same time as an Air France Boeing 747 took off from Paris in France. Crossing above the Atlantic, 002 landed in Paris and set off back to Boston, where it arrived 11 minutes before the 747. Aboard these two flights were 500 businesspeople from Brazil, the US, West Germany, France and Britain, while a crowd of 100,000 people came to see Concorde in Boston, jamming the highways. The aircraft was still a hit with the public, even if the airlines had changed their minds.

Finally, on 15 January 1976, British Airways took delivery of its first Concorde at Heathrow Airport, followed six days later by its first scheduled flight, from London to Bahrain, while Air France simultaneously flew from Paris, with a fuelling stop in Dakar, to Rio de Janeiro. A Tri-State Port Authority ban on Concorde flying into New York meant that the original trans-Atlantic flights came into Washington Dulles, starting in May 1976, while the French developed a route from Paris to Caracas in Venezuela from April 1976. On 22nd November 1977 both airlines were allowed to land at JFK in New York and the era of supersonic passenger flight on the routes Concorde was born to serve could truly begin.

Brian Walpole was at the helm of the aircraft. The test flight had all the noise abatement equipment ready to condemn the aircraft as per the anti-Concorde campaigning that went on at this time. The genius strike of turning sharp to the left after take-off from New York's JFK Airport meant the needle didn't move on the noise monitors. And as Walpole was doing the press conference afterwards, they towed the aircraft into the hangar and that was it - the Americans fell in love with her almost more than what we did. They checked the noise monitors on every departure.

Singapore for a Season
Back in the late 1970s, when British Airways and Air France were trying to win custom for Concorde around the world, they struggled initially to persuade the Americans to accept the plane on American turf. So they looked around for other routes which might prove popular.

For BA, the idea of connecting British people to former colonies such as Hong Kong, Singapore and Australia was very attractive. Hong Kong had become a massive financial centre, with very wealthy individuals and businesses. Singapore was on its way to a similar status. Since Concorde could fly between London and Singapore in just nine hours (including a fuel stop in Bahrain), compared with 13 hours on a subsonic carrier, BA decided it was on to a winner.

As far back as 1972 the Singaporeans had their first glimpse of Concorde, when it made an appearance during a promotional tour of Asia, visiting Hong Kong, Tokyo and Australia, drawing thousands of spectators wherever it went. By 1975, plans for a regular weekly service were in progress, with cabin crews handpicked for trials. Singapore Airlines took a great interest in the project, telling the media that it was negotiating to buy two Concordes to start flying in 1977, operating between London and Australia via the Lion City.

In 1976, with Concorde still barred from flying to New York, British Airways negotiated a deal with Singapore Airlines (SIA) where the airline would lease 20 seats out of 100 on each flight, to compensate it for the loss of First Class passengers on its own aircraft. So far so good. Singapore Airlines launched a global advertising campaign in December 1977 telling the world: 'SIA has gone supersonic'.

Then politics intruded, as so often in the Concorde story. Possibly spurred by the American refusal to allow Concorde to land, India refused permission for the aircraft to fly over its airspace, unless it could have more landing slots at Heathrow and 'fifth freedom' traffic rights from the London airport. ('Fifth freedom' is where an airline can carry passengers between two foreign countries, so long as it's part of a larger route including the carrier's home country.)

British Airways wasn't in a position to grant these rights to India, so it had to detour around Indian airspace, adding time and expense to the trip. But never mind, that wasn't a deal breaker. Getting through to Singapore, however, was trickier. Flights from Bahrain would typically cross over the Straits of Malacca and over a small part of Malaysia. But now Malaysia joined in the bargaining game, arguing that Concorde posed a risk to its environment. Everyone knew very well that this was fiction, and that Malaysia was up to the same tricks as India: trying to win more Heathrow slots and fifth freedom. This news came from Malaysian authorities on 7 December, just two days before the first flight was due to arrive in Singapore from London via Bahrain.

A Malaysian government minister was quoted saying that they had to "look into matters affecting the people's interests and environmental factors." Aviation experts decoded this as meaning that they didn't like Singapore Airlines operating a Concorde service, because it made Malaysia look bad.

British Airways executives and UK government agents tried to reason with the Malaysians, to no avail. The Singaporean government, however, struck a deal with Indonesia, to allow Concorde to fly through its airspace in return for support over East Timor – a region of Indonesia calling for independence. That saved the day, even if the flight was a little longer.

The initial flight took off from Heathrow on 9 December, on schedule, with a traditional Singaporean lion dance. It touched down the following morning, 25 minutes early, having successfully refuelled in Bahrain. Was that the end of the troubles? Of course not! Indonesia then said it had only agreed to allow flights for one week. Like Malaysia, and like India, it too wanted more Heathrow landing slots and, in addition, didn't want to aggravate its neighbour Malaysia by undercutting its position on Concorde. Back to the drawing board.

Only three flights made it from London before the project was postponed, and negotiations with Malaysia restarted. It took a further 13 months before flights could recommence, on 24 January 1979. In the meantime, Singapore Airlines benefited from a load of free publicity, since its livery had been painted onto one side of the Concorde used for the route, which then flew all over the world on BA routes.

For the next 21 months, until the service was finally cancelled on 1 November 1980, Concorde flew three times a week between London and Singapore, taking British business people out on the nine hour flight, alongside a handful of Singaporean residents and a similar number of Australians and New Zealanders, almost half of them connecting with flights to other cities. HRH Princess Margaret, the younger sister of HM Queen Elizabeth II, made the return trip in April 1980 during an official visit, which included the Philippines and Malaysia. Apparently, Her Royal Highness was invited onto the flight deck for the landing at Heathrow and mentioned to the pilot that 'her sister' was at home, as they flew over Windsor Castle.

Besides the politics of Concorde's route over various countries and jealousies between nations, there were more practical concerns. Extremely hot and humid weather had an impact on Concorde's performance, meaning that it could only take 86 passengers when departing from Singapore. Passengers were happy to cross the Atlantic in three hours in the Concorde cabin and put up with the noisy environment. They were less happy to spend nine hours in these conditions, despite the vintage champagne and salmon en croute they received en route.

Whether for political or practical reasons, the anticipated connections from Singapore to Hong Kong, Tokyo, Manilla, Seoul and elsewhere simply didn't materialise. It would have saved passengers an awful lot of time: Singapore to Tokyo on Concorde would have taken three hours instead of seven.

In the end, economics had the final say, as British Airways came under pressure from the UK government of Margaret Thatcher to balance its books. The route was losing an estimated S$20 million (equivalent to £24 million today). There were stories of friction between British Airways and Singapore Airlines and reports of flights being only half full. The cost of aviation fuel was rising, to add to the route's troubles. In September 1980 the airlines announced that the service would end on 1 November and a short but glorious chapter in Concorde's history came to an end.

The tale of Alpha Foxtrot

Concorde Alpha Foxtrot (G-BOAF) started life as Concorde 216, the last of the famous aircraft to be built. It was completed in April 1979 and initially registered as G-BFKX, an American registration given to it because the plan was for 216 to fly to Washington Dulles, then taken over by Braniff Airlines which would fly it to Dallas and back, ready for the return flight to London. In the event, this didn't happen and in June 1980, 216 became G-BOAF and was bought by British Airways.

Flying the well-worn route from London to JFK, G-BOAF did a great job for several years, achieving a record crossing time from New York to London of 2 hours 56 minutes and 35 seconds in January 1983, a record that stood for thirteen years. I was on this record-breaking flight. In 1989 the aircraft did a circumnavigation of the world, flying 38,343 miles in total.

Following the Paris crash in 2000, G-BOAF was selected as the development aircraft to get all the new modifications: improved tyres, fuel tanks lined with Kevlar and armoured wiring in the landing gears. BA went further with their return to service investment by commissioning Sir Terence Conran to design a new interior with new lighter seats that reduced BA's fuel bill by £1 million per aircraft. On 17 July 2001 G-BOAF flew out of Heathrow, the first British Concorde to fly after the fleet was grounded 11 months earlier. This was a flight to seek reinstatement of the Certificate of Airworthiness and was captained by Chief Concorde Pilot Mike Bannister with the CAA's pilot for Concorde onboard. The aircraft effectively did a Bay of Biscay pleasure flight in terms of routing and touched down at RAF Brize Norton where the world's press awaited the outcome of this test flight. It was a complete success.

Weeks later, a full test flight simulating the new RTF service that BA were launching was carried out. The cabin was filled with BA staff for the occasion and it was a rip-roaring success. When the flight landed, phones and pagers starting ringing like a fairground attraction to the news that was breaking. It was 11 September 2001 where the terror attacks in New York and Washington were unfolding. This delayed the restart of Concorde services until 7 November 2001 where, in a sign of confidence towards Concorde's return to flight, Prime Minister Tony Blair was encouraged to fly Concorde to a meeting with President George W Bush to discuss the recent commencement of the 'War on Terror'. Then in November, the aircraft flew Blair to Scotland where he once again met Bush.

On 26th November 2003 Alpha Foxtrot became the last ever Concorde to fly anywhere, landing at Filton Airfield, where it remains, on display for visitors in a purpose-built hangar.

Weird and Wonderful Concorde Facts

In its 27-year career, Concorde witnessed some crazy scenes, hosted hundreds of wild and wonderful guests and achieved things that no other aircraft could have attempted. Here's a selection of some of the most extraordinary stories.

1. A French Concorde once took a rare anti-venom medicine to Africa where a snake-bite victim had just two hours to live. The medicine arrived in time and the victim survived.
2. In 1999 Victoria Beckham took three return Concorde flights from London to New York and back to have her Vera Wang wedding dress fitted. I also did three transatlantic Concorde flights in a single day to get contracts signed.
3. Singer Rod Stewart had his hair stylist flown over to the United States on Concorde to fix his Barnet after another hairdresser had made a right mess of it.
4. Concorde had a special safe in its rear hold for valuable items. It regularly transported diamonds and large amounts of currency. It also took human organs for transplantation, saving numerous lives.
5. Soul diva Diana Ross once assaulted a customs officer who was attempting to search her, then was arrested when police boarded Concorde. She was eventually cautioned and released, then promptly booked another Concorde ticket and flew home.
6. Phil Collins played the 1985 Live Aid concert in London, jumped onto Concorde and crossed the Atlantic before taking a helicopter to Philadelphia (which I arranged via New York Helicopters) where he played a second set, this

time with Eric Clapton, on the same day.

7. TV presenter Terry Wogan (RIP) was thrilled to report that he could eat breakfast in London, fly across the Atlantic on Concorde and then eat another breakfast in New York. Because of this, I became a guest on the Wogan show, and was able to make Terry a life honorary member of the Mount Kenya Safari Club, founded by William Holden that I was a member of the International Executive Committee.

8. In 1993, the lead singer of the band Madness, Suggs, hit the longest ever putt in the history of golf while flying on Concorde. His ball travelled five miles in two seconds as it rolled along the aisle. Later, the Ryder Cup team beat his record with another longest putt.

9. The British Royal Family were frequent guests on Concorde. HM The Queen, HRH Prince Philip (who once took the controls of the aircraft), HRH The Queen Mother for her 85th Birthday, HRH Prince Charles (now HM King Charles III) and Diana, Princess of Wales flew on the aircraft. Also HRH Prince Andrew and Sarah, Duchess of York.

10. Concorde's bright white paint was twice as reflective as the paint used for other aircraft, in order to mitigate heat at extreme speeds. When an Air France Concorde was painted blue as part of a sponsorship deal with Pepsi, the plane had to fly slower than usual, so that it didn't overheat or the paint burned off.

11. The fastest transatlantic crossing took place on 7 February 1996 when captain Leslie Scott flew Concorde G-BOAD from JFK to Heathrow in two hours, 52 minutes and 59 seconds. This is still a record for any passenger aircraft.

12. Before it was certified ready to fly, Concorde was subjected to more than 5,000 hours of wind tunnel testing, making it the most tested aircraft in history. This is the kind of detail that future supersonic aircraft manufacturers tend to ignore, because it would cost them far too much to replicate.

13. Over its 34-year lifespan (including the seven years leading up to the first commercial flights) Concorde carried out just under 50,000 flights, carrying two and a half million passengers.

14. In 1976, one of the first commercial Concorde flights took a haggis to Bahrain so that Scots over there could celebrate Burns Night with a traditional feast. Forty years later in 2016, another haggis was taken on board Concorde

G-BOAA at the National Museum of Flight near Edinburgh, to commemorate the occasion. Staff at the museum recited a new version of Robbie Burns' poem to the haggis, mentioning Concorde. They also announced an £80,000 renovation project for the aircraft.

15. In 1998, Concorde welcomed its oldest ever passenger. Eva Woodman was 105 when she boarded the aircraft at Filton near Bristol for a 90-minute flight over the Bay of Biscay.

16. On Christmas Eve 1985 four Concordes, piloted by Brian Walpole, John Eames, John Cook and my friend David Leney took off from Heathrow to celebrate 10 years of service. They made a series of formations over the south coast of England, including a diamond shape and all four in a row, before returning to the ground. British Airways allowed 65 of its other Concorde staff to go up as passengers on the flights. This was the only occasion that Concordes flew in formation and it produced some of the best images of the aircraft that you'll ever see.

17. The only picture of Concorde flying at supersonic speed was taken from an RAF Tornado in April 1985 by the official Concorde photographer, my great friend Adrian Meredith. Although it could match Concorde for speed, the Tornado couldn't maintain this for longer than four minutes, because it started running out of fuel. So Concorde had to slow down to allow the jet to get a good shot.

18. Concorde had an extra wheel on its tail, to make sure that its tail fin didn't scrape along the ground on take-off or landing. This was because it had such a high 'angle of attack'.

19. A Concorde freighter, 'B' Model and medium-range version of the aircraft were all designed, but never built.

20. Sir Richard Branson initially offered to buy some of the retiring Concorde fleet for £1 each. He then upped his offer to £1 million and eventually to £5 million a head, but the deal fell through because Airbus refused to continue maintenance of the aircraft.

21. Inspiration for Concorde's wing shape came from 13th century gothic architecture: the 'ogee' arch, which has two flattened 's' shapes meeting in a point at the top, appears in buildings such as Beverley Minster in East Yorkshire, as well as ancient Persian and Moroccan buildings. It proved to be

ideal for supersonic flight.

22. According to aviation design experts, BA's oldest Concorde, G-BOAC, which first flew in February 1975, weighed around a ton more than its youngest model, G-BOAF, launched in April 1979, thanks to the lighter materials used in its construction.

23. When the last passenger Concorde flight left JFK on 24 October 2003, water canons sprayed jets of red, white and blue-coloured water onto the fuselage as it taxied onto the runway. In and around Heathrow, a crowd of 100,000 spectators saw two take-offs in the morning and three landings. I was commentating on Sky News and Windsor Castle was lit up to commemorate the plane's final commercial journey.

Paris 2000

It was a mild July day in Paris. A well-heeled group of German holidaymakers gathered in a special lounge at Charles de Gaulle Airport on the outskirts of Paris, chatting with the captain who would pilot them to New York aboard Concorde on Air France flight 4590. From there, they would board the cruise ship MS Deutschland for a 16-day voyage to Manta in Ecuador. The group included a well-known soccer coach, a multimillionaire businessman, several children and guests aged from seven to 91.

Captain Christian Marty was extremely well known in France and among the aviation community. A long-serving Air France employee, he had flown as a commercial pilot since 1969 on Boeing 727s and 737s, Airbus A300s, 320s and 340s, before being appointed as a Concorde captain in August 1999. Outside his stellar aviation career, Marty was also a star of extreme sports, particularly windsurfing. On 12 December 1981, he set off from Senegal on the west coast of Africa on a specially designed sailboard, accompanied by a supply boat. Despite falling off at one point and having to swim back to the board, he arrived in French Guiana in Central America on 18 January 1982, having covered a distance of 4,222km and becoming the first person to windsurf across the Atlantic. However, his licence to fly had expired.

Just before the plane was about to set off, it emerged that 29 items of luggage had to be loaded onto Concorde, weighing 500kg in total. These hadn't previously been declared on the aircraft's manifest and they took the total weight of the plane up to 186 tonnes, one tonne more than its certified maximum structural weight. Just at this time, the wind direction changed, giving Concorde an 8-knot tailwind for its direction of take-off. The official guidance in these circumstances is to taxi to the other end of the runway and take off in the opposite direction, against the prevailing wind. But to save time, Captain Marty decided to stick with the original direction. When you take off with a tailwind behind you, it reduces the amount of weight you can carry safely. Instead of 185 tonnes, Concorde should have weighed no more than 180 tonnes – meaning it was now six tonnes too heavy.

Added to the luggage and the tailwind, Air France 4590 had 1.2 tonnes of extra fuel in its rearmost tank, which shifted its centre of gravity to the back, beyond the safe operating limit of 54 per cent set by Concorde test pilots. Looking at the flight with the advantage of hindsight, there seem to be a catalogue of problems. But at this point, after 24 years of unblemished flying taking in many thousands of flights all over the world, Concorde was one of the safest planes ever to take to the skies. Nobody had any fears that this record would end.

Or did they? As long ago as 1981, the American National Transportation Safety Board raised concerns that Concorde's tyres could cause a 'potentially catastrophic' problem. It had examined four Air France Concorde incidents between 1979 and 1981, including one at Washington Dulles International Airport where two tyres blew out during take-off, damaging an engine and puncturing three fuel tanks, hydraulic lines and electrical wires and tearing a hole in the top of a wing. Just a month later, another tyre blew out, leading to new procedures and inspections for wheels and tyres.

Between 1981 and 1993 there were at least another five serious incidents with burst tyres on Concorde, often damaging fuel tanks, wings and landing gear, each of them on British Airways flights. Aviation experts think that this vulnerability was partly due to Concorde's high take-off speed, which increased the risk of tyres blowing out. In turn, any debris from the burst tyre would be travelling at such a high speed, it could cause the fuel tanks to rupture.

All this was far from the minds of the 100 passengers, three flight deck crew and six cabin crew on 25 July 2000. They were excited to fly up and out across the Atlantic and reach Mach 2 as they headed towards their luxury cruise.

Flight 4590 lasted just a few minutes. After what seemed a routine taxi and acceleration along the runway at Charles de Gaulle Airport, the air traffic control tower contacted the flight deck. "Concorde 4590, you have flames behind you." This was the first that pilot Christian Marty, his first officer Jean Marcot and flight engineer Gilles Jardinaud knew about the impending disaster. They had not yet taken off, but since they were already speeding along at 328kmph, it was too late to abort the take-off. There was only 2km of runway left, and it would have taken 3km to come to a halt. All of this was being witnessed by an Air France Boeing 747 that had just landed from Tokyo with President Jacques Chirac on board.

As flames shot out from behind them, the flight crew tried everything they knew to avert catastrophe. When Concorde was just 25 feet into the air, flight engineer Jardinaud closed down engine 2 without the authority of the captain, which he should have had. The engine was by now showing a fire warning. Damage to the undercarriage meant that they couldn't retract the landing gear, causing drag which prevented the aircraft gaining altitude. Engine 1 lost all power, probably because it was taking in hot gases, before it recovered slightly, but by this time there were multiple problems to deal with. The left wing was starting to disintegrate because of the fierce fire underneath it. The right wing tipped up into the air because there was more thrust from engines 3 and 4 on that side.

As they fought to stabilise Concorde, the crew reduced power on engines 3 and 4, aiming to bring it level again, but this just stalled the engines and caused a complete loss of control. In a frantic series of calls to the control tower, co-pilot Jean Marcot and captain Christian Marty tried to come up with a plan. "Le Bourget, Le Bourget, Le Bourget," pleaded Marcot, meaning that they should try to land at Le Bourget Airport, 9km away. Captain Marty disagreed: "Too late," he said. The control tower had another idea: "Concorde is returning to runway zero nine in the opposite direction," it commanded the crew. "No time," said Captain Marty.

He was right. There was no time. It took just one minute and 17 seconds from the moment that the control tower alerted captain Marty to the moment that flight 4590 crashed into the Hotelissimo Le Relais Bleus in Gonnesse, killing four employees in the (mercifully) otherwise empty building along with all 109 passengers and crew on board.

How did it happen? The most popular theory, which gave rise to a series of court cases and criminal investigations, was that a strip of titanium alloy from the engine cowl of a Continental Airlines DC-10 had fallen onto the runway during take-off, five minutes ahead of Concorde's departure. When Concorde ran over this debris, travelling at a speed of 300kmph, it punctured the right-front tyre of its left main wheel, sending a 4.5kg lump of rubber into the underside of the left wing at a speed of 500kmph, or 140 metres per second.

This in turn sent out a pressure shockwave through the body of the aircraft which ruptured tank number 5, just above the landing gear well. Fuel flooded out of this hole and was ignited by an electric arc in the landing gear bay, caused by debris cutting the landing gear wire, or else simply through contact with the extremely hot engine.

This titanium strip formed the basis of years of legal battles, as Air France argued that it had been wrongly installed and wasn't even an officially sanctioned part. Beginning in 2005, a court case eventually decided in 2010 that a mechanic called John Taylor, who had replaced the strip on the DC10, was guilty of manslaughter due to negligence and Continental Airlines was fined €200,000 and ordered to pay Air France €1 million. The French appeals court then overturned these verdicts, while ruling that Continental would have to pay 70 per cent of any compensation claims to the families of those who died in the crash. Air France had by this time already paid out €100 million.

Once investigators had looked in fine detail through the crash scene, they discovered that a 12-inch spacer that should have been fitted to Concorde's left side landing gear, to keep it in alignment, was not installed properly after a service three flights before. This meant that a particular strut could wobble from side to side, made worse by the uneven fuel loading. Some observers believe that drag marks on the runway prove that Concorde was veering to the left during its take-off, as a result of this missing part.

The official investigation, carried out by the French Bureau of Enquiry and Analysis for Civil Aviation Safety (BEA) decided that this missing spacer didn't cause or contribute to the crash, whereas an independent report by a former Concorde pilot and flight engineer argued that, without the problems caused by the missing spacer, the aircraft would have taken off earlier, and would therefore not have run over the titanium strip.

An even more unlikely theory, really more of a conspiracy theory, was that Concorde veered to one side in order to avoid a Boeing 747 carrying French President Jacques Chirac which was on the runway, thus putting it into the path of the titanium strip. Alternatively, some posit that Captain Marty continued trying to take off in order to avoid the 747, when he should have aborted.

Although it is very hard to see how any pilot could have rescued flight 4590 once it was burning so fiercely, some Concorde captains argue that, by shutting down engine 2 so quickly, which still had about 30% of thrust which would have saved them, they hampered the aircraft's ability to manoeuvre and made a crash more likely. Official guidance recommends getting to 400 feet in altitude before closing off an engine, whereas the crew did this at 25 feet. "The pilot should have been able to fly his way out of trouble," said one former Concorde captain.

Like so much of the Concorde story, the Paris crash became intensely political as the years rolled by. Blaming Continental Airlines for the accident, due to this titanium strip, "shows the determination of the French authorities to shift attention and blame away from Air France, which was government-owned at the time and operated and maintained the aircraft, as well as from the French authorities responsible for the Concorde's airworthiness and safety," said Continental's spokesman.

They do have a point. A runway inspection prior to take-off, which was 'protocol' for Concorde flights, did not happen after the Continental flight. That would probably have spotted the titanium strip.

These are all hypothetical arguments though. Following the crash, a series of mandatory modifications were commissioned, fuel tanks were lined with Kevlar to make them stronger, the aircraft's tyres were replaced with harder-wearing alternatives and wiring in the landing gears was armoured. British Airways invested an additional £14 million in a return to flight programme that far beyond the requirements of the mandatory modifications.

But the public, especially French passengers, began to choose other planes. September 2001 and the dot.com crash didn't help, nor did various issues with Air France Concorde's, including an engine surge and failure to shut an engine down in February 2003 that almost caused the loss of another aircraft. Some believe that collusion between Airbus and Air France hastened the demise of Concorde. Donald Pevsner, in his expose '*The Betrayal of Concorde*' argues: "the premature retirement of Concorde, at least a decade before this would have been technically necessary," was a "saga of the secret betrayal of Concorde by senior executives at Air France and the senior engineering director at British Airways, and the secret collusion between the Chairman of Air France and the President of Airbus to ensure that AF would not have to suffer the 'loss of face' that would ensue from its unilaterally retiring its Concorde fleet, thereby leaving BA with a monopoly on supersonic transatlantic passenger service." He concluded that the deal was a "nasty litany of hypocrisy, cowardice and corporate politics." The arrangement was that if either wanted to continue to fly they could take up the option of paying the others maintenance fees around $40 million as I was informed and Airbus more than doubled this that's what put 5 recently converted Concordes ready to fly until 2010 maybe into museums.

Here are the five reasons for the crash. Plane overloaded by 5 tons due to extra fuel and baggage not on manifest. The spacer dropping off, the engine being cut without command, fuel tanks overloaded not allowing movement of fuel so the tanks imploded, lastly the captain refused to go to another runway because of wind change.

Where are they now?
One of the unique things about Concorde: public fascination with the aircraft has never gone away. If anything, it's grown over the decades as new generations have come to recognise what a phenomenal achievement it was, how beautiful it looked and what a treasured place it has in the history of aviation. I can think of no other type of aircraft which has so outlasted its flying days, attracting hundreds of thousands of people every year to see it for themselves. Most aircraft are scrapped once they're grounded. Only two of the 20 Concorde models built are no longer intact – one was scrapped by Air France after a heavy landing and the other crashed in Paris in July 2000.

Even six of the prototype Concordes, which never flew commercially, can be seen in air museums. Three of them are in England: G-BSST, the first prototype built in the UK, was constructed to prove that it could fly supersonically and

1. Concorde flew into space on virtually every voyage, something we passengers sometimes took for granted. This is the only picture of Concorde flying at supersonic speed, taken by my good friend Adrian Meredith from an RAF Tornado that was trying its best to keep up.
© Adrian Meredith

Sonic Boom

2. Sitting in my seat 9a onboard G-BOAE in Barbados being interviewed by The Nation Newspaper with my copy of Executive Travel magazine - this cover is the most reproduced magazine cover in history!

Sonic Boom

3. Seat 9a with Sally Cordwell CEO of Aerospace Bristol.

4. My favourite seat 9a with an old boarding pass for one of many trips to JFK. Concorde windows were small and triple-glazed to protect you from the kinetic heat of friction generated by the speed which reached 100ºc.

5. On a visit to the Runway Visitor Park at Manchester Airport, I was asked to give a short presentation to during one of the popular tours onboard G-BOAC.

6. Back where it all began! Sitting in what would become 'my seat' - 9a - onboard G-BOAC - the very first Concorde I flew on May 25th 1976 for the inaugural Washington Dulles-London Heathrow service.

Sonic Boom

7. Anyone who flew on Concorde can tell you how different it was from regular flights, it started with the departure lounge. Photo (left and below) courtesy of Adrian Meredith.

8. Receiving my ticket in person at the Concorde check-in back in 1978.

9. Fred Finn, Captain Brian Walpole and David Springbett on press trip around UK to celebrate BOAG return to flight.
© Adrian Meredith

57

Sonic Boom

10. My Concorde leather baggage tags (front and back) that flew as much as me.

```
>UR..
RESERVATIONS MODE ENTERED

>*BA194/22AUGJFKLHR-FINN..
 1.1FINN/FREDMR
NYCBAOQ 10AUG RZIZGS
 1  BA  194 R    22AUG   JFKLHR  HK1   1015 1900
 2  BA   55 F    22AUG   LHRNBO  HK1   2140 0800
 3  KQ  173 F    24AUG   NBOMBA  HK1   1000 1050
 4  KQ  188 F    24AUG   MBANBO  HK1   2130 2220
 5  UY  801 F    26AUG   NBODLA  HK1   0930 1440
 6  UY  706 F    26AUG   DLALOS  HK1   1700 1835
 7  ET  780 F    28AUG   LOSFIH  HK1   2215 0055
 8  UT  335 F    30AUG   FIHJNB  HK1   0115 0545
 9  BA   HTL     30AUG   JNB     HK1   OUT 30AUG SGLB SOUTHERN SUN AP HTL NN
DAYROOM
10  SA   36 Y    30AUG   JNBSAY  HK1   1300 1430
11  BA   52 F    3SEP    SAYLHR  HK1   2045 0545
12  BA  193 R    6SEP    LHRJFK  HK1   1115 1014
FONE-NYC-H 201 665 1660
2.NYC-B SAME
TKT-021AUGNYC000KO WILL CALL JFK 0845/22AUG
GEN FAX-SSROTHSET NN COMPLI HTL FIH 29AUG
2.SSRRQSTBAHK1 9A BA194R22AUG
3.SSRRQSTBAHK1 9A BA193R6SEP
4.OSIBA VIP MOST FREQUENT CORCORDE TRVLER
5.OSIYY VIP MOST IMPORTANT BA ACCT
RMKS- FQ H13416
 2. NYC BA-XLON Q156.00R BA NBO(-(DLA)PA LOS(DLA)496.60RTF)
 3. ET-XNBO KQ SAY 25M 1971.30F BA LON BA NYC Q331.00R 1577.00F PLUS U
SD6 P 265.00........FARE USD4687.00
 4. FQ H 13416 ADVSD/MRS FINN NYCBVGS13AUG
 5. ATTN RATES/NOTE PSGR NOW TRVLG NBO/MBA/NBO/DOES FQ STILL APPLY NYC
KOGS18AUG
 6. ADVD PAX HK UT335/30AUGFIHJNB SEG11 NYCBLGS20AUG
 7. FQ H13987...3SEP TKTS AS FOLLOWS
 8. NYC BA LON BA NBO PA LOS ET FIH M25 (SAY) 2090.00F NYCLON Q 165.00
 9. F/USD2255.00 NYCNMGS20AUG
10. SEP TKT....
11. NBO KQ MBA KQ NBO KES1500 BR 8.8664 USD169.00
12. 3RD SEP TKT....
13. FIH UT JNB SA SAY BA LON BA NYC M25 (FRW) 1971.30 LONNYC Q 311.00
ZAI1112.00 P 25379.20 FCU27661.50
14. F/ZAI13831.00 BR 5.5661 USD2485.00 NYCNMGS20AUG
15. JFK ADVSD TAW NYCKOGS21AUG
16. PAX MR ADVD ALL FQS AND WAS FFC AS WELL NYCSGGS22AUG
```

11. A challenging itinerary, but not for me!

12. There were no TV screens on Concorde, just a display panel showing how fast we were travelling. © Adrian Meredith

58

13. One of the most thrilling and scary experiences of Richard Branson's life, flying with the Red Arrows at their training base in Lincolnshire.

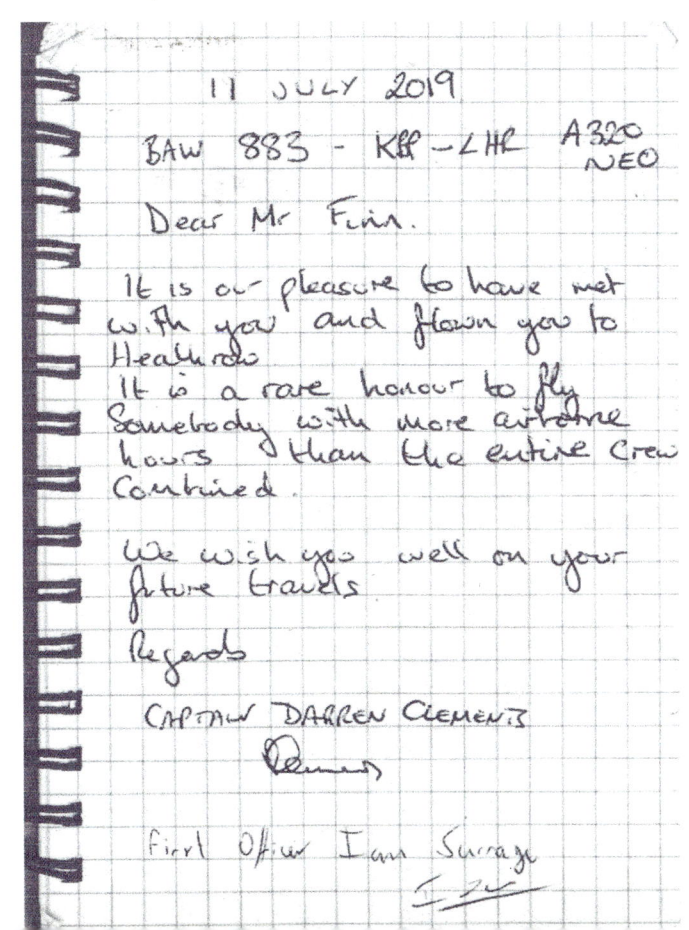

14. With my dear friend - Sir Richard Branson who has always been a loyal supporter to me.

15. A personal note from Captain Darren Clements and First Officer Ian Surrage.

> 11 JULY 2019
> BAW 883 - KEF - LHR A320 NEO
>
> Dear Mr Finn,
>
> It is our pleasure to have met with you and flown you to Heathrow.
> It is a rare honour to fly somebody with more airborne hours than the entire crew combined.
>
> We wish you well on your future travels
>
> Regards
>
> CAPTAIN DARREN CLEMENTS
>
> First Officer Ian Surrage

Sonic Boom

16. Mike Bannister, BOAC's youngest qualifying pilot flew 9,600 hours on Concorde including flying in formation with the Red Arrows over the London Eye on Millennium Eve.
© Adrian Meredith

17. A personal thank you from the Red Arrows for their team dinner at my home.

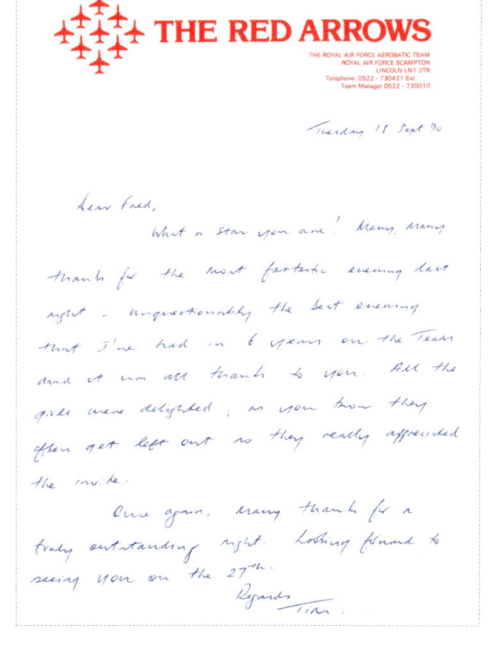

18. My Ticket to Moscow to meet Gorbachev.

19. Mikhail Gorbachev in our Moscow office.

21. Sabre, my Alsatian dog at Maison Victor Hugo. I had to leave him on Jersey and never saw him again.

22. Dame Virginia McKenna.

20. Stood next to the famous Concorde nose cone in the Concorde Room at London Heathrow Terminal 5's 'Concorde Room'
© Ben Lord

61

23. As I approached my fourth birthday, a fleet of 77 Luftwaffe aircraft dropped 40 tons of bombs on Canterbury.
© Iliffe Media

24. An early picture of my family, I was five and my sister one, with my Mother and Father.

25. At 11 years old all I wanted to do was play cricket.

26. My home town Canterbury from the air in 1942 following an air raid just before my second birthday in June of that year.
© Iliffe Media

27. Bewildered pedestrians in Burgate Street, Canterbury following an air raid in 1942
© Iliffe Media

28. Doris (RIP), Fred and Kate just as it was in 1942 - the best pint of mild anywhere.

29. Reunited with some of my British Airways Concorde friends with G-BOAD in New York in May 2024. I was onboard the fastest transatlantic crossing of Concorde until Captain Leslie Scott (to my right) broke that record with this aircraft on February 7th, 1996 in 2 hours, 52 minutes, 59 seconds!

perform as it should. Today it's at the Fleet Air Arm Museum in Yeovilton, Devon; G-AXDN was a pre-production model, which introduced a new wing plan, more fuel capacity and a new engine intake system. It's now at the Imperial War Museum in Duxford, near Cambridge; G-BBDG was another pre-production model that was reassembled at Brooklands Museum in Surrey by museum volunteers in recent years. There are another three in France: the prototype F-WTSS which did the same job as its British equivalent and is now at the Museum of Air and Space at Le Bourget Airport in Paris;the pre-production model F-WTSA, now at the Musée Delta, Orly Airport, also in Paris and finally F-WTSB at Musée Aeroscopi in Toulouse.

Concorde in Britain

Besides the prototype models, there are four other Concordes still in the UK, three of them open to the public.

At the Runway Visitor Centre at Manchester Airport, G-BOAC sits in a purpose-built hangar, kept in immaculate condition by a dedicated team of museum staff, with daily guided tours, a small cinema room showing a history of the aircraft next to a gift shop and café. There are other planes on display at the Centre, but Concorde is very much the prize exhibit. Corporate events and private parties can book the space and mingle beneath its magnificent fuselage.

It's due to Heritage Concorde that John Dunlevy – former British Airways Concorde engineer and the longest serving British Concorde engineer, became involved with G-BOAC. John has been connected with Concorde since 1965, when he became an apprentice with the Bristol Aeroplane Company and streamed for test flight avionics and production avionics. He specialised in the aircraft air intake development at Fairford on the prototype and preproduction Concordes, and was involved with the British prototype 002 tours and British pre-production 101 endurance flying. He left Fairford in 1977 to join British Airways. John is the one, together with Graham Cahill, Head of Heritage Concorde, who have done all the work on this and other Concorde's nose dropping, cabin lighting, flight deck instrument lighting, landing lights etc. G-BOAC became the first semi-live Concorde since retirement and all of these efforts have been undertaken voluntarily. Peter Ugle, former Concorde engineer, is also part of that remarkable team and the official photographer.

This is my favourite Concorde today, housed in the ideal way, giving visitors not just the chance to see it but to go inside, sit in the seats and even watch the nose cone rising and falling. On a recent visit, they even let me operate the mechanism for the cone. While we were there, I gave a brief talk to the guests telling them stories from my days flying on the aircraft, my favourite seat, the celebrities I'd met and so on. It's a real pleasure to be part of Concorde's legacy, all these years after it stopped flying. flying. During the tours of Concorde they always tell people my name and which seat I sat in except when I flew in the flight deck because I had given my seat up to someone like Bob Guccione.

G-BOAC was always British Airways' flagship Concorde, named after its predecessor company British Overseas Airways Company. It was among the first production models, meaning that it's slightly heavier than the later versions, which used lighter components and different designs.

The first production Concorde that BA received, on 14 January 1976, was G-BOAA. It was also the first to fly commercially for the airline, taking off from Heathrow on 21 January 1976 at the exact same time as an Air France equivalent in France. Today, the plane rests at the National Museum of Flight in East Lothian, a few miles outside Edinburgh in Scotland. This has a very impressive collection of military and civilian aircraft – more than 50 in total. They keep Concorde in a special hangar, which I always like to see.

Aerospace Bristol in Filton is home to G-BOAF where since 2017, the aircraft sits in a hangar these days, although it spent several years outdoors before it was finally housed undercover. This was the last Concorde ever built and made the final flight of any Concorde, on 26 November 2003. The museum offered a special Anniversary Tour in 2023 to celebrate 20 years since the last flight.

The fourth production model still in the UK is G-BOAB, situated at Heathrow Airport and used by British Airways for training. After the Paris crash, this aircraft had pushed back from the gate at Heathrow to take-off for an outbound JFK flight on 15th August 2000. There was then a radio message from BA Operations for the aircraft to return to the stand and it was at that point the CAA rescinded Concorde's Certificate of Airworthiness. All passengers onboard were transferred to 747 services to New York and the aircraft never flew again.

Concorde in France

As the hub of France's aviation industry, you'd expect Toulouse to have a Concorde. And indeed they have two. The Aeroscopia Museum next to Toulouse Airport houses F-BVFC, built in Toulouse and first flown on 9th July 1976. It flew more than 14,000 hours and completed Air France's final Concorde flight on 27th June 2003 when it was delivered to Toulouse. Its final commercial flight was 31st May 2003. The aircraft is kept outside and you can walk around it but not go inside except by special permission, which was granted to a group I was with just before the COVID-19 pandemic. It was kept alive for purposes of the crash investigations until 2009/2010. Aeroscopia also has the pre-production F-WTSB, kept indoors and accessible to visitors, who can see the flight deck, test equipment and interior features.

Aeroscopia is a fantastic facility. It opened in 2015 so it's still very new, with 26 civilian and military aircraft including the two Concordes. Definitely worth a visit if you're in Toulouse.

The Musee de l'Air et l'Espace at Le Bourget in Paris has Concorde F-WTSS, one of the prototypes, along with F-BTSD. This was the first Concorde of any in the world to be returned to a resemblance of life after retirement in 2003 when in 2006, a group of ex-Air France engineers managed to be the first to 'lower the nose'. This happened in France ahead of the UK due to the ownership differences post-retirement between BA and Air France. This Concorde had the dubious pleasure of being painted blue in a promotion with Pepsi Cola in 1996. This had the incidental effect of slowing the aircraft down, because its normal white colour helped keep the aircraft cool, whereas the dark blue meant it risked over-heating. Or the paint just burned off.

Concorde F-BVFF was undergoing maintenance at the time of the Paris crash in 2000 and never flew again. It had more than 12,000 flying hours and is now at Charles de Gaulle Airport in Paris, where it sits on some metal poles inside the airport perimeter, gradually rusting away (although the airport staff give it a wash down from time to time).

Concorde in the United States

In tribute to Concorde's stateside home, New York City hosts G-BOAD, the Concorde which flew from New York to London in 2 hours 52 minutes and 59 seconds. It was also the aircraft with the most flying hours, an amazing 23,397 hours. Now at the Intrepid Sea, Air and Space Museum in New York City, G-BOAD flew the London-Bahrain-Singapore route from 1979 to 1981, which probably accounts for its massive accumulation of hours.

G-BOAG entered service in 1980 and flew for British Airways until October 2003. It flew until October 2003 commercially. Its ferry flight to Seattle took place on 5th November 2003 where special clearance to fly supersonically over Canada after a refuel stop in New York had to be granted. It had a patchy life, being used for spare parts for some years before getting a refit and coming back into service. Today it lives at the Boeing Museum of Flight in Seattle (a major location for aviation history, given that Boeing started there) and is in excellent condition, according to the museum director.

The Smithsonian National Air and Space Museum in Chantilly, Virginia, has Air France Concorde F-BVFA, which took the airline's first Concorde passengers to Rio de Janeiro in 1976.

Germany

There is just one Concorde in Germany, housed at the Auto Technik Museum in Sinsheim. F-BVFB was built in Toulouse and is accessible to visitors, despite being mounted as though it is in flight. The unique thing about this museum is that it also has an example of the Tupolev Tu-144, the only other supersonic passenger jet to have entered commercial service.

Barbados

Another exceptionally well-used Concorde, G-BOAE ended up at the Grantley Adams International Airport in Bridgetown, Barbados, where it has a special hangar. It is considered that this Concorde is the most complete of the entire BA fleet, and is understood to have every single piece of cutlery and crockery in place. Her Majesty Queen Elizabeth II flew to Barbados on this Concorde in 1977. Although the centre has been closed to visitors since 2018, I had the priviliege of being invited by the CEO of Grantley Adams International Airport to visit this Concorde in January 2024 together with my dear friend, Ben Lord. She looks absolutely sensational and we're looking forward to working with Barbados to resume this Concorde as a tourist attraction where I was mindblown by how much love and adoration there is on the island amongst Barbadians.

The final curtain
In the end, the many forces that were keeping Concorde in the air, from its loyal fan base to the British and French national pride, the money that British Airways was making from its operation and the time it continued to save businesspeople, were not enough to save it from retirement.

Concorde was an expensive aircraft to operate and maintain. The high operating costs, including fuel and maintenance, made it challenging to operate profitably, especially for Air France, which had barely any profitable routes. Ticket prices were high compared with subsonic flights, limiting the number of passengers who could afford to fly on Concorde. With budget airlines like Ryanair and Easyjet flying all over Europe for as little as a few pounds, it made the prices seem even more exorbitant.

The aircraft had a relatively small operational range, compared with several wide-bodied jets such as Boeing 747s, 777s or Airbus A380s that could fly non-stop from London to Tokyo, Cape Town or Los Angeles. Concorde was limited to flying between major cities like London, Paris and New York which further limited its customer base.

Despite many efforts, nobody had managed to rid Concorde of its sonic boom, which meant that it couldn't fly over most populated areas of the world, once again restricting its operations and preventing it from linking many cities.

The crash of Air France Flight 4590 in July 2000 near Paris raised safety concerns about Concorde which never went away, despite modifications to its wheels and fuel tanks and a full investigation which showed that it was caused by a piece of debris on the runway that punctured one of the aircraft's tyres, leading to a catastrophic chain of events. Even though fault for the incident wasn't ascribed to Concorde, it had a lasting and most undeserving impact on the aircraft's reputation.

By the time Concorde retired, its fleet of aircraft had become quite old, with the earliest models entering service in the late 1960s. The cost of maintaining and upgrading these ageing aircraft became increasingly prohibitive. Airbus, which acquired Concorde manufacturer Aérospatiale in 2000, said in 2003 that it would no longer supply replacement parts for the aircraft, which was a significant blow to its future. The high-tech, advanced systems which Concorde introduced in the 1970s were no longer cutting edge in the 21st century. Part of the problem was that Concorde had little incentive to modernise, given that it had no competitors. Subsonic planes like the Boeing 747 were constantly challenged by rivals such as the Airbus A380 and invested in upgrades. With such a relatively small fleet, Concorde stuck with its existing systems, even though they were going out of date.

As the aviation industry evolved in the early 2000s, with newer, more efficient subsonic aircraft that could carry more passengers at lower costs, greater range and fuel efficiency, airlines and passengers began to vote with their wallets. Environmental concerns about the pollution and climate change caused by jet fuel meant that airlines were under pressure to reduce their CO_2 emissions. There was very little scope for Concorde to do this.

Finally, the September 11, 2001 terrorist attacks had a significant impact across the aviation industry, causing a sharp decline in air travel demand. This further reduced the already limited demand for Concorde flights at a time when it was already facing criticism on other levels. It's understood that Concorde lost 40 of its frequent customers in the 9/11 attacks.

Given all these factors, the two airlines operating Concorde services, Air France and British Airways, simultaneously announced the retirement of the Concorde fleet on 10th April 2003. While Concorde remains an iconic symbol of aviation history, its retirement was ultimately determined by Airbus exponentially inflating the product support costs in order for Concorde to have a certificate of airworthiness at a time where Air France intended to cease its Concorde operations leaving British Airways bearing all of those costs. When the news came through in 2003 that Concorde would be retired, there was a surge in interest from aviation enthusiasts and loyal customers. Airlines organised farewell flights that allowed passengers to experience Concorde one last time. These flights were highly sought-after and often sold out quickly. BA made £54 million net profit in the final six months following the retirement announcements. BA wanted to operate until Spring 2004 but Airbus wouldn't grant permission for it to fly to Barbados for one last winter season.

The final British Airways commercial flight took place on Friday 24 October 2003, carrying 100 passengers, including Piers Morgan, Jeremy Clarkson and Joan Collins – from New York to London. I had the pleasure of welcoming them all home while commentating for Sky News on that day. Five weeks later, on 26 November 2003, the very last flight of any Concorde – BA's G-BOAF 'Alpha Foxtrot' - landed at Filton Airfield near Bristol. It truly was the end of an era.

Concorde's legacy
At the height of the fierce debates over whether Britain should invest in Concorde in 1959, Sir Morien Morgan wrote a letter to the government urging it to go ahead with the project.

"We must emphasise that a decision not to start detailed work fairly soon on the transatlantic aircraft would be in effect to opt out of the long-range supersonic field. Since we would never regain a competitive position this could have a profound effect on the pattern of our aircraft industry and on our position as a leading aeronautical power."

It would take another 17 years before Concorde made its commercial debut, and Morgan kept making this point with consistent urgency all the way through. Although he died in 1978, Morgan did at least see Concorde through to completion. But did his vision of Britain as a 'leading aeronautical power', building on the heroics of the Battle of Britain and on Concorde itself come to pass?

In 2023, the UK has the world's second-largest aerospace industry, second only to the United States. It employs well over 100,000 people and the civil aerospace sector alone is worth £32 billion per year.

Rolls Royce is the world's second-largest maker of aero engines, with more than 13,000 engines in service globally; BAE Systems is the world's fourth-largest defence contractor. Airbus, Boeing, General Electric, Lockheed Martin and dozens of other corporations have major operations here.

Today, 40 per cent of all the small satellites orbiting the Earth were made in the UK and the industry says it wants to capture 10 per cent of the global space market by 2030. Drones are already big business for UK companies: in 2022, the world's first urban drone airport opened in Coventry, paving the way for autonomous air taxis. By 2030, drones could earn the UK an extra £45 billion a year and create 600,000 new jobs.

I think we can say that Sir Morien Morgan was right.

Chapter 3
My Childhood

On the 1st June 1942, as I approached my second birthday, Hitler paid a visit to my home. A fleet of 77 Luftwaffe aircraft flew over from Germany and dropped 40 tons of bombs on Canterbury, killing 43 people and destroying hundreds of buildings as part of the 'Baedeker' raids of historic English towns. Although one of the bombs flattened my aunt's house next door, there was no-one home at the time and I was safely in an air raid shelter in our garden.

Even though I was too young to be aware of this horror, I do have some fleeting memories of the Second World War. Later, my Mum and I lived in a basement flat in Leeds, where I remember meeting American airmen in a nearby Nissan hut. They offered me chocolates (which were at a premium because nobody had any) and were kind to me. I sat with them in the evenings and they'd tell me stories. I was probably aged four at the time.

Of course you don't think about it at the time, but could that experience have drawn me towards America, and flying?

Another distant memory is living in a house with a nice old man called Mr Diamond in Bradford during the War, who was a long-distance train driver and taught me about steam trains. And then one day a tram came off its rails coming down a hill next to Headingley Cricket Ground in Leeds. Nobody died, but it was a shocking sight. It actually ran somehow into the entrance of a stately home.

When I was five, after the War I was sent to live with my grandparents in Canterbury, Kent. There was a Mosquito plane, made out of wood, with two engines, reassembled in the old moat surrounding the city wall. My grandmother would hold me up so I could climb into the hole in the belly of the fuselage. I can still remember the smell of oil on leather. The Mosquito was the fastest propeller plane of the War. What an impression this made on me! The fastest plane in the skies!

Here again, you can see the start of something that would shape my life in later years.

These days, when I go back to Canterbury, it's a journey back into time. Not only into my family's history, but England's. There's an ancient feel to the city, with its Roman walls, its cathedral and castle, and the country's oldest church still in use – St Martin's, built in 597 where my mother is buried, alongside generations of Finns.

Funnily enough, when I visited St Martin's in 2011, Cannon Noel had retired. Noel introduced me to the vicar who asked me if I would do one of my talks about my life and career to his parishioners, since I was born and lived around the corner from the church. He then asked if had I thought where I was going to be buried? If I was going to be cremated, I was welcome to a spot along with my Mum in the churchyard. I am now planning to have a stone saying: "I started here, travels led me away, then I came back here."

I suppose because Canterbury is on the River Stour in a fertile part of England, with mild weather and plenty of materials for building, it was one of the earliest settlements in the country. Historians think it was occupied in prehistoric times, and there's certainly evidence of an iron age settlement, which the Romans took over in the 1st century.

Then, since it's not far from the coast and the nearest crossing to France, invaders and English armies would fortify it, develop towns and build churches. St Martin's was founded in 597 by St Augustine, who had been sent by the Pope to re-establish Christianity in Britain. He also built a monastery and Canterbury Cathedral – together, they now form a UNESCO heritage site.

I like to do little tours, starting at St Martin's Church in Canterbury on the Hythe, then taking the world's smallest public railway (built in 1920) down the coast to New Romney, and the Red Lion Inn at Snargate, which has been in the same family for over 100 years. It has no food, it's just a traditional English pub with unique games and the best pint of mild anywhere, just like it was during the Battle of Britain. It has welcomed visitors since the 1500s. Then Dungeness, one of the best places in the UK for fish and chips, with the fish usually caught the same day. And finally, the Mermaid Inn in Rye, East Sussex, which was rebuilt in 1420, with cellars dating to 1156. The Mermaid Inn provides accommodation in genuine Tudor rooms, a restaurant and a bar with one if not the biggest fireplaces in the UK. Visit here and you're following in the footsteps of Queen Elizabeth I who stayed here in 1573.

That part of Kent is criss-crossed with travellers' paths. The Danes pillaged across the countryside in the 9th century, William the Conqueror made his way through Kent in 1066, Chaucer published his account of pilgrims walking to Canterbury in 1387, Belgian weavers arrived in the 16th century, the railway arrived in 1830, the Luftwaffe in 1942 and an army of students descended on the town after the university was founded in 1962.

No wonder I developed a love of travel and adventure, with all these echoes of exploration, pilgrimages, battles and emigration.

By the mid-20th century, the travel routes that caught a young boy's attention were in the air rather than on the ground. I would cycle over to the airfield at Lympne, where I'd watch the Bristol Freighters of Silver City Airways taking off and landing on its grass runway.

They were big old planes, the 747s of the propeller world, with room enough to put cars in the hold. They'd fly passengers and their cars across the channel to Le Bourget in France for the handsome sum of seven shillings and sixpence. For a time, I had a carefree existence, cycling around the countryside, climbing apple and oak trees and getting as close as I could to these awe inspiring machines at the airfield. After pestering many times, I guess they wanted to get rid of me, so a very nice pilot who had a Tiger Moth plane with an open cockpit from the First World War agreed to give me a flight "OK, get in," he said and I jumped into the front seat, held in by nothing more than cloth straps. He took me up for a spin and did some stunts, turning us upside down, thinking it was just hilarious being a bit of a daredevil. And I loved it too – it was better than any fairground ride.

My grandfather was an ex-policeman who was also an adventurer. He'd cycle miles out into the countryside, well into his 50s and 60s. As far as I know, his family before him were tenant sheep farmers – there are more than a dozen Finn's in the graveyard at St Martin's Church in Canterbury. I remember him as a strict disciplinarian. He'd give me a taste of his stick if I did anything wrong when we went out on a walk and if the dog did anything wrong, he got the stick too.

If you tour Canterbury, the guide might point out where the 'public cage for talkative women' could be found in the 16th Century, next to the town pillory – where offenders would be locked so that the public could throw things at them. There was a ducking stool for the same purpose there too. Women didn't have such a nice time of it in those days.

The generations just before mine had enormous families: my mother was the youngest of 17 children! Her father ran a furniture shop in Canterbury, meaning that he was a minor local dignitary. He was a member of a Masonic Lodge and would go about his business in a pin-striped suit with a gold watch in his pocket. For years, I'd hear stories about my mother's siblings and my cousins – how one had emigrated to Singapore to become a hotel manager, then he became a missionary in Brazil. Another worked for Lotus Cars (very glamorous in my eyes!) and became a preacher in USA and another was a padre in the prison service: you can imagine the prayers before food was served in my auntie's house. There were so many of them, I suppose it opened my eyes to the possibilities of working overseas, of doing all kinds of different jobs, following your passion.

When I was nine years old, I began to find my father's strictness very tough. He was a schoolmaster and expected high grades from me, which didn't always happen. Whereas today you might hire a tutor to help a young boy who was struggling, his approach was to beat me when I didn't get my homework right. He'd hit me over the head and slap my ears, just because I couldn't work out fractions.

My mother was more sympathetic, but she couldn't do anything because my father dominated her completely, always making fun of her. I came to feel that she was almost held prisoner by him for decades. She wasn't allowed to drive or go out on her own. The only money she had was an allowance from him. Yet her self-worth was so low that she felt herself lucky to have him. I thought it was the other way around.

From the vantage point of more than 70 years, I now think I had a kind of breakdown at the age of 10. I simply couldn't cope with my father and how cruel he could be to me and this coincided with a bout of rheumatic fever. I was in bed for days. On one occasion I hit him back, punching him in the nose. Of course that didn't do me any favours. But it built up in me a fierce determination to escape as soon as I possibly could. Those planes down at Lympne Airfield seemed all the more attractive as a means of getting away. Or the enormous steam trains rattling towards London, or fast cars. Anything!

Occasionally I caught a glimpse of what lay beyond my life in Kent. At the age of 13 I went on a school trip to Belgium and Holland to see the tulip fields and tour Amsterdam. It was really my first taste of freedom and opened my eyes to the excitement of travel and adventure. The teachers in charge generously turned a blind eye to our furtive drinking and smoking. One schoolmaster in particular was very good for me. His name was Clifford Ball and I regarded him as more of a father than a teacher. We stayed in touch for many years and later I managed to arrange trips to Kenya for him.

In my early teens, my father moved jobs and began working at a grammar school in Windsor. We lived in nearby Feltham and from there it was a short bike ride to the London Flying School and the very early version of Heathrow, which had begun operations in 1946. In those days, security was very light so I'd crawl under a wire fence and sprint across the runway, dodging the airport police on their water-cooled Velocette motorbikes. I managed to sit in the flight decks of all kinds of aircraft and watch the engineers doing their maintenance work. It was a risky business. One time I was almost run over by a French Languedoc plane with three engines.

In my mid-teens, we moved down to Exmouth in Devon, where my father taught at another school. He was very well respected in the education business, not only in his school, where he was head of English, but more widely. He wrote something like 40 textbooks and collections of poetry and prose, so people thought very highly of him. You can still buy his books on Amazon today (look up Frederick E.S. Finn), some of them are more than 50 years old, which is pretty incredible. Most books disappear within a few years. He had a rare talent for understanding literature and explaining his passion to other people, something that a whole generation of students and teachers appreciated. When you think of all the stories of terrible families, happy families, warm relations and awful breakdowns between fathers and sons in literature, it seems crazy to me that he wasn't able to see the damage he was doing to his own family.

My aunties used to say to him: "Why are you jealous of your son?" I couldn't answer that question at the time and I can't now either. He was a successful teacher and celebrated author, why would he envy the life of an unacademic teenager? Maybe I represented something to do with freedom that he felt he had lost. Or else there was such an unbridgeable divide between school life, where children did as he said, and he was admired and respected, and home life where – like in just about every family in history – children can be unruly, difficult and disobedient. Did he think my lack of academic achievement reflected badly on him? Certainly he had a Jekyll and Hyde personality.

My friend Elaine, who lived just across the road from us, remembers him as an extremely well-liked schoolmaster. In later life she became a teacher herself and used his textbooks in her work. So it was a big surprise to Elaine, and other people at school, to find out what a different person he was at home. She remembers that, at school, my Dad was regarded as some kind of saint. But then she'd find that he'd locked me out of the house and I would come over to her place and ask if I could stay. This happened quite a few times. When I spoke with her recently, she recalled how different I seemed from most of the boys that she knew at the time. She thought I was a free spirit, who always wanted to try something different, something that nobody else had done. Always looking to move on.

For me, this was still a troubling time because of my relationship with my father. At least in Kent, he and I had shared an interest in cricket and would go to see matches together. When we got to Exmouth, he was so aggressive towards me – I think mainly because I wasn't academic like him and left school before taking A levels – that he purposefully prevented me playing cricket. He would tell the team captain that I wasn't available when they phoned me. Can you imagine how awful that was? The one thing that I really loved, and he was trying to undermine me?

Somehow, I managed to keep playing cricket and eventually won a place in the Somerset and Gloucestershire Second XI team, which was a paid role. My father never congratulated me or encouraged me. But it gave me a sense of possibility, that I could make a life for myself outside the family.

Elaine also remembers how I would get a brainwave and dash off to do a training course – I spent a few weeks in a Merchant Navy barracks – or apply for all kinds of jobs, at a grocer's shop called Liptons, working in Exeter… It's funny to hear her side of things, how appalled she was that a young boy could be locked out of his own house by his father. It does seem like child abuse, in retrospect.

Even in later life, once I'd been working for many years and established myself in a good career, my father and I never saw eye to eye. When I lived in America he and my mother came to visit, but he seemed very uneasy. I remember him pacing up and down outside the restaurant we had booked. When my mother was quite old, I took her to the United States for an operation. Then she died in 2003: she was suffering from oedema, then contracted MRSA, which was causing havoc in hospitals all over the country at the time. I took her ashes back to Canterbury, to be interred at St Martin's, where I plan to end my days.

When my father died, nobody even told me for quite some time. I didn't attend his funeral and wouldn't have wanted to. All he left me was a cheap watch and a bit of money to repay my mother's medical trip to the States. I sold the watch and left his memory behind me. My sister Joan was much closer to my father being four years younger than me. We see each other every so often and I enjoy these visits to Exmouth now to see my family.

If there was one good thing that came out of my relationship with my father, it was that I survived his hostility, his aggression, his anger. I realised that I had to stand on my own feet and make something of myself, without any help from him. It reminds me today of my friend Johnny Cash's song 'A Boy Named Sue.'

When I look back at the Devon part of my childhood, I remember Exmouth as quite a small town, and it still is. There were about 26,000 people there in the 1950s and today there are 35,000. It's a pretty little place, just around 10 miles downstream from Exeter and (as the name suggests) at the mouth of the River Exe. There are some lovely beaches nearby, like Budleigh Salterton and Sandy Bay. People come from all over the country to spend their summers here, as they have done since the 19th century when the train first arrived. In the 1950s, barely anyone took holidays overseas. The South West of England was the most popular place in the country to visit in the summer.

But for a teenager, holiday resorts are never that much fun, especially in the winter. So I was in a hurry to leave. The Merchant Navy gave me a job and that was my passport to travel.

A world of possibility

When the 1950s dawned, I was about to turn 10 years old. Unhappy at home, I dreamed of travel, planes, trains and automobiles, foreign countries, adventures.

For a young boy, there was plenty of material to feed these dreams. The Festival of Britain in 1951 presented a futuristic blossoming for the country, as it recovered from the ravages of World War II, incomes rose and people's options multiplied. The Festival, timed to be 100 years on from the Great Exhibition of 1851, featured the Skylon sculpture, which shot 300 feet up into the air on London's South Bank, like a frozen rocket headed for the moon.

In 1952, HM King George VI died and there was a further burst of optimism and possibility with the accession of HM Queen Elizabeth II at the age of 25. So young, so beautiful, so adventurous! She famously received the news of her father's death while staying on safari in Kenya. These details held such meaning for an 11-year-old boy – Kenya must be some kind of paradise to attract British royalty. I think my later fascination with and love for Kenya stems from this early impression.

When HM Queen Elizabeth II was crowned on 2 June 1953, it coincided with three events that struck a chord with me: the launch of the DH.106 Comet – the world's first commercial jet airliner – the ascent of Everest by Edmund Hillary and Tenzing Norgay, and the publication of Ian Fleming's first James Bond book, Casino Royale. At that time, Fleming lived in St Margaret's, just a few miles from Canterbury – something I probably didn't know as a child, but it makes sense that his works were popular there, just as they became worldwide.

If you combine these three things: making it possible for regular passengers to travel by jet; pioneering a new human achievement by going as high as it's possible to go on dry land; and launching a new fictional hero on the world, you can see how exciting it could be for a young boy. What possibilities were opening up. The sky was literally the limit.

Soon there was more: Roger Bannister ran the first sub-four-minute mile in 1954, once again showing that Britain was the best! Closer to home, rationing for petrol, meat and sugar finally ended, nine years after the end of the war. Now the post-War era could really begin. In the remainder of the 1950s Britain gained its first motorway (a bypass around Preston in Lancashire, which became the M6), the Mini was first seen on British roads, helping to bring affordable motoring to a wider public, and television ownership had jumped to 57 per cent of the country, from just 2 per cent in 1950.

Like my family, most British people didn't travel far from home, if at all. Only one in 14 families went overseas for their holidays and only just over half made any kind of trip. Even so, the seeds of long distance flights were germinating in the 1950s. Whereas at the start of the decade, there was only one class on passenger aircraft, from May 1952 a 'Tourist class' fare was introduced, at around two-thirds of the regular price, on routes across the Atlantic. This helped to put the journey into more people's budgets, but only just. It still cost the equivalent of more than £3,000 in today's money for a return fare, instead of £4,500.

Pan Am was among the early adopters of this deal, in which passengers had to buy their own lunches and weren't served alcoholic drinks – even if they offered to pay for them. No boozing for the common people! (BOAC was more generous. It offered a full four-course meal included in its tourist fare). Despite the high prices, these flights became hugely popular and by 1957 more than two-thirds of all air travel was made up of 'tourists'.

The first scheduled passenger jet flights across the Atlantic set off on 4 October 1958 in DH.106 Comets – one flying from Idlewild in New York to London and the other going west, from Heathrow to New York. In this case, there weren't any tourist class seats, with passengers having to fork out the equivalent of more than £10,000 for their First Class and Deluxe tickets.

When I read about these early flights today, it makes me realise how strong an impression it must have made on me. One flight attendant on the BOAC service to New York gave an interview to The Independent newspaper in 2018, where she remembered: "It was marvellous. We were used to travelling to New York on Boeing Stratocruisers which took up to 20 hours. We couldn't believe flight was possible in such a short time. There were all sorts of dignitaries on board, press and the chairman of BOAC. It was a thrilling experience. We served customers Madeira biscuits and coffee when they came onboard, followed by cocktails and canapes, and then a five-course lunch with wines. Passengers ate and drank from when they got on board until the time they got off."

This is such a close relation of the Concorde experience – just 20 years earlier and taking twice as long (these first trips took six hours 20 minutes). I recognise all of those feelings, all the excitement, the disbelief, the luxury. It seems amazing in retrospect that this was all developing next door to where I lived as a teenager, near to Heathrow, passing over my head as I cycled to and from the airport, filled with curiosity and hankering for adventure.

It seems funny to think of it now, but in the 1950s, air travel had a lot more risk attached to it. The Comet, while it became a popular plane by the end of the decade, had a terrible time in 1953/54, when it suffered three crashes within a year. First, a BOAC de Havilland Comet took off from Calcutta in India on 2 May 1953, hit some bad weather and disintegrated, with the death of all 43 passengers and crew on board. Then in January 1954 another BOAC Comet with 35 on board, flying from Singapore to London, suffered an explosive decompression and fell into the sea near the Italian island of Elba. Finally, yet another BOAC flight, this time from London to South Africa, crashed in similar circumstances. Wisely, de Havilland took the Comet out of commission and redesigned it.

It wasn't just passenger planes that caused problems. On 6 September 1952, when I was 12 years old, a de Havilland DH.110 fighter jet disintegrated during a display at Farnborough Air Show, killing not only the pilot and test flight observer on board, but 29 people in the crowd below, hit by falling debris. A further 60 people were taken to hospital. If this is what happened to planes that were supposedly at the top end of the military's engineering expertise, how safe could the public feel in any old passenger plane? A gust of wind seemed to be able to bring down some of these aircraft.

Stories like this one gave the whole population a taste of the danger inherent in flying. They're terrible accidents and you can imagine how scared people become. But when someone well-known dies in a plane crash, it takes the level of horror up to a new level.

In 1958, just as I was beginning to seek out ways to escape my problematic home life and travel the world, three big air crash stories dominated the news headlines. The first came on 6 February 1958 when a British European Airways Airspeed Ambassador plane carrying the Manchester United football team, its staff and some journalists, crashed during an attempted take-off at Munich Airport after playing Red Star Belgrade in the European Cup quarter finals. Twenty people died at the scene and three more later.

This was a national tragedy of enormous proportions. How could almost a whole football team, the best in the country, be wiped out in a plane crash? In the aftermath of the disaster, some people thought that it was slush on the runway that caused the problems – something that a small snow plough should have been able to sort out in a couple of hours – but I think that ice on the flaps was a more likely cause. A plane can't take off if these don't work.

From the most famous sportsmen of the age, to one of the world's great actresses. Elizabeth Taylor was pure box office. Her movie Cat on a Hot Tin Roof was among the biggest hits of 1958. Yet on 22 March of that year, she came within a cat's whisker of death, when the twin-engine Lockheed Lodestar she was meant to be flying on crashed in New Mexico, killing her husband Mike Todd and three others on board. It was only a heavy cold that had kept Taylor from making the flight. An investigation found that the aircraft was overloaded, it was flying in icy conditions at too high an altitude and it suffered engine failure. You have to wonder how some of these planes ever got off the ground!

The final disaster of this trio came on 3 February 1959, when American pop legends Buddy Holly and Ritchie Valens, along with another singer J.P. Richardson and their pilot died when their Beechcraft Bonanza light aircraft crashed into a cornfield in Iowa, en route to Minnesota. Once again, poor weather was a big factor, with light snow, heavy winds and poor visibility. Other passengers had pulled out, having been warned about the conditions, but Buddy Holly and his friends went ahead anyway.

Whenever I hear the Don McLean song American Pie, written about this crash, I think back to my teens and how these early flights could send a shiver up the world's spine, just thinking about getting into an aircraft. In the 1950s and 1960s, US airlines each had five or six crashes a year, most of them fatal to all on board.

Even when their flights landed safely, for a lot of people, flying in the 1950s was a miserable affair. Because many of the aircraft were unpressurised, they couldn't fly above 12,000 feet. This, in turn, meant they couldn't avoid bad weather simply by going higher. Today, it's rare to see anyone using an air sickness bag. In those days, it was a common sight, as they flew through far more turbulence than we'd expect today.

The space race

Instead of German bombers and missiles flying overhead, by the time I was 17 there was another kind of object whizzing through the skies above my home in Devon. The USSR launched Sputnik, the first man-made object in space, on 4 October 1957, sparking what was to become a decades-long contest between them and the United States to put satellites, people and all kinds of technology up into space.

Even as a small kid, I had been vaguely aware of how important it was that we somehow made it into space. The Eagle comic launched in April 1950, when I was 10, with its main character Dan Dare, the 'pilot of the future'. It sold 900,000 copies and made a generation of kids like me into instant fans of space travel. At the weekends, we'd go to the cinema and pay 6 pence – the equivalent of 2 and a half pence today – to see films about Flash Gordon, another spaceman who travelled the galaxies.

Kids in the USSR and America were devouring the same kinds of comics and dreaming of the day when we could board a rocket to Mars or take our hovering saucer-shaped personal planes for a spin through the cities of tomorrow. We all assumed that these advances would arrive pretty soon. After all, Germany had managed to invent bombs that could cross Europe and America had invented the H-bomb, powerful enough to destroy major cities. The era of space travel was surely just a few years away.

Although Russia had quickly taken advantage of the post-War political vacuum to move into Eastern Europe and expand the USSR, nobody in the West considered Russia to have as advanced a scientific capacity as America. Nor did the Russians make much noise about their plans. I discovered more recently that they were worried that America would steal its secrets, or that any failures would be highlighted by the West, to denigrate it. But the USSR was making bigger strides in space technology than anyone knew.

When Sputnik launched, it caused an immediate sensation. It "shattered the perception created by American propaganda of the United States as the technological superpower, and the Soviet Union as a backward country," as the New York Times put it. What made it feel very immediate and almost threatening was that amateur radio enthusiasts could pick up the 'beep…beep… beep' transmitted by Sputnik – which translates as 'traveller' or 'companion' in Russian - as it passed overhead once every hour and a half. This "thrilled and terrified" listeners, the American media reported. "As a result of great, intense work of scientific institutes and design bureaus the first artificial Earth satellite has been built," announced the USSR's official media network, TASS.

As a teenager, it thrilled me to think that, for the first time in history, the human race had managed to shoot something that far into the sky, and that the laws of nature meant that it just stayed there, circling for months on end, as though it had become a new kind of moon. I wanted to find out as much as I could.

Sputnik was dreamed up by the Chief Soviet Rocket Scientist Sergei Korolev in 1954. He persuaded the USSR's Minister of the Defence Industry Dimitri Ustinov to fund an orbital satellite project, building on the achievements in rocket technology that the German military had made during World War II. First, they had to build a rocket powerful enough to launch the satellite – and they called it R7. Then, they formed a committee of four industrial Ministries (Defence, Radio Technology, Ship Building and Machine Building), along with the USSR Academy of Scientists. They decided that Sputnik should try to collect information about the density of the atmosphere, solar wind, magnetic fields and cosmic rays.

These were all phrases out of the pages of the Eagle comic, as distant and mysterious to me as fairy dust and unicorns, but they only served to intensify my fascination with Sputnik and the Soviet programme. For the Americans, Sputnik caused an immediate reaction. President Dwight Eisenhower poured money into the US space programme in a desperate attempt to catch up, but in December 1957, the first American satellite attempt ended in disaster when Vanguard exploded on the launch pad. Not only was America falling behind in the space race, its technology was a conspicuous failure.

Fortunately for American pride, it didn't take long for its boffins to solve the problem and complete a successful launch, in January 1958 – this time called Explorer, a satellite that went further into space than Sputnik had. Take that, Soviets! But then the USSR launched a second Sputnik and the race went on.

Because these rockets could not only launch satellites but missiles, there was always an edge of danger to the competition. Soviet leader Nikita Krushchev boasted to the world about how many Intercontinental Ballistic Missiles his country owned, so American felt it had to respond and build even more. It wasn't just a race to conquer space, but to potentially wipe out a whole country, if not the human race.

Besides these build-ups of technology and weaponry, Sputnik's launch spurred the US to create the Advanced Research Projects Agency (ARPA, which later became DARPA, with 'Defense' added at the front) in February 1958, followed in October of the same year by the National Aeronautics and

Space Administration (NASA). In the final couple of years of the 1950s, these dramatic developments had a limited impact on the space race. The US did manage to broadcast a human voice from space – President Eisenhower sending a Christmas message – and take the first pictures of Earth from space, but the Soviets responded by sending an unmanned spacecraft to the moon, landing it in September 1959 and then sending another which orbited the moon in October. Significant parts of the Soviet space program took place in Ukraine, by the way, as well as the development of the Soviet Antonov aircraft.

Even though the USSR put the first man into space, when Yuri Gagarin made a single orbit around Earth in April 1961, the United States slowly but surely pulled away from the Soviets in terms of funding, expertise and achievements, coming to dominate the field in the 1960s, especially once President John F Kennedy had issued his famous challenge to the nation, to put a man on the moon. In the United States, as in Britain, there was a new mood of determination to figure out how things worked. Schools on both sides of the Atlantic introduced more science and technology teaching. There were government incentives for innovation and design.

For me, all this astronomical development just served as inspiration and motivation at a time when I was hankering to leave home and travel. Maybe one day I could fly at the kind of speeds that I was reading about, way up above the clouds, where I could see the circumference of the earth and stare out into the inky black universe...

Breaking the speed of sound

There are some events in history which make a huge impression on a child. For me, one of the biggest was the news that US Air Force pilot Chuck Yeager had broken the speed of sound, flying his Bell X-1 rocket-propelled plane at 700 miles per hour above the Rogers Dry Lake in California, the first manned flight to reach this extraordinary milestone.

I was seven years old at the time, and the idea of travelling at 700 miles per hour seemed completely out of this world. During the War, which had only ended two years earlier, there was a national speed limit for cars of 35 miles per hour. It was almost impossible to imagine travelling 20 times as fast as this, even with a rocket attached to your plane. I wasn't the only one who found this feat incredible. Scientists warned that supersonic flight was impossible, because an invisible force would destroy any aircraft that attempted it.

What also captured my imagination was the difficulties that Yeager and his team had to overcome and the risks they took. On their first attempts, the X-1 had encountered terrible buffeting when it approached the speed of sound, so Yeager had abandoned the flights. Back on the ground, his team of engineers adjusted the aircraft's stabiliser, so that he could make small changes to the angle of attack, which helped smooth out the airflow around the plane. It was constructed with extremely thin, strong wings and a horizontal stabiliser that could be adjusted in tiny increments, to overcome extreme aerodynamic forces.

Does this description remind you of another long thin aircraft that would come along a couple of decades later?

Then on October 14th, 1947, on its ninth powered flight, the X-1 edged up from Mach .965 to Mach 1.06, finally breaking the speed of sound and putting Yeager into the record books. From the moment his plane left the Boeing B-29 bomber, which flew it for 30 minutes up to 20,000 feet, to the moment it touched down on the lakebed, the flight lasted just 14 minutes. But it was a record-breaking, historic 14 minutes which stayed with me for a long time.

Yeager became one of my childhood heroes. He was already a big name in America, after a fantastically successful wartime record where he won 11 air battles and became the Air Force's most experienced test pilot. When I read about how he instinctively understood machines and could describe how an aircraft felt at speed, helping his engineers to improve the technology, I was starstruck!

The pioneering efforts of Yeager and his team, and the performance of the Bell X-1 in 1947 were a hugely important step forward in the journey towards supersonic civilian flight. Without his bravery and expertise, Concorde might never have flown at all.

Chapter 4
Starting Work

Going out into the world as a young man with few qualifications was tough at first. I'd grown up in a part of Kent where many of the neighbours were sales representatives, who lived in nice houses and drove nice cars. So this gave me an idea of it being a good career.

But like many young people, I was caught in a catch 22 of applying for work and being told I needed experience. But how could I get experience until someone gave me a job? Undaunted, I worked in grocers' shops, for a decorators' business, in an electrical supplies shop, all the time applying for sales jobs with various companies. I really just wanted to try out something new, nothing I tried was what I felt right about, my life was only about cricket then.

There were a few false starts. I spent a few days in Glasgow on a trial for a sales position. But they didn't offer me a job because (they said) 'You're no good with people'. Then I found a job in Bristol, but had a terrible bout of flu on the day I was supposed to start work, I was told by the manager that if I didn't come in I didn't need to start work at all. I did go in to tell the manager Victor that he could stuff his job. Many years later the role was reversed, but that's for later in my story.

To get around, I bought a 1934 Austin Seven Ruby one owner for £25, after passing my driving test on my 18th birthday, thanks to the tolerance of the aptly-named Mr Passmore. He had a reputation as a grumpy old man, but I suppose my years of driving around on parade grounds and private roads was enough to convince him. And coincidentally, his daughter was friends with my girlfriend at the time.

In my late teens, I decided to sign up for my first voyage, from Exmouth docks over to Cork in Ireland on a flat-bottomed boat which pitched and rolled all the way over, leaving me sick as a dog for three days.

The trip was with the company F T Everard, one of Britain's largest merchant fleets with a history going back to the 1880s, when Frederick T Everard started building and renovating sailing barges on the Thames. The company's vessels took part in both World Wars, ferrying people away from Dunkirk and taking refugees from St Helier in the Channel Islands just before the Germans invaded.

Over the years, it had a fleet of more than 450 sailing, steam and motor ships, together with tugs and harbour craft.

Three days of misery was enough for me, however. So, I took a train across Ireland and an overnight ferry from Rosslare to Fishguard, then back to Exmouth to plot my next escape.

I did a Merchant Navy training course, which was based in Aldershot, in Hampshire. I stayed there for six weeks and enjoyed it. Heading to London armed with a 'Seaman's Discharge Book', which gave me visa-free travel, I went to Esso's offices in Thames House North in London, across from Lambeth Bridge, and applied to work with them. They said yes.

This job was the first that I really settled into. I stayed with Esso for four years, working my way up the Merchant Navy hierarchy from deck boy to Navigator and Officer of the Watch, after taking my Second Mate's certificate. The trips would last anywhere from four to six months, taking me all over the world: all along the Eastern Seaboard of the United States, to the Caribbean and Venezuela.

One thing that particularly stood out from this time was my first commercial flight. Esso wanted me to join a ship in New Jersey, so they flew me from Blackbushe (now a private airport, sitting in between Heathrow Airport and the town of Basingstoke on the A30 main road). From here, I took a four-engine propeller-driven Douglas DC4b to Prestwick in Scotland, then Keflavik in Iceland and Bangor in Maine, United States. Then there was a final leg to Idlewild in New York, the airport which became John F Kennedy International Airport in December 1963, in memory of the assassinated President Kennedy.

The whole journey took 19 hours and was completely eye-opening to me. OK, it wasn't the space race experience of Yuri Gagarin or Chuck Yeager, but it was about as adventurous as British people could get in civil aviation terms. Touching down at Idlewild, I felt a sense of destiny. This was the New World, the land of possibility. I was only a few years out of school – my whole life was in front of me and here was a chance to make something of myself.

This feeling grew even stronger on a later trip, when I went ashore with three shipmates at Mattituck on Long Island, New York state. Somehow, we missed the ship's departure and ended up marooned on Long Island for three weeks before we could get back on board. Even though the local police gave us stern warnings about how we would be in big trouble, Esso was fine about it. The company paid for our lodging and food and nobody really said anything about it afterwards.

After all it wasn't our fault, the ship sailed earlier than expected. But it planted a seed in my mind of where and how I wanted to live. In a nutshell, I fell in love with America and the way of life over there.

Once I'd finished a trip with Esso, I'd return home and wait for a telegram from the Post Office boy giving me instructions for my next journey. This was a nice routine, spending half of my life on the West side of the Atlantic, visiting new places, meeting new people and progressing up the Esso chain of seniority. In fact, there was always plenty of spare time during the voyages, so I took the opportunity to study marketing and international law – subjects that I figured would help me find a good sales job in future.

Having earned the right to sail as a Quartermaster, I could now find work with a whole new range of companies. This led to long sea voyages with P&O and with City Line, where I had a chance to visit Australia, South Africa, Canada and many other far-flung places. Docking one time in Montreal, Canada, I met a young Canadian singer called Paul Anka, who was barely out of his teens at the time. We chatted for a while, then he went his way and I went mine. (He later wrote the hit My Way, recorded by Frank Sinatra, Elvis Presley and many more).

Leaving Southampton for Australia in 1962, we made several stops during the month-long voyage, including the Suez Canal, where I was fortunate to take the controls at one point as we steered through the narrow passage. We were on an old steam turbine ocean liner called SS Stratheden, built in 1937, which had taken passengers from Britain to Australia for three years before serving as a troop ship during World War II. She mostly ferried soldiers to and from Britain and the Far East, with a couple of trips to the Caribbean and Canada. By the time I served on Stratheden, she had been taken over by P&O and refitted as an ocean liner for 1,200 passengers, sailing once more from Southampton to Australia.

On another trip, I visited Cape Town in South Africa on the Pendennis Castle. This was a Royal Mail Ship, with both passengers and cargo, operated by the Union-Castle Line. She was built in 1955 by Harland and Wolff to replace the old Arundel Castle and came into service on the UK to South Africa route in

1959, sailing from Southampton to Las Palmas in the Canaries, then on to Cape Town and round the cape to Port Elizabeth, East London and Durban, delivering mail. I was Quartermaster for this trip and very much enjoyed sailing on the Pendennis Castle, with its magnificent magenta colour – the corporate signature of Union-Castle.

In its time, the Pendennis Castle was a tiny bit similar to Concorde. It slimmed down the voyage time from Southampton to Cape Town from 13 to 11 days and set a record time for a Union-Castle vessel on the route. It also had high standards: air conditioning and private showers in the first-class cabins, and a new breed of female staff known as the 'stewardettes', who made life more entertaining for the guests, particularly the younger ones. The 1960s, when I was sailing, were the heyday of this kind of travel. Air transport was so expensive and infrequent that far more people travelled by sea outside Europe. These weren't the cruise liners of today: people weren't so much on holiday as getting somewhere for work, to relocate or visit relatives. It's a lost form of transport now. But at the time, the companies took great pride in offering high quality service, sailing faster than their rivals and making life as pleasant as possible for passengers. Sadly, the oil crisis of the early 1970s together with increasing air travel and containerisation of cargo meant that ships like the Pendennis Castle were no longer viable. She retired from service in 1976 and was scrapped in Taiwan in 1980.

By 1966 I started work for a paint distribution business, selling mostly to wholesalers, when I had a call from a guy called Harry Lapidus. He and I knew one another from some business trips to Jersey, where he owned a string of hotels, and from playing cricket out there. He was keen to lure me over to Jersey full time, to play in the local team, so he offered me a job running one of his hotels.

Harry was a shrewd and energetic businessman. He'd managed to buy one hotel, then remortgage it to buy another, then another, until in the end he had 17 hotels. The place he hired me to manage was Maison Victor Hugo in Grève d'Azette in the St Clement district of St Helier, the capital (and basically the only town) of Jersey. St Clement has wide sandy beaches and an old tower at Le Hocq. The town gets really packed in summer with tourists, though there's not much going on in the winter.

I soon discovered that Maison Victor Hugo was very popular with visiting rugby teams. They would turn up for the weekend and create all kinds of havoc. I remember seeing mattresses floating away in the sea. It was my job to meet them on arrival at the hotel and let them know, before anything else, that they would be paying for any damage before they left Jersey.

In between my work at the hotel, I played a good deal of cricket over in Jersey. Sussex County Cricket team were regular visitors. They used to stay next door; however, my great friend John Snow would bring his team mates over to my hotel much to the annoyance of the hotel where they stayed. There was a well-kept ground just along from Maison Victor Hugo in a sports complex called FB Fields, named after Florence Boot, the Jersey-born wife of Jesse Boot, the first Baron Trent. Boot's father founded Boots the Chemist and then Jesse built it from 10 stores in the East Midlands into a national retailer with more than 500 stores. He sold the business in 1920 then died in Jersey in 1931 after donating money to establish the Fields and a magnificent pavilion for the cricket pitch.

Maison Victor Hugo was thriving, so I needed an assistant. A chap named Ernie wrote to me from England saying that he'd worked in the entertainment industry and could do this and that. So I took him on, and in all fairness, he did a pretty good job. The trouble was that, after Ernie had been at the hotel for a few months, I fell ill on my holiday: I had a terrible virus and couldn't return to Jersey for a while. This holiday left Ernie with the temporary licence until I got back. In my absence, Ernie took the reins of running the hotel and began spreading rumours to David Lapidus (Harry's son) that I wasn't interested in returning, which was certainly not true. The upshot was that Ernie was appointed manager and I was out. In the end it turned out to be a great favour.

Given that it was David Lapidus's decision, I can't really blame Ernie for what happened. He took advantage of the situation and good luck to him. What upset me most, funnily enough, was that I had a lovely Alsatian dog at Maison Victor Hugo called Sabre. I had to leave him on Jersey and never saw him again. I did see Harry again, many years later, when I was giving a lecture on the QE2 ocean liner and he was a passenger, travelling with a 20-year-old wife and their baby. We had a chat and he said he was thinking of moving to Florida, so I recommended that he try Palm Beach. And I had the chance to explain to him the circumstances - we were still good friends.

After the disappointing end to my Jersey adventure, I was looking for new opportunities and had a call from a guy named John Dix, who I'd met while working in Jersey. He offered me a job at the Pair of Shoes nightclub and casino in Mayfair, central London, as a car parking jockey. Basically this meant parking clients' cars each evening. Now one of the unwritten rules of the club was that the 'door' belonged to the doorman – in other words, whatever tips or extras were earned on the door were kept by the doorman. So for every car that I parked, I would hand over payments to the doorman, whose hand was outstretched as soon as I returned from parking the car. Then at the end of the night, he would share the proceeds out evenly between us.

Even though it was a pretty lowly position, the money I made from simply parking cars could be fantastic – as much as £100 a night, which in 1968 was a huge sum, the equivalent of more than £2,000 today. I do remember seeing many well-known people coming into the Pair of Shoes, and apparently it was a favourite hangout for all kinds of movie stars. There are pictures of Charlotte Rampling at a roulette table, and reports that Sophia Loren, Ursula Andress and many others would flock there when in London. The actor Telly Savalas would be there, playing backgammon with Omar Sharif. "If my wife shows up, tell her I'm not here," he instructed me. Much later, I bumped into Savalas in South Africa on a cricket tour, when he was playing in a celebrity golf tournament.

These were the days when stars and wealthy British aristocrats enjoyed the thrill and danger of associating with gangsters, whether in the United States, where Frank Sinatra was infamous for the company he kept, or in London, where Barbara Windsor married the convicted criminal and nightclub owner Ronnie Knight. Many of London's nightclubs had dodgy owners, none more so than El Morocco, bought by the notorious Kray twins in the mid-1960s. Barbara Windsor and Ronnie Knight were regulars.

Little did I suspect but the Pair of Shoes had a starring role in this carousel of crime. Just before I started working there, a meeting took place in Wimbledon, southwest London, between American kingpins from Las Vegas including Benny Huntman, Dino Cellini, Meyer Lansky, Angelo Bruno, Charlie the Blade, together with representatives of gangster groups from across Europe. They concocted a plan to bring planeloads of American gamblers to London, where they would bet on the roulette tables of the Pair of Shoes, the Colony Club and elsewhere, while staying at the Dorchester hotel. Everyone concerned would make a huge amount of money out of these rich but foolish Americans.

"Every minute of the way, there was a profit to be made," said Mark Sykes, who worked for the owner of the Pair of Shoes, Eric Steiner. Sykes was an aristocratic chancer who enjoyed the buzz of celebrity nightlife. He had many colourful stories about Steiner and the Pair of Shoes. "It was an amiable environment," he recalled. "Eric organised what he called the junket for high rollers from Las Vegas who were flown over to London and stayed for a week at the Dorchester, all expenses paid. It was a staggering business. It was wonderful," said Sykes. "All these people would come over and they all took over the floor of our casino. They would open big lines of credit each and the gangster guy at the other end would guarantee this money. We were paid everything within two weeks. Tremendously efficient, the Americans."

Sykes remembered the Pair of Shoes owner Eric Steiner as being "absolutely nuts" but with impeccable taste. He would wear alligator skin shoes, drive a 1959 sky blue Ford Thunderbird car (like Sinatra) and typically have a model on each arm, taking them to London's most exclusive shops to buy a new pair of shoes. "That was part of his patter," said Sykes. Steiner was originally Swedish and had built up a reputation cruising around Southern California living on the earnings from playing poker. In London, he'd borrowed the money to buy the Pair of Shoes from Charlie Matthews, an Irish gypsy bookmaker. "Afterwards, he wouldn't let Charlie into the club because he said he was too rough for the place," said Sykes. "I soon understood what a complete lunatic he was. He was terrified of being kidnapped and had two ferocious looking Alsatian dogs, Lucky and Gangster." I should have asked him to let me have one of them.

Sykes thinks that most of the staff at the Pair of Shoes were stealing from him, and that Steiner knew it. "When anybody is an out and out thief, they always think that everybody else is thieving from them," he pointed out. Eric apparently installed a sophisticated eavesdropping system all around the club, so he could hear what the dealers were saying while he lay on his bed in the apartment upstairs. But Sykes reckoned that the dealers knew this and would prank Steiner by saying something outrageous, just to see him charge downstairs in his pyjamas to find out what was happening. "Crazy as he was, he made it work," said Sykes. "It was an elegant club. It was small, but it was very elegant." Steiner would always find out which stars were in town and send them a bunch of red roses, with an invitation to come to the club.

From the Pair of Shoes, I moved on to the Penthouse club and casino in Shepherd Market, Mayfair, owned by Bob Guccione, the American owner of Penthouse magazine. At least Guccione owned the Club, but franchised the casino to a syndicate which also owned the Pair of Shoes. Guccione had a string of casinos in the States, including one in Atlantic City, which he built for $15 million. Like many nightclub and casino bosses, he had running battles with the authorities over licensing and permits. In one legal case, Federal law enforcement agencies accused him of doing deals with an associate of Angelo Bruno – one of the mob bosses who gathered in Wimbledon in 1966. "We don't investigate people we buy property from," responded Guccione's lawyer.

In London, Guccione had similar troubles with the UK authorities, especially following the 1968 British gaming-control legislation, which aimed to stop organised crime infiltrating the casino business. That actually sounds quite naïve – the whole casino business was based on organised crime, as far as I could work out! Guccione opened the Penthouse casino in the late 1960s in Whitehorse Street, between Shepherd Market and Piccadilly. This was where I started off as a car jockey, but was soon promoted to Maitre d', welcoming guests to the restaurant, bar and casino. Trouble eventually erupted when the Commissioner of the Metropolitan Police alleged that both the Pair of Shoes and the Penthouse Club had violated a rule that guests had to wait for 48 hours after joining a casino before they could gamble. The New York Times covered this story, reporting that Guccione felt that the "real reason" for closing down the casino was the junkets arranged by American travel agencies. "The board contended that some junketeers extended credit to players and resorted to strong-arm tactics, with the aid of organised crime, to recover their investment." This was exactly what Mark Sykes had described at the Pair of Shoes. Guccione responded that anything amiss was the responsibility of the manager of the Penthouse casino (fortunately not the Maitre d'), not his fault of that of Penthouse International.

In any case, by the time this dispute was resolved, I'd met one of the Penthouse Club's regulars, a Canadian guy called Steve Herchoff. "You're wasting your life here," he told me. "Come over to Canada." I thought: "Why not?"

I later became a life member of the Penthouse Club by giving up my seat on Concorde to Bob Guccione and sitting in the flight deck.

Chapter 5
The New World

With just a business card in my pocket and a head full of dreams, I boarded a flight to New York in the middle of November on British Caledonian, arriving in the middle of a snowstorm.

"Who's this?" asked Steve Herchoff on the phone in Toronto.

"It's Fred, Fred Finn."

"Are you in London?"

"No, I'm actually in New York and I've taken you up on your kind offer to come to Canada."

I think Steve was a bit surprised to find a Brit behaving more like an American and acting on impulse like this, flying half-way around the world after a chance conversation. But he straight away offered me a place to stay and my North American adventure began!

I flew on American Airlines into Toronto Airport and Steve picked me up, taking me back to his vast mansion in St John's, just outside Toronto, where he lived with his wife, a former Miss Australia, and daughter. This was a pleasant introduction to Canada, giving me a couple of weeks to catch my breath and get used to the environment. After that, I found a room in a Swedish couple's house and started looking for work.

First off, I repeated my progression from parking jockey to Maitre D' at the Four Seasons 'Inn on the Park' in Toronto, with the main difference being that the temperature was minus 30 degrees. Welcome to Canada! Before long I met the general manager of the Holiday Inn, Ontario, who asked me to go and work for him as full-time food and beverage manager. This felt like a step in the right direction, meaning I could draw on my experiences as a hotel manager in Jersey and working in hospitality in London.

Things were going really well at the Holiday Inn, especially in the bar, where I succeeded in packing out the place in the evenings, partly thanks to a policy of hiring great looking staff. Sadly, the finance director of the hotel picked a fight with me and started telling me how to run my side of the operation. I told him to stick to the accounts – which were very healthy, thanks to my efforts – but the hotel manager took his side, so I headed back to Toronto and onto the next endeavour, briefly working for Dictaphone, recording messages on a tape machine (not my cup of tea).

Once again, Steve Herchoff came to my rescue. This time, we came up with a novel idea. Instead of buying a separate car to use commercially, tradesmen and other small business owners could buy a magnetic sign to stick to the side of their vehicles, transforming it into a moving advertisement and corporate branding. Then they could simply take it off in the evening, saving the expense of signwriting and all the other costs of a second car. (If only we'd patented this design – the royalties would have been worth having!)

I was so confident of this plan that I flew back to the UK one Friday evening on an overnight flight, hopped out of the plane on Saturday morning and walked down Staines High Street in West London, into a butcher's, a baker's and probably a candle-stick maker's, to demonstrate the idea. Everyone agreed that it was a great product and I proceeded to take four orders back to the States on Sunday afternoon, ready for Monday morning in the office.

This schedule worked so neatly, so efficiently and effectively that it made all kinds of lights flash in my head. There must have been a thousand products sold across the United States in the late 1960s which had yet to reach Britain. Just like Elvis had built up a massive following in the States before becoming a sensation in Britain, just as Coca Cola had taken off, there were any number of new innovations ready to be popularised. And personally, I loved nothing more than flying, staying in smart hotels, selling great new products and meeting people. I felt that I'd found my vocation.

For a few months, I concentrated on setting up this new business, which meant renting an office in Highgate in North London, overseeing the manufacturing and hiring salespeople. It went well, so once it was properly established, I returned to Toronto and found a new job at a company called Napa. What Napa did – and still does, because you can see from the website www.napacanada.com that it's alive and well – is very simple. It makes small pumps that you can fill with lubricant, or ketchup, or anything you like, then squeeze the handle and out comes the liquid. I worked for Napa for a few months in Toronto before they appointed me Sales Director and asked me to move to New York.

What a sight awaited me! They set me up in an apartment on the West Side, on 71st Avenue, from where I'd scoot downtown to Napa's offices on the 26th floor of a block on Fifth Avenue opposite the Flatiron building. From this lofty perch, one day in late February my boss gestured down to the street below. I could just make out a tiny rectangle: a dark green, almost British racing green Oldsmobile Cutlass. This was to be my ride on a 17-week tour of the States, taking in Pittsburgh, Milwaukee, Minneapolis, Denver, Seattle, Las Vegas, Los Angeles, San Diego, San Francisco, Phoenix, Dallas, New Orleans, Nashville and Miami.

This was one of the craziest and most fun times of my life, quite apart from being the most tiring. I had to visit as many automobile and hospitality outlets as possible, in every major city in the country, demonstrating this Napa pump and persuading them to put in orders.

It was an amazing adventure, setting off in this lovely car with a credit card loaded with $400 a week (worth something like $3,200 today) and the best currency you can possess in the United States – an English accent. Women would say things like "I could listen to your accent all day!" and sometimes they'd want to follow me around the country, flying down to whichever new city I was visiting next. What a way to spend four months, with a pile of cash in the bank, doing a salesman's version of a rock band's tour of America, just like a rolling stone…

Whenever I arrived in a new city, I'd choose a couple of districts and visit the biggest automotive and hospitality places I could find. It was a receptive market: this pump meant that people could measure the amount of ketchup (for restaurants) or lubricant (for garages) they were using, which saved them money and made their lives easier. You can imagine the advertisements of the time, with a suited presenter saying: "Say goodbye to wasted ketchup misery!" as he demonstrated the pump, which let out a nice jet of ketchup. It was low-tech but effective, and just fitted with the spirit of the age – convenience, speed, utility.

Every place I went gave me a distinct impression that has stayed with me ever since. Detroit felt like it was in despair, I didn't feel safe there, it wasn't comfortable. In Seattle I met a lovely girl who invited me back to her home. Then in the middle of the night her ex-boyfriend arrived and started threatening to kill himself. Denver was high up in the Rocky Mountains, so high in fact that you had to alter your carburettor to deal with the altitude. You'd come across cowboy towns with horses tethered outside and watch people dancing in a bar. I remember standing there and remarking to a stranger: "I've never seen anything so beautiful in my life." It never hurt to say you liked what they did. Then the next thing you knew, they'd invite you in for a drink.

It was the same thing in Las Vegas. Everyone treated me extremely well, just for being English. I managed to catch Elvis Presley singing at the Hilton while I was there. That was a real highlight. He gave you the feeling that he was singing just for you. This truly was the greatest show on earth! Elvis was beyond fantastic. What a showman, what a voice! It's easy to see why they made a film about his Las Vegas shows.

Los Angeles was less friendly, I didn't enjoy the city, whereas Santa Monica was much more to my taste. Florida too. I prefer it to California. In Dallas I was invited by someone I met back to his ranch, where I got on very well with his daughter, but soon discovered that she was a drug addict. Another time in Dallas, I was invited to a bar, then to a show. A lady walking with a stick came out onto the stage – it was Ella Fitzgerald, one of the greatest singers of the 20th Century. Then down in Puerto Rico I was in the front row at a Tony Bennett concert: another of the icons of the age. I was sad to read that he died in July 2023, at the age of 97. He was still taking to the stage at 95 and recording new material. What a trooper (which he was, in the Second World War, in Europe).

My Cutlass did really well, all the way round, driving across mountain ranges, through deserts, across the whole country. It was an amazing car, built by General Motors and with a heritage going back to the mid-1950s when Oldsmobile decided to release a sports coupe with a boat-tailed fastback roofline and a V8 engine. During World War II, General Motors stopped making cars and instead manufactured fighter aircraft and bombers for the war effort. In 1962, GM called the next generation of its Oldsmobile Cutlass the F-85 Jetfire, after the North American F-86 Sabre fighter jet. They were clearly linking their foray into fast, powerful aircraft with the cars they produced afterwards, making drivers like me feel like we were in the cockpit of a fighter jet! When you look at the language GM used to describe various Cutlass models – "Turbo Hydra-matic 350 transmission", "Rocket V8" and "Jetaway" – they really went to town on the aviation buzz.

My final trip in the Cutlass was almost like a plane ride. I set off from

Jacksonville, on the Atlantic coast of Florida, and only left the car once to refuel before I hit the George Washington bridge in New York, a distance of 940 miles.

The national tour for Napa was deemed a success, so I carried on working for the company for another four years, setting up an office for them in London. Once again, I adopted a neat routine, leaving New York on a Friday evening and arriving into Heathrow around 6.30am on Saturday morning, quick shower and shave then into the office near Hammersmith in West London and working all day. Then I'd spend my evenings at the Penthouse Club in Shepherd Market, where I now had honorary life membership, or at the Pair of Shoes in Mayfair. On Sunday, I'd have lunch at a pub near Heathrow where lots of flight crew would hang out, then catch a 4pm flight back to New York and roll up to the office there first thing on Monday morning.

Generally, I flew with Pan Am or BOAC on Stratocruisers, Constellations, Britannias, 707s, Corvairs and 747s. The Corvair was actually the fastest commercial airliner in the skies until the VC10 and then, of course, Concorde came along. Elvis Presley bought a Corvair from Delta Airlines in 1975 as his personal jet, refitting it and naming it after his daughter Lisa Marie. You can pay it a visit at Graceland, in Memphis, Tennessee, where it sits next to his home, kept (like the house) in perfect condition for millions of visitors.

After four years of weekly subsonic commuting across the Atlantic, I was offered two jobs in a week, just at the time when I moved out of New York and into New Jersey. By this time, I'd built a little bit of a reputation in sales, taking on jobs that others would find daunting. Companies would headhunt me, recognising that I could get results.

The next phase of my professional life started at the Regency Hotel, Park Lane, New York. Harold Hassenfeld of the Hasbro Corporation wanted to talk to me and offer me a job licensing a new manufacturing process for pencils around the world. Hasbro owned Empire Pencils – one of the biggest pencil making operations in the world at the time. I explained how I could help them, but admitted that I'd just accepted another position the previous day. Hassenfeld asked me who had offered me the job and when I told him, he replied: "Oh, they're one of our main suppliers, I'll have a word." Sure enough, the following day I found myself employed by Empire Pencils and having breakfast with

Harold Hassenfeld and his sales director Arthur Vandekar. Over eggs and coffee Hassenfeld laid out exactly what my role would be for the following years. I would relocate right away to Murfreesboro in Tennessee to be close to the manufacturing plant in Shelbyville, a town known as 'the pencil capital of the world'. It was also close to the home of Jack Daniels whiskey in Lynchburg.

Hasbro paid for the move, found me a house and set up a 'rent to buy' deal where my monthly rent went towards a deposit for the property. It was all very smooth and reassuring. Soon, I found an even nicer house across town, a beautiful 5,000 square foot ranch that was only four or five years old, with a huge driveway and rear garden with a patio, then just miles of fields. Every six months or so a giant harvester machine would come and cut the grass. I lived here with my second wife Susan, our four children and a nanny from 1974 to 1978, getting to know local people like my colleague at Hasbro, George Buchanan and his wife. We'd visit their place and they'd come to ours, our kids played together, it was all very neighbourly. We'd have lunch together most days, if we were both in town. We'd drive over to the Jack Daniels distillery. Unfortunately laws forbid buying of liquor even though it was made there, except from local bootleggers, delivered in brown paper bags. You'd go into a restaurant, pour it into a glass with a mixer, then they'd charge you the full amount.

George lived just a quarter of a mile away from me, and we'd travel together for work, going to trade shows or to the company office in New York. We went to a trade show in Chicago in 1979, in one of the worst blizzards in American history. We were only supposed to be there for three days, but we ended up staying for almost a week, unable to move. The hotels ran out of food, there was no clean linen. But on the upside, we got to meet Muhammad Ali who was in town, which was an experience neither of us will ever forget. He was just as pretty as everyone said, including himself, and had the biggest hands I've ever seen. All the better to hit you with…

George and I hit it off right away. We just clicked and really enjoyed one another's company, something that's carried on all through the years. He and his wife Valerie have come to see me in London a couple of times and it's been a great pleasure to show them around and introduce them to parts of the city that tourists don't often see, as well as going to iconic British places like Stonehenge in Wiltshire or Canterbury in Kent, where my family comes from.

He also remembers how, not long after he joined the company, some Hasbro marketing people came down from New York and talked to us about their plans. I came up with some ideas and – since the company hadn't really done much marketing before – they were impressed. Or at least that's what George thought at the time. He says that I seemed to know what I was talking about, which is the main thing in sales. You've got to sound convincing. The managers of Jack Daniels appreciated what I did, in any case. They made me a 'Tennessee Squire' on account of the amount of business I brought to the state and would send me hampers of barbecue gloves, beautiful glasses for all drinks and BBQ aprons.

As an Englishman in New York (and Tennessee), I think people considered me a bit of a curiosity. I'd already travelled around the world in the Merchant Navy, visiting places that many of them had never heard of, never mind visited, but also around the States, which relatively few Americans did at that time. So I guess it gave me an aura of experience, but I never felt I was superior to the people I met or worked with, I treated them just like anyone I'd meet in England. Maybe I could see things in a different way, from having visited so many countries and worked in different industries. Some people found it very difficult to talk to the boss, Harold Hassenfeld, but I had no problems with him, or him with me. Once you've had to deal with a bad-tempered sea captain on a long voyage, or a casino customer who's just lost a fortune on the tables, you can talk to almost anyone.

Around this time, I bought a Cadillac Coupe de Ville, one of the most comfortable cars I've ever owned. It was almost 19 feet long and would turn heads as you cruised down the street. One of the heads that turned was a police officer, who accused me of speeding. Fortunately, when I mentioned the name of my boss, he let me off with a caution. That's the way things used to work down there – maybe it still does. You'd hear about the rolls of banknotes passed to policemen at the annual ball. One day at a party I met the local police chief. He gave me his card and said that if I had any trouble, or needed anything sorted out, I should give him a call and he'd take care of it for me.

Owning a Coupe de Ville was like getting an injection of Americana into your veins. This car made its debut in 1949 and was among the most popular power cars of the century. General Motors President Charles E. Wilson drove one for years, before finally gifting it to his secretary. Up until then, she'd been in the back seat, where there was a special pad in the rear armrest for her to take dictation, along with a vanity case, while the glove compartment had a telephone in it. By 1951 more than 10,000 Series 62 Coupe de Villes were sold across the United States, and after becoming a full model in its own right in 1959, the Coupe de Ville continued wowing customers for another 46 years, finally bowing out in 2005 when it was GM's largest sedan. What I liked about it, among other things, was the way that the side light stayed on when you shut the door, so that you could see your way to your house at night.

For the first few years of my time at Hasbro, I'd travel up from Murfreesboro to the company head office in New York, where I'd stay at the Plaza on Central Park and Fifth Avenue. This was a hell of a hotel. Opened in 1907 and modelled on a French chateau, it was one of the most expensive hotels ever built, costing $12 million dollars, which would be more like $500 million today. "Nothing unimportant ever happens at the Plaza," as the saying goes, and I'd see stars like Burt Lancaster, Cary Grant, Elizabeth Taylor and many more from my favourite table in the Edwardian restaurant, with a view looking out over the park. On one memorable night, I checked in and was handed the keys to the penthouse, which had 15 rooms and a golf driving range on the roof. Unbelievable!

You knew you were following in the footsteps of some of the world's biggest stars when you walked underneath its crystal chandeliers (there were 1,650 of them in the hotel). The Beatles stayed here on their first crazy tour in 1964 and Marilyn Monroe was a frequent guest. Writer F Scott Fitzgerald lived here and wrote The Great Gatsby, followed by Ernest Hemingway. Later, Donald Trump bought the Plaza and lived here between 1988 and 1995 with his then wife Ivana, alongside celebrities like Mariah Carey and Tommy Lee Jones. These days, it can cost $100,000 a month to rent one of the residencies.

I spent 25 years working for Hasbro altogether, living in Tennessee, then in New Jersey. So much happened during that time: here are just a few of the events that stand out in my mind.

Gas rationing

In 1973, the combination of OPEC reducing production and the Yom Kippur War between Syria and Egypt on one side and Israel on the other caused the price of gasoline to rocket and its availability to plummet. All across America, lines formed at gas stations, sometimes miles long. You had to work out in advance how to secure your next tank full before you set off to drive anywhere. I remember having to put my car in line for two or three days, just waiting to get some gas. You'd tour around the town and watch out for flags on service stations – green meant they had gas, yellow meant they were rationing and red meant they were dry.

Luckily, I had a friend in New Jersey who owned a gas station, who was fond of malt whisky and had access to a ready gas supply. I gave him a couple of bottles of the finest Scotch, parked my car behind his old school bus, and he'd fill me up and load extra cans of gas into the trunk. I had to take care not to get shunted up the backside! You make some interesting friends when you have to.

It was an example of the way that things can get out of hand in the States. I read later that there really wasn't much of a gas supply crisis in the 1970s, especially since the US was producing almost 10 million barrels of oil per day at the beginning of the decade, which still made up two-thirds of its consumption by 1973. A few scare stories appeared in the media and suddenly there was a national panic, everyone needed to fill their tanks at the same time and that's when the trouble started. You'd see this mass crowd behaviour in all sorts of ways. There's a minor disturbance and suddenly you'll see 12 cop cars descend on the same spot.

I guess it's because America had such a widespread broadcasting network, with hundreds of millions of people getting the same news and reacting the same way. What it meant for an executive like me was that, if you could harness the media in the right way, you had access to a huge and very lucrative market.

Race relations

In the 1970s, things were pretty tense between the races down in Tennessee. I met white people who ran businesses in New Orleans and were brought up in sugar plantations, with black nannies, but then they hated black people once they grew up. That seemed weird to me, how you can grow up with black people and then dislike them as an adult.

In the south at that time there were still remnants of the brutality of slaving times. Someone once pointed out the place in Shelbyville where the last black man had been lynched. Although I wouldn't say that I witnessed police brutality to black people.

President Nixon's 'war on drugs' in the late 1960s and early 1970s was really an excuse to criminalise the black community and anti-war liberals. At least that's what his domestic policy chief John Ehrlichman said, when he spoke about it years later. "The Nixon campaign in 1968 and the Nixon White House after that had two enemies: the anti-war left and black people. We knew we couldn't make it illegal to be either against the war or black, but by getting the public to associate the hippies with marijuana and the blacks with heroin, and then criminalising them both heavily, we could disrupt those communities. We could arrest their leaders, raid their homes, break up their meetings and vilify them night after night on the evening news."

Personally, I never went near marijuana or heroin. A glass of Jack Daniels was about as racy as I got. But there was one night in Murfreesboro when Elvis was performing and I went along with my wife Susan. Everyone says it was a terrific concert but we could hardly see the stage because there was so much marijuana smoke that we began to feel ill and decided to leave the venue and listen to it from outside. Not very counter-cultural!

Although lynchings no longer happened, the spirit of the Ku Klux Klan, which originally formed in Pulaski, Tennessee in 1866, lived on. Pulaski was only about 60 miles from Murfreesboro. Even if you didn't see people going around in pointed white hats, you'd certainly see a lot of Confederate flags, with images of crossed rifles, even on the police vehicles. The old practice of white Americans in the south banding together to catch runaway slaves had been replaced by a pretty racist police force.

After-Effects of Vietnam

Nixon's prosecution of the war on drugs as a way to attack the left showed how divided America was at that time over Vietnam. As the only war that America ever lost, there was a deep sense of guilt about it. What had the country gained in return for 58,000 dead soldiers? You would see it in the streets, with homeless veterans begging for money, especially in New York. I visited a hospital in the city once and, while I was there, a car backfired outside with a loud bang. Half the people in there jumped out of their skin, their nerves shredded by having fought in that awful war. There were parades against Vietnam, movies about it, and Jane Fonda going over there and getting known as 'Hanoi Jane'.

All this felt very different to the post-War Britain in which I grew up, where we suffered privation and death and destruction, but somehow the experience brought us closer together rather than tearing us apart. Maybe it's the difference between winning a justifiable war and losing one which never had such a strong basis. As Muhammad Ali said: "I ain't got no quarrel with them Vietcong. No Vietcong ever called me a nigger."

As someone who supported black people's rights and couldn't see the rationale for the Vietnam war, I agreed with Ali on this one.

American Presidents

From my first visit to the States at the end of the 1950s to my most recent, in the 2020s, I've lived through 13 US presidents: Eisenhower, Kennedy, Johnson, Nixon, Ford, Carter, Reagan, George HW Bush, Clinton, George W Bush, Obama, Trump and Biden.

Of these, I'd rate Reagan as the best and Trump as the worst.

Here's some thoughts on some of them:

Lyndon B. Johnson – 1963-1969

Taking over in the wake of JFK's assassination wasn't easy. The country was still in mourning and shock, and this good old boy from Texas carried on many of Kennedy's reforms, which made sense, given that he'd been vice president under Kennedy for almost three years by the time succeeded to the top job. Then he won a landslide election in 1964, giving him the political tailwind to enact tax cuts, the Clean Air Act and the Civil Rights Act in that same year. He was a liberal reformer, who advanced voting rights for black people and introduced Medicare and Medicaid. He kept faith with NASA and funded the Apollo Missions to carry out JFK's promised moon landing.

On the other hand, he sent hundreds of thousands of Americans to Vietnam, which turned popular opinion against him and led to mass protests across the country. It also meant that the Democrats lost the White House at the next election when 'Tricky Dickie' Richard Nixon beat Hubert Humphrey in 1968.

Like JFK before him and Boris Johnson in our time, Lyndon Johnson was a prolific womaniser. The former president used the White House as his own private harem. Official biographies of the president talk about his domestic reforms and Vietnam, but there's a whole other story of secretaries, friends of his wife, female politicians and others who ended up in his bed, many of them secretly having his children.

Richard Nixon – 1969-1974

The Watergate scandal of 1974 was one of the oddest things that I experienced in my time in America. Richard Nixon had just recently won re-election in 1972 with an absolutely enormous mandate. He won 520 of the Electoral College votes to 17. His first term had been a triumph: he'd withdrawn American troops from Vietnam, saving the country further bloodshed, loss of life and expense. He'd been president when Apollo 11 landed on the moon and Neil Armstrong stepped down the ladder on 20 July 1969. He'd calmed tensions with both Russia - signing a treaty to reduce the chances of nuclear war – and China, where his meeting with Chairman Mao went down as a historic event, along with 'ping-pong diplomacy', as an American table tennis team visited Beijing. In the Middle East, Nixon's Secretary of State Henry Kissinger negotiated peace between Israel and Egypt.

At home, he'd successfully implemented desegregation of schools, particularly in the southern states, and increased the number of women working in government. What more did a guy have to do to catch a break?

It turned out that, even though he was a highly skilled politician, nobody really liked him. He wasn't prepared to smooth-talk Congress into cutting deals. Instead, he just vetoed their objections, or used special powers to defund programmes. As one biographer put it: "Nixon often adopted a stance of confrontation rather than conciliation and compromise. This attitude would later turn on him during the Watergate scandal."

This was Nixon's tragic flaw. The country was doing well, living standards were rising, there was money to spend, but Nixon was so singular that he couldn't get along with anyone. The irony of Watergate is that the Republicans really had no need to break into the Democratic headquarters because Nixon was miles ahead in the 1972 election. The crime that did for him was covering up his tracks and denying that he knew anything about it, rather than the break-in itself. They even lost the tapes with all the recordings on them. When you think of how many lies Trump has told and his constant practice of covering up, you have to feel a bit sorry for Tricky Dickie. He was born too soon.

Ronald Reagan – 1981-1989

Like most people in America in the early 1980s, I was a big fan of Ronald Reagan. Even if British people back home derided him as a B-movie actor who was just doing what big business told him, I could see that Reagan knew what he was doing. He was certainly nobody else's mouthpiece.

He benefited from having Jimmy Carter as an opponent in the 1980 election, after Carter had made such a mess of the Tehran hostage crisis – something I saw from very close quarters, as I describe elsewhere in this book. Carter was a perfectly nice guy, but Americans don't always choose presidents for their niceness. Reagan was personable, but he had a tough side, like some of the characters he played in his movies.

Reagan's idea was to reduce taxes and take America in a more right-wing direction, rolling back some of the more liberal measures of Democratic presidents and cutting regulations in areas like environmental protection and civil rights. Just as in the UK under Margaret Thatcher, unemployment rose sharply under Reagan, but economic growth increased, helping the country to emerge stronger in the long run.

Overseas, Reagan was fiercely anti-Communist, replacing the mass mobilisation in Vietnam with a series of smaller interventions: he invaded Grenada to overthrow a communist-backed government and supported right wing movements across Latin America, with mixed results. The biggest outcome of Reagan's foreign policy was the end of the Cold War in November 1989 with the fall of the Berlin Wall. He had just left the presidency, but you can link that epic historical event directly to his policies of opposing the Soviet Union and convincing its people that freedom was better than an obsolete Communist ideology.

My life under Reagan was one of almost constant travel, as I criss-crossed the Atlantic and ventured into Africa, the Middle East and South America licensing American products. I think his brand of optimistic capitalism worked well for my work. There was a general feeling of support for what we were doing – spreading the benefits of free trade, innovative businesses, enterprise and energetic consumerism.

And of course Concorde was a symbol of how great it was to be Western

– a living example of what you could aspire to in the free world, where the advances of science and technology were accessible to everyone (or at least anyone who could afford to pay).

Donald Trump 2016-2021

My personal pick as the worst president in living memory. By almost any measure, I'd say his tenure was a failure and in many cases a disaster. America's reputation in the wider world has been tarnished and it will take years to repair. His greed and dishonesty are quite staggering and it was only the cowardice of his fellow Republicans that prevented him being impeached and thrown out of office.

On some level, you can trace this historic nightmare back to Ronald Reagan: like Reagan, Trump rose to political prominence on the back of a national media profile and his presidency featured tax cuts and rolled back environmental protections. Yet there is a world of difference between Reagan's drive for a more prosperous America and a safer world and Trump's naked self-interest.

From his earliest business ventures, Trump would fail to pay his suppliers and then threaten them with lawsuits until they went away. He lied to get out of the Vietnam draft, falsely inflated his wealth, swindled millions of Americans (something he's still doing today, by getting them to donate to his political funds, then using the money to defend himself against legal challenges).

It's hard to connect the Republican Party of Donald Trump with that of the 1980s – having lived in the United States for most of that decade. I guess we were still living somehow in the aftermath of the Second World War, where people were forced to stick together and take on a common enemy. It switched from Germany to the Soviet Union, but there was the same sense of unity and standing up for American values. Today, Americans spend more time fighting each other, with Trump and his followers desperate to annoy liberals, at whatever cost. Among his many failures, Trump's decision to downplay COVID-19 and cast doubt on vaccines was one of the worst, costing thousands of lives.

Even in terms of travel and trade, Trump made things worse, provoking a trade war with China, withdrawing from international treaties and praising the brutal dictatorship – against the better advice of the FBI - of Vladimir Putin. As far as my beloved Ukraine goes, this was the worst possible approach to the horrors of Russia's invasion. Trump could have taken a much firmer line against Russian aggression (and not messed around with Ukraine in an attempt to smear Joe Biden). Reagan must have been turning in his grave when Trump cosied up to Putin, in such a betrayal of American values.

God help America if he gets re-elected in 2024!

Chapter 6
Licencing to the World

The longest period I worked for one employer was for Hasbro and its Empire Pencil Company, with a factory based in Shelbyville, Tennessee and its offices in Manhattan and Pawtucket, Rhode Island.

The story of Empire is a fascinating one, so let me take you back to its origins, in Providence, Rhode Island in 1923 when three brothers arrived from Poland seeking their fortune. Henry, Hilal and Herman Hassenfeld were Jewish emigres and – like many others coming to America in those days – found work in the textile business. Using leftover remnants of cloth, they made hat liners and pencil box covers.

From this tiny business, the three brothers used their imagination, commercial flair and energy to build one of America's largest and most profitable companies, earning huge revenues and selling into almost every household in the country. It's a story of spotting and seizing opportunities, never staying still, being prepared to take risks and staying ahead of the competition. You could say that my career has followed something of the same pattern!

A very early example happened in the mid-1920s when the brothers found their pencil box covers were big sellers. Why not make pencil boxes themselves, they wondered? From a family enterprise of eight people (all of them relations), the business soon expanded under the shrewd and foresightful Henry Hassenfeld. In 1926 Hassenfeld Brothers incorporated and by 1930 there were 200 employees and sales of $500,000 a year from pencil boxes and zipper punches for school supplies.

Faced with a potential crisis when its pencil supplier raised its prices and decided to sell pencil boxes to undercut Hassenfeld's, Henry responded in typically robust fashion. He went into pencil manufacture and ditched the old supplier. Crisis averted, and the company gained a new product line that would be one of its best sources of income for decades to come.

Hassenfeld's genius for reinvention and diversification didn't end there. By the end of the 1930s, the company added toy manufacture to its product list, figuring that parents and children that liked its pencil cases might buy medical sets for children playing at doctors and nurses and modelling clay for budding artists. This direction also proved to be a big hit, especially after World War II when it introduced makeup kits for young girls, advertised its toy Mr Potato Head on television, licensed Disney characters for toys and turned itself into one of America's largest toy companies.

On the pencil side of things, the brothers originally called their business Providence Pencil Company, then in 1946 they acquired Empire Pencil Company based in Shelbyville, Tennessee, and decided to keep the Empire name for the merged operation. Shelbyville was by then the pencil capital of the United States, with as many as five or six manufacturers all based there, including Musgrave, National Pencil Company and the US Pencil and Stationery Company. They used the local red cedar wood to make pencils.

On a side note, Harold Hassenfeld's parents Henry and Marion travelled to Jerusalem in 1951, looking for an opportunity to invest in Israel and help the newly-formed (just three years old) country to thrive. They decided to start a pencil factory, as a sister company to Empire, based in Jerusalem and named after the city.

The Jerusalem Pencil Company did very well. It had a big range of graphite and coloured pencils, appealing particularly to the Jewish community in the United States, with names like Park Avenue, Yamit (meaning 'small sea' in Hebrew), Sabra ('a Jew born in Israel') and Masada shall not fall again (Masada was an ancient town, besieged by the Romans in 74 AD).

When Henry Hassenfeld died in 1960, his son Merrill took over the parent company which ran the toy business while older brother Harold looked after Empire Pencil Co. For a time, this arrangement worked out fine, as the toy side prospered with products like G.I. Joe – an action figure based on a US Marine. The parent company rebranded as Hasbro in 1968 and offered shares on the stock market. But in the 1970s, as some of the company's toys struggled (it had some disasters, with 'Javelin Darts' withdrawn after the government said they were unsafe, and a water gun shaped like a hypodermic syringe that newspapers called 'junior junkie' kit), tensions mounted between Harold's pencil operation and Merrill's toys. Harold resented that Merrill had most of the capital investment, even though his pencils were more profitable.

One day when I was working on a licensing deal in Rome, it turned out that Merrill was there too. He invited me to dinner at one of the city's best restaurants, ordered the best wines and said: "Fred, you're doing a fantastic job for the company. From now on, you stay in first class hotels and you fly first class." The company was definitely pleased with how things were going. I had to sign legal contracts on behalf of the company as an officer of the company (which is the same status as a director in UK,) which was fine because I have a master's degree in international law, and so my title was VP of Licensing and Marketing.

Later, other Empire Pencil directors also followed the precedent I set and had flights on Concorde.

Eventually, when Merrill died in 1979 at the age of 61, things came to a head between the brothers. Harold refused to work with Stephen Hassenfeld, who took over from Merrill, and Hasbro spun off Empire Pencil in 1980, giving Harold independence. Hasbro went on to great things under Stephen's leadership, introducing a fantastic range of extremely popular toys including the Transformers, Cabbage Patch Kids, Tonka Toys and the licensing rights for the Star Wars movies. By the mid-1980s, Hasbro overtook Mattel to become the biggest toy company in the world.

Empire Pencil, meanwhile, under Harold Hassenfeld, saw how successful Hasbro had been with its licensing operations and decided to follow suit. This is where I came in.

Today, licensing is a massive, global activity, with brands licensing everything from Marmite to Formula 1 cars. Back in the 1970s, when I first started, it was relatively new. In the 1960s, there were some notable licensing deals. For example, the animated TV series Flintstones, produced by Hanna-Barbera Productions, ran from 1960 to 1966. It spawned a whole industry producing chewable vitamins, breakfast cereals that looked like pebbles, and much besides. Even now, you can buy Flintstones mugs, bags, tee-shirts, socks, posters and toys.

Next came a licensing phenomenon from England that swept the United States. In 1964, the Beatles song '*I want to hold your hand*' sold 2.6 million copies in two weeks and 74 million people watched them perform on the Ed Sullivan show. That year, American teenagers spent $50 million on Beatles merchandise. Reliance Manufacturing paid £100,000 for a licence and sold more than a million Beatles tee-shirts in three days.

Soon, the licensing craze spread to sports, with first the National Football League (NFL) then Major League Baseball and the National Basketball Association getting in on the action. Hasbro played a central role in the growth of licensing, especially with G.I. Joe, which the company licensed for movies and (later) for video games.

In parallel, goods producers grew increasingly aware of the potential rewards of licensing overseas companies to manufacture their products. In the same way that the Flintstones creators or the Beatles didn't have to make tee shirts or mugs, they simply licensed their intellectual property to companies that would do this, so manufacturers could grant other manufacturers a licence, without the bother of making things overseas themselves.

There were so many advantages to this process, compared with starting up a new factory in another country, along with a sales, marketing and distribution network. You picked an existing manufacturer with a good reputation, gave them the licence, they produced, sold, marketed and distributed the goods and paid you a royalty for each sale. For the licensing company, it was cheap, it was flexible (you could get out relatively easy if you wanted to), it meant you could get into markets that were otherwise closed to imports, maybe for political reasons, you avoided taxes that you might otherwise have to pay on exported goods, and the arrangement was more likely to appeal to overseas governments, since it boosted local employment and often meant a transfer of technology and increased skills.

None of this means that setting up a licensing agreement was easy. I had to negotiate with the licensee company itself, with my own bosses, with various ministries in the country where we planned to operate, and with the foreign trade department of the United States government, not to mention law firms in the licensing country and the US. Getting all of these ducks in a row would take two or three years on average. That's one big reason why I had to fly to and fro so often. There were always ten sides to every negotiation and I had to make sure everyone understood one another.

The issues we had to agree on included currencies. An overseas company (and its government) would typically want to pay royalties in local currency. This was more predictable for them, since it removed the danger of foreign exchange movements, which could prove expensive. Governments always want to pay in local currency because their foreign currency reserves are precious – especially dollars. But my company wanted to be paid in dollars, so that we didn't suffer from currency fluctuations.

Then there were issues of quality. We didn't want to licence production of Empire Pencils if the end result was going to be sub-standard. A pencil may look like a pretty straightforward thing to make, but there are 17 stages to its manufacture. In complexity, making a pencil is on a par with making a watch.

Even before you get to the manufacturing stage, there are a hundred different parts to the negotiations: everything from training a new workforce to importing machinery, agreeing royalty payments and accounting standards to the messy business of what should happen if the relationship doesn't work. Simply deciding whether an American or a Kenyan court should adjudicate any dispute can take months to resolve.

In some countries where I worked, we also faced political risk. There may have been a history of military coups, or sudden nationalisations. Empire Pencils didn't want to spend five years and millions of dollars on a project, only to find that the government had seized everything and refused to give any compensation, as happened to some companies in Venezuela for example. It's a minefield!

Even now, with the advantage of decades of experience and precedent, companies have to be careful when negotiating licensing deals. Imagine how much trickier it was in the 1970s, when the practice was only just getting started. You risk losing control of your product if the licensee decides to take it in a new direction. You rely on them being able to sell your product effectively, and you rely on their professionalism and quality of management. If they mess up, it could affect your reputation back home – and in other markets. If they do well, you could even create unwanted competition for yourself.

Where we had an advantage was in our technology. Empire had developed a new manufacturing process through which wood fibres were mixed with plastic, producing a better-wearing, more easily manipulated material, which improved profit margins. It was my job to convince overseas pencil manufacturers to adopt this new system and licence Empire's technology.

Once I'd succeeded in convincing a company in Kenya, for example, then it would mean that I could conclude similar deals in other countries in the region. Uganda and Tanzania all used schillings for currency, and it was quite straightforward to supply to those markets from Kenya. The same applied in the UK and Ireland, or in Argentina and Chile.

Besides the formal negotiations, you would find that the bosses of the manufacturing companies were always looking for backhanders. They knew that American companies were wealthy and they expected you to cough up. By law, however, the most we could pay as a 'service charge' was $25. When you're dealing with a multi-millionaire, $25 is insulting. So we would put them on a plane to Hamburg and let them loose on the night-time entertainment there. This worked a treat. They were far happier than if we'd paid them cash. We called them 'educational trips' and everyone was happy.

It was all about personal contacts, rather than based on figures and marketing projections. Securing the deal in Kenya took years, as I mentioned But in the end it came down to a trip I made out to Limuru in the countryside, to track down the Kenyan Finance Minister. I heard he was there playing golf, so I took a chance and drove out there, armed with refreshments for him, in case I managed to find him. By chance, he was there. I met him, we arranged to meet and the deal went ahead. Golf courses are good places to discuss business, I've always felt. There are barely any trees for spies to attach microphones to.

This chap agreed the deal with me for Kenya and we both went on to better things. The deal became my calling card, it opened the door for similar negotiations all over the world.

So after Kenya, which took three and a half years to complete, I was able to expand the licensing agreement over similar deals in Canada, in Nigeria, Argentina and Iran. In each place there were different challenges, of course, but the framework of the licensing agreement was the same.

What helped in the negotiations was that pencils qualified as an educational product, because they're so often used in schools. And I can say that, overall, the Kenyan government was very happy with what we did. They earned foreign currency through selling the product elsewhere. As part of the negotiations, I tracked down the Minister of Industries, Eliud Mwanga. Later he wrote to Harold, the chairman of Hasbro, saying how pleased he was with the relationship. "It's a shame that more companies don't send people like Fred Finn to Kenya, to get the job done," he wrote, which definitely put me in the chairman's good books.

I remember Eliud as a very kind and generous man. He and his wife took me around a safari reserve almost in the City of Nairobi where you could photograph a cheetah against the backdrop of Nairobi in his ministerial car. Then 20 years later, when I was delivering clothes to an orphanage in Kenya, he sent me a lovely letter saying how sorry he was that he couldn't meet on that occasion. Then, when the Hasbro chairman came to Kenya to see how things were going, Eliud arranged a safari for all of us, where we visited the Masai Mara and Serengeti, where four million animals migrate every autumn, one of the most spectacular sights in the animal kingdom – it's even visible from space.

My introduction to Kenya

The first time I remember being aware of Kenya was in February 1952 when a young Princess Elizabeth who left London as a Princess went there on safari with her husband Prince Philip. They stayed in Treetops Hotel, a tiny game-viewing lodge where their room was built into the branches of an old fig tree overlooking a waterhole. She returned as the Queen in February 1952 following the death of her father King George VI.

I was 12 years old and the whole idea of living in a tree, surrounded by exotic, magical wildlife, in the middle of a jungle, was impossibly romantic and adventurous to me. It seemed like the perfect trip. That day they had reportedly seen rhino, baboons and a herd of elephants, pink from rolling in the dust.

Then the news broke that her dear father had died and she was now Queen, with all the weight of an Empire on her young shoulders, meaning that she had to flee that idyllic scene and return to the British winter. This only added to the allure of the Kenyan countryside, a paradise that had been snatched away from our princess and her prince. I grew determined to visit this place one day.

Treetops is close to Sagana Lodge, a villa next to a trout stream that was given to Elizabeth and Philip as a wedding gift from the Kenyan state. It lies just a few miles from Mount Kenya, close to the spot where years later I would form great friendships and then arrange for numerous people to visit. The original Treetops burned down many years ago.

Kenya was a British colony in 1952, so she was visiting as a representative of the Head of State, HM King George VI, her father. The couple were on the first stop of a six-month tour of the Commonwealth, taking in Australia and New Zealand, cementing her role as a senior royal, forging relations with this empire upon which the sun never set.

At the time, staying in a place like this was extremely rare. It was also dangerous, with threats from both animals and humans. A hunter stood guard at the entrance to Treetops Lodge with a shotgun, in case any leopards should come too close. Further protection came from local men armed with spears to deter journalists keen to get a glimpse of royalty, but also in case of attack from the Mau Mau rebels, who opposed colonial rule. It would be a further 11 years before Kenya became a republic, but the seeds of discontent were already growing.

Aviation played a role in the story as well. Newsreels showed Princess Elizabeth arriving in Kenya on a BOAC Argonaut plane, stepping onto the runway in a print dress, while Prince Philip wore a white naval uniform replete with medals. Too soon, they flew home again and the historic, longest-ever reign of a British monarch began.

Before Queen Elizabeth's reign was 10 years old, I'd visited Kenya myself. As a merchant seaman, my voyages would often stop in Mombasa, on Kenya's east coast, on the way to India. And while you're away at sea, you get plenty of chance to read up on the places you're going to visit, so I'd immerse myself in books about the history and culture of Kenya.

After my days in the Merchant Navy came to an end, I worked in London for a consultancy called Montague Kent, which specialised in helping companies improve their operations and find new markets. This also involved dealing with Kenya, as it was a popular overseas location for companies aiming to expand into Africa.

Since those long-ago days, I've spent years of my life in Kenya, travelling there perhaps more than 600 times, and never regretted a moment of it.

Chapter 7
Narrow escapes

As our car with darkened windows raced towards the airport in Tehran, I was with my colleague Bob Ferguson, the catering manager from BA who would later become Catering Director of Emirates Airlines. People were burning effigies of American President Jimmy Carter, chanting 'death to America'.

It was December 1979 and I was in a hurry to leave Iran, now that the Islamic revolution was in full swing. Not only was I an American resident, but I was there as an American citizen, to help me put a licence deal together with Shah's government.

Bob and I had been held after a mob of students invaded the American Embassy in Tehran, situated right across the street from our office and seized 66 hostages. First, we were locked up for a few days, then pushed onto the floor of a car which took us across town, where we were held under house arrest. Our captors said it was for our own safety, but we weren't sure what to believe. The atmosphere was volatile and unpredictable. At first the Ayatollah tried to stop the students, then supported them. We felt we could be bundled in with these Embassy hostages and never seen again.

At the airport, I kept my American passport buried deep in my luggage and flourished my British one. "This was issued in New York. Are you American?" the Revolutionary Guard demanded. "Of course not, I'm British!" After inspecting my bags in great detail – fortunately they didn't spot my other passport – they let me through. As the BA VC10 crossed the Turkish border, the entire plane burst into cheers and applause as the Iranian clocks had turned back 2,000 years.

This situation had been brewing for decades. Western governments had meddled in Iran's politics since the 1920s, when Britain imposed a monarchy on the country and placed Reza Shah Pahlavi in power. Then Russia and Britain kicked him out and installed his son Mohammed Reza Pahlavi on the throne in 1941. When the Shah's Prime Minister Mohammad Mosaddegh threatened to turn against the West in 1953, Britain and the United States once again orchestrated a coup.

In the 1970s, Mohammad Reza Shah's 'White Revolution' caused huge unrest across Iran, made worse by the oil crisis and his harsh domestic regime of detentions and torture. Even though the Shah was close to the American, Israeli and British governments, he had a shrinking circle of supporters at home. The clerics, left wing intellectuals, farmers and students all combined to demand change, accusing the shah of pandering to the West.

In September 1978 the Shah imposed martial law and troops massacred hundreds of protestors on the streets of Tehran. By January 1979, he and his family had fled Iran and by the beginning of April, Iran was an Islamic republic.

All through this time, I was busily setting up a licensing agreement for Empire Pencil Co, so that an Iranian company could manufacture our products in the country. A change of regime didn't necessarily mean we couldn't work here, so we kept plugging away. Besides, we'd invested tens of thousands of dollars and many months of time and effort. Things were progressing well, as far as we could tell.

Life in Tehran began to change in subtle ways. Before the revolution, you could walk down Pahlavi Avenue in the centre of the city, past beautiful restaurants, wine bars, pubs, hotels. One by one, these began to close, as the Ayatollah imposed his Muslim regime. At first, people didn't take it very seriously. Young people would put roses in the muzzles of Revolutionary Guards' rifles, believing that they would never fire on their own people.

Then gradually, the mood darkened. In late 1978 all the talk was of the Shah leaving, as his regime became ever more repressive. Each time government forces shot a protester, there would be a big funeral march; the government would try to suppress the march and shoot more protests, so then the next funeral would be even bigger. Once the Shah eventually fled, more than a million people took to the streets of Tehran to welcome the Ayatollah back from exile in February 1978.

Women could no longer walk through the streets dressed as they pleased. Westerners were all under suspicion of being agents of the Americans.

I would walk up and down the street next to the Embassy, taking pictures of whatever was going on, including women burning effigies of Jimmy Carter. One day a Revolutionary Guard demanded my camera, but I refused, saying that I was filming the demonstrations, which were on their side.

I look back on my experiences in Iran with bittersweet memories. Being taken hostage was indeed a close shave – the Embassy hostages weren't released until January 1981, after 444 days of captivity on the day that Ronald Reagan became president – but there was another close shave in my personal life.

In Tehran I'd met a beautiful Iranian woman who worked for the Shah as his personal assistant. She would fly all over the world with him. Sometimes I came too. We took the Shah's kids to Disney World in Florida, for example, where Disney shut the whole park for half a day so they could visit in peace. We visited Tennessee and New York together.

Then came the revolution. Our proposed marriage didn't go ahead because it has to be conducted under Muslim law. I couldn't stay in Iran and she couldn't leave, so that was the end of the relationship. I did send her $1,500 to cover the cost of her wedding dress. But being married to an Englishman was probably not a good move for her at the time.

I did return briefly a year later to try and repatriate funds blocked by the Iranian government. I was able to negotiate an agreement that if our claim wasn't on the Jimmy Carter claim for funds blocked in Iran, they would transfer the funds to Bank Melli in London, part of the central bank of Iran. Of course, various commissions had to be paid to allow this to happen, but in the end a large part of those funds - over $200,000 - were transferred back to the USA to the Empire Pencil account.

The whole Iranian experience was quite surreal. It was the most intense example in my life where politics and business have intersected, putting me in the middle of a dangerous, potentially life-threatening situation. As a representative of an American company, licensing American products in a developing country, you generally feel protected, secure and are well-treated by the local people you meet. You're there to improve their standard of life and provide them with things they need. In Iran, none of that applied. I represented a hated, aggressive foreign power that wanted to dominate them and effectively enslave them.

Part of it was to do with oil and money. The United States economy had expanded wildly in the mid-20th century: between 1940 and 1980 its population rose by 70 per cent and its GDP by 500 per cent, so it needed vast supplies of cheap oil to feed this growth. Geographically, Iran sat between the Soviet Union and the oil-rich Middle Eastern states, so America desperately wanted to keep it independent and stable. No such luck!

America's enemies, including the Palestinian Liberation Organisation (PLO), Fidel Castro's Cuba and of course the Soviet Union clubbed together to support the Ayatollah, realising that – even if they disagreed with his extreme Islamic code – he could be useful to them by kicking the Americans out of Iran.

So quite by accident, I ended up at the centre of the most dramatic and fiercely fought diplomatic stand-off of the time, replacing the equally divisive Vietnam campaign, and one which contributed to Jimmy Carter's loss of the US presidency in the 1980 election, as the hostages languished in Tehran and his attempts to rescue them were embarrassing failures.

It was a moment in history where things changed very suddenly. Under the Shah, people might end up in prison, but then they could walk out. Under the Ayatollah, you never got out.

Who would have thought that being a licensing executive would be such a hazardous career?

Hijacks on land and in the air

When I first began flying in the late 1950s, hijacking airplanes (or 'skyjacking') was very rare. There hadn't been a single mid-air hijacking in the United States at this time - the first took place in 1961 when an airliner flying above Florida was forced to land in Cuba.

Yet by the end of the 1960s it had become quite the fashion. Between 1968 and 1970 there were almost 200 hijackings, often by Middle Eastern political militants who demanded ransoms or wanted to free their comrades from prison. In September 1970 there was an 11-day crisis where four aircraft were destroyed on the ground and 300 passengers were held captive for a week. Flying was becoming a riskier business.

Next came my favourite story. In 1971 a man known as D.B. Cooper boarded a Northwest Orient 727 flight from Portland, Oregon, to Seattle. Soon after taking off, he beckoned an air stewardess to look at his briefcase. It had a bomb in it, he told her, and if he didn't get $200,000 in $20 bills (worth $1.5 million today) and four parachutes, he was going to blow them all to smithereens. Landing in Seattle, Cooper received his money and the parachutes, allowed all the other passengers to leave, then instructed the pilot to fly to Mexico, nice and slowly and not too high. Somewhere over Oregon – maybe back where he started, in Portland – Cooper jumped out of the plane with his loot and was never seen again. The case became a fixation for a generation of Americans and has never been solved. No-one knows if he survived the jump, who or where he is, or what prompted him to undertake such a crazy mission. Netflix released a TV series '*D.B. Cooper: Where are you?!*' in 2022.

Inspired by D.B. Cooper and hundreds of others, the spate of hijacking eventually persuaded more than 50 countries to coordinate a response. Countries that were seen to sponsor hijackers could have their air permits rescinded. But still they happened. In June 1976 an Air France flight from Tel Aviv to Paris with 103 passengers and crew was hijacked by two PLO members plus a couple of Germans from the extremist Red Army Faction. They forced the pilot to fly to Libya, then on to Uganda, where the dictator Idi Amin welcomed them. Apparently he was in on the plot from the beginning. Then in one of the most dramatic and daring rescues in aviation history, an Israeli commando taskforce raided the plane, shot several of the hijackers and released all but three of the hostages, who were killed in the crossfire.

The story gripped the world's imagination and was quickly made into three action movies: *Victory in Entebbe* (1976) starring Burt Lancaster, Anthony Hopkins and Elizabeth Taylor, *Raid on Entebbe* (1977) starring Peter Finch and Charles Bronson, and *Operation Thunderbolt* (1978) starring Klaus Kinski and Sybil Danning. Even if you'd never worried about hijackings before, you were probably obsessed with them now. They took over from sharks, thanks to *Jaws* (1975) as something for people to get irrationally scared of. Quite possibly, the sensation over Entebbe encouraged more people to attempt hijackings.

It certainly didn't dissuade the three members of the Palestinian militant group Abu Nidal Organisation, who hijacked an Egypt Air flight in 1985. This incident was far more horrific than the Entebbe hijack and rescue, probably too much for movie audiences to bear. Things went badly wrong almost as soon as the plane took off from Athens on its way to Cairo. After only a few minutes, the hijackers took control and began separating Israeli and American passengers from the others. An Egyptian security guard then shot and killed one of the hijackers, whereupon the others shot back, causing the plane to lose pressure. The captain made an emergency landing in Malta, where the captors said they would kill one person every 15 minutes if the Maltese government didn't allow them to refuel. Five people were killed, one after another. Then a team of Egyptian commandos blew a hole in the plane, accidentally setting it on fire, before shooting indiscriminately inside the plane, killing more passengers but missing the main hijacker, who disguised himself as a hostage and was taken to hospital. Absolute shambles.

Ethiopian Airlines had a way to cure hijacking on their planes: on one attempted hijacking on a Boeing 727 the hijackers were overcome, had their throats cut and thrown out of the rear door. From then on they always had an air marshal in all classes and on all flights. They would shoot anyone attempting to enter the flight deck. I know this as I was a consultant for the airline and the crew wanted me to join them on the flight deck to witness a star phenomenon. They informed the air marshal that it was ok for me to enter the flight deck.

Not long after the Entebbe crisis came my own brush with hijacking. In 1977 I flew out of Heathrow with British Airways on a plane for Hamburg in Germany to meet my then wife Susan for dinner. As we arrived at Hamburg Airport, we noticed a jam of tanks near the runway, along with guys with guns. We were nowhere near the arrivals gate, so I asked one of the flight crew: "What's this welcome committee about when we're so far from the gate, surrounded with tanks - we're not being hijacked are we?" "Certainly not Mr Finn, we're just waiting for the gate."

Within seconds the forward and aft doors flew open and armed police stormed in and dragged two people off the aircraft. I'll never know what they were up to and why they didn't actually hijack the plane, but it certainly looked like they were in big trouble.

When I finally met my wife at the hotel, she asked why I'd arrived at 2.00am instead of 7.00pm the previous evening, as we'd arranged. I proceeded to explain what had happened but she wouldn't believe me. It was only when we watched the news the following evening, then read the papers later that she could see I was telling the truth.

Honestly, you'd think that having terrorists about to blow your plane out of the sky was a good enough reason to be late, but you just can't reason with some people!

One other mid-air drama: I used to have a complimentary pass on the JFK to Newark helicopter service, run by New York Helicopters. One time, I was sitting up front with the pilot and he asked if I'd like to fly over downtown Manhattan. So we flew over to the World Trade Center and looked into the Windows of the World restaurant, then off to the Statue of Liberty and back to Newark. As we landed, the only other passenger in the back of the helicopter took a swing at the pilot for taking this scenic route, which wasn't in the approved flight plan. I ended up as a witness in the court case brought by this passenger, which was thrown out.

Having this free pass meant I could go shopping in New York by landing on the Pan Am Building at 200 Park Avenue, until one day a helicopter blew over in the wind and a rotor fell off in the wind and killed people 60 floors below. It also played a role in me becoming a US citizen many years ago. I had to appear before a swearing in ceremony at 10:30 but needed to be on Concorde at 13:45 that day, so I did the ceremony, jumped in the helicopter to collect my US passport, then took another helicopter to JFK and was in London at 16:45 New York time the same day.

Trouble on the border

A few years earlier, I was actually taken hostage. Not in a plane this time, but in a Mexican bar of all places.

It was the early 1970s and I was demonstrating Napa's ketchup and grease pumps in San Diego. With a couple of days to spare, I decided to take a bus trip to San Ysidro, a suburb of the city bang on the border with Mexico. In those days, you could simply jump on a bus and cross the border, so I decided to check out Tijuana, right on the other side of the line.

At a bar, I met some friendly guys and started drinking. One drink led to another and soon it was evening. We all decided to go to another bar, but on the way there I became separated from them and suddenly, in the middle of the street, a stranger approached me and stuck something into my ribs. Whether or not it was a gun, I didn't know, but it sure as hell felt like one. He led me down an alleyway to an old room where there was just a chair, table and a large, miserable-looking Mexican woman who the guy said was his daughter. He wanted me to marry her and take her across the border so she could become an American citizen.

What he didn't realise was that I wasn't yet an American citizen myself, but I wasn't about to tell him that. He kept me in that dingy room overnight and by the morning I was desperate for the loo, so I persuaded him to take me to an outside toilet. I saw my chance to escape and made a run for it. I didn't look back until I reached a bus – I didn't care less where it was heading for, as long as it was away from this guy and his ghastly daughter. As it turned out, the bus took me back across the border to San Diego. As you can imagine, I've never gone back there again.

On the other hand, I do love the music of Herb Alpert and the Tijuana Brass. So I'm not completely against that little piece of Mexico.

Fire in the mountains
Staying at the Mount Kenya Safari Club was always a pleasure and a privilege. Set in 100 acres of manicured gardens, with a pool, spa, animal sanctuary and restaurants overlooking Africa's second highest mountain, it's one of the continent's finest resorts.

I would normally stay in one of the Club's lovely cottages, but on one occasion they were all booked, so they put me in the Presidential Suite. It was extremely luxurious, so I felt honoured and privileged (though I secretly preferred my little cottage). Arriving in the suite, an open log fire was already alight. I noticed that the firewood next to the hearth looked a bit different to the regular wood they provided – very white in colour.

Since the Club is in Nanyuki at an altitude of 2,150 metres, it gets pretty chilly in the evenings. So as the temperature dropped, I threw some of these white logs onto the fire. As soon as they ignited…WHOOSH! The flames leapt up and set fire to the chimney. "Oh no! This isn't good!" I thought. It scared me to death, thinking that the fire was going to engulf the wooden beams supporting the entire roof and burn this extraordinary building to the ground!

The resort security officer ('Askari' in Swahili) was soon on the phone alerting me to the flames shooting 20 feet into the sky and asking if I could 'please turn off the fire'. Easier said than done. Another member of staff arrived and opened the balcony window, which was the worst possible thing to do, simply adding oxygen to the blaze.

Eventually after several hours it burnt itself out, to my great relief. I remember staying up all night with the manager Eddie Hourau drinking cognac to settle our nerves as the flames slowly extinguished themselves. If things had turned out differently, I feared I'd end up in a Kenyan jail for the rest of my days.

Crash landings and other mishaps

Most of the time, I find it easy to forget or ignore how much inherent danger there is in flying. An engine or mechanical malfunction, a terrorist, a crazy pilot, a couple of bird strikes or even a stray bolt on the runway could spell disaster.

In more than 60 years of flying, I've experienced most of the near misses and emergencies that it's possible to have in an aircraft. Here are my top five:

1. Belly landing

Flying from London to JFK one time in the 1980s, we were flying low over New York for an hour, wondering why the pilot didn't land. There was no announcement of any problem, so we grew concerned that there was a bomb on board. Eventually, we touched down belly first, with a great deal of screeching noises and plenty of screaming among the passengers, but no harm done. The plane was in one piece and we all left safely.

I expect the pilot cruised around for so long to burn off fuel, which made the landing safer and with less likelihood of a fire. Although it's a dramatic way to arrive, belly landings are relatively common and barely ever result in injury or death. Sometimes they happen because the landing gear malfunctions and sometimes because the pilots forget to deploy the landing gear! In the United States, where there are around 200,000 private aircraft, landing gear mishaps happen eight times a week on average.

As long as the pilot lands in as straight and level a way as possible, with enough airspeed to retain control, belly landings are generally safe. If there are major complications, like strong crosswinds, low visibility or malfunctioning instruments – for example if the pilot can't tell their altitude – the aircraft could possibly flip over, disintegrate or catch fire. Fortunately, my experience was in the majority: scary but safe.

2. Wild rides

When flying, you have to put your trust in the captain. My attitude is that they're professionals, they're extremely well-trained and experienced, so I let them get on with it. Sometimes, though, you have to wonder about them. One time we were flying from Pretoria, the capital of South Africa to Lilongwe, the capital of Malawi, a thousand-mile flight of about three and a half hours. Lilongwe is a beautiful city, surrounded by mountains and – in sunny weather – one of the loveliest places to visit. But on this particular day, there was torrential rain, terrible visibility and we were skimming the tops of the mountains as we made our approach to Lilongwe. I could see the ground beneath us. For once, I really felt that we shouldn't have landed. For the one and only time I was pushing up from my seat, we were so close to the ground. It wasn't safe. After we arrived, the captain cheerfully said: "I've got a party to go to!" And off he went.

Another time, we landed in an absolute gale, with gusts of wind up to 100 miles and hour. You could tell how tricky it was because two planes up ahead of us aborted their landings. But our pilot decided to go for it. We landed on a taxiway, bouncing all the way along, before finally coming to a standstill and everyone breathing again. It was very sporty.

In the days when I was licensing products around the world, I'd fly down to Buenos Aires in Argentina. On one of those trips, there was a panic that someone had a bomb on board, and the pilot decided to make a very fast landing at Ezeiza Airport. It meant that one set of wheels was on the runway, the other on the grass, which made for an extremely bumpy ride. We were convinced the plane was breaking up, but happily we were wrong.

Sometimes it all kicks off inside the plane. You'll see rock and roll bands having food fights and getting so drunk they assault the cabin crew. One guy slapped a stewardess and picked a fight with three people all at once! Needless to say, I'm not a fan of this behaviour. Flying can be a wonderful experience if you just relax and enjoy it.

One final close shave in a plane. I was booked onto a flight to Hong Kong when I was on my way to Singapore to stay with Concorde captain John Hutchinson. I couldn't make the flight for some reason. I later discovered that the man in my seat was stabbed in the head by a woman in a wheelchair sitting behind him, missing his brain by 2mm.

With 65 years of flying behind me and 15 million miles, I consider myself lucky to be alive, in all kinds of ways.

Sonic Boom

30. With Bryn Williams and Patricia Hodge presenting one of my prizes at a charity evening.

32. My good friend Murray Walker and Noel Edmonds receiving their Honourary Memberships to the Mount Kenya Safari Club at a Save the Children charity event.

31. Making Terry Wogan an honorary member of Mount Kenya Safari Club after appearing on his prime-time BBC chat show "Wogan".

33. I flew in a BOAC DC4b on my first trip across the Atlantic in 1958.

34. My tent whilst visiting my beloved Kenya, overlooking some of the most beautiful nature on God's earth.

129

35. These pencils have a story to tell.

36. I was delighted to be invited to visit G-BOAE in January 2024 and meet Hadley Bourne, CEO of Grantley Adams International Airport, Barbados with my dear friend, Ben Lord.

37. Returning home! Avis have always been great to work with and they looked after me superbly during a recent trip to what was once my former home - New Jersey in May 2024.

Sonic Boom

38. With my parents before leaving for New York in 1980.

39. Me with some Masai ladies on a trip to Kenya in 1990.

40. Gemima the beautiful orphan giraffe at Ol Pejeta Kenya, taking a biscuit.

41. The two most beautiful seats on earth outside my room La Dique Island Seychelles.

42. Following my own advice - setting my watch to the local time zone I'm travelling to once I've boarded a flight.

43. My well-worn passports, bearing the marks of their extensive journeys.

44. Richard stumbled out of the Red Arrows Hawk T1 aircraft looking distinctly green around the gills but he absolutely loved it.

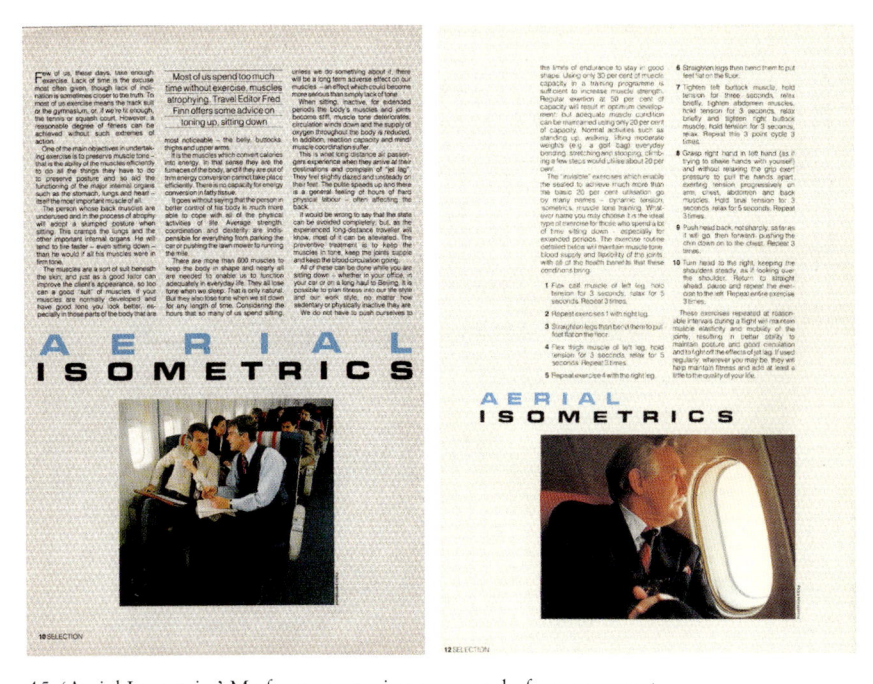

45. 'Aerial Isometrics' My famous exercises you can do from your seat.

46. Photo shoot for the Daily Mail travel article. Photo by Adrian Meredith.

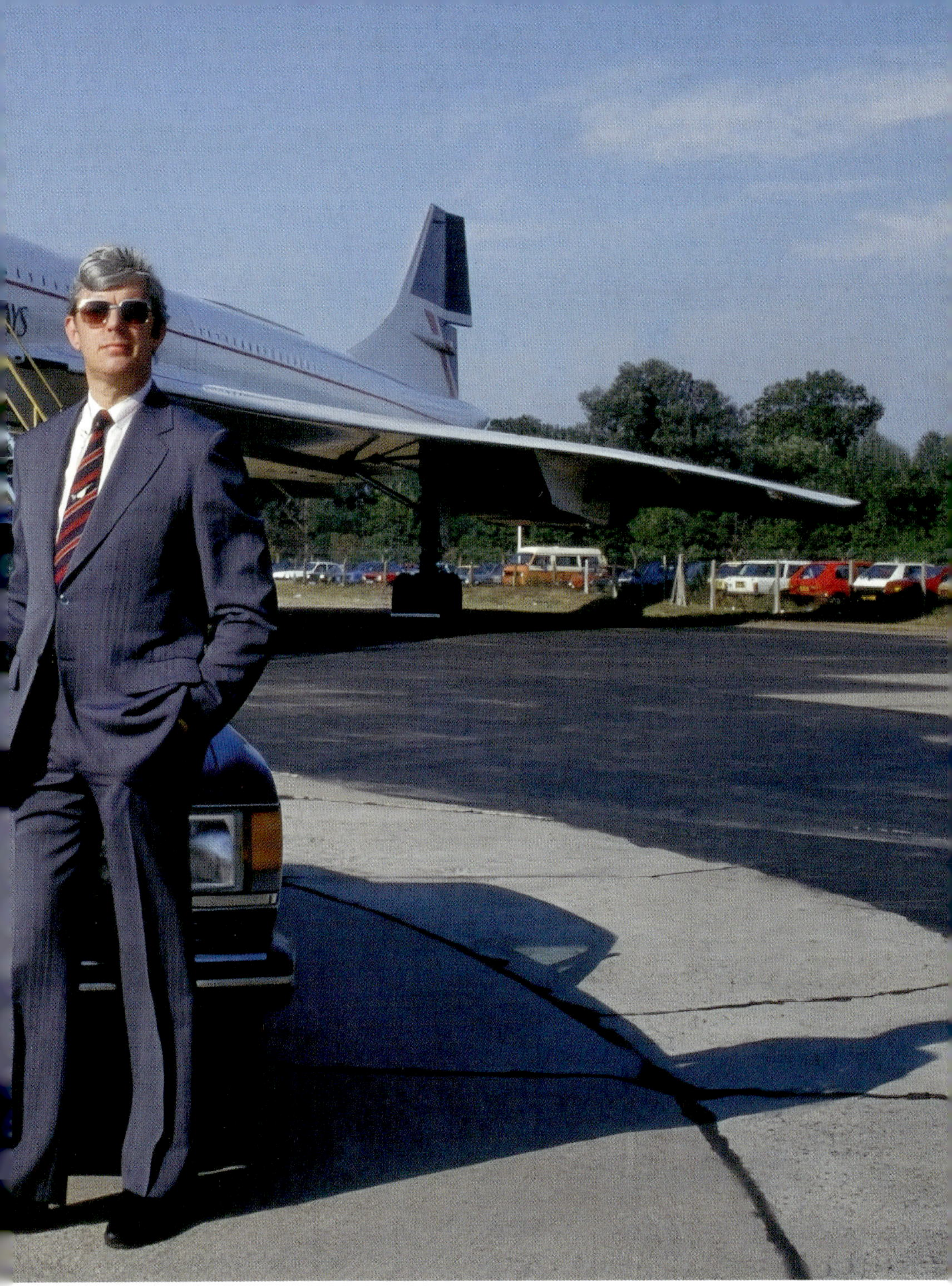

Sonic Boom

Transport

Delta Air Lines' jet base on a 56.6ha *175acre* site at Hartsfield International Airport, Atlanta, Georgia, USA has 14.5ha *36acres* roof area. A recent addition to the hangar gives it a high-bay area of 317 × 74 × 27 m *1041 ×242 ×90ft*.

Chalk's International Airline has flown amphibious aircraft from Miami, Florida, USA to the Bahamas since July 1919. Albert 'Pappy' Chalk flew from 1911–75.

Edwin Shackleton of Bristol, Avon has flown as a passenger in 538 different types of aircraft. His first flight was in March 1943 in D.H. Dominie R9548, and other aircraft have included helicopters, gliders, microlights and balloons. Here he admires the hot-air balloon in which he made flight number 459.
(Photo: Charles Breton)

Airlines

Busiest airline The country with the busiest airlines system is the United States, where the total number of passengers for air carriers in scheduled domestic operations exceeded 481.3 million in 1994.

On 31 Dec 1994 British Airways operated a fleet of 253 aircraft. It employed an average of 51,164 staff, and 30,595,000 passengers were carried in 1993–4 on 644,000km *400,000miles* of unduplicated routes.

Busiest international route The city-pair with the highest international scheduled passenger traffic is London/Paris. More than 3.4 million passengers flew between the two cities in 1992, or nearly 4700 each way each day (although London-bound traffic is higher than that bound for Paris). The busiest intercontinental route is London/New York, with 2.3 million passengers flying between the two cities in 1992.

Largest airline The former Soviet Union's state airline Aeroflot, so named since 1932, was instituted on 9 Feb 1923 and has been the largest airline of all-time. In its last complete year of formal existence (1990) it employed 600,000 — more than the top 18 US airlines put together — and flew 139 million passengers with 20,000 pilots, along 1,000,000 km *620,000 miles* of domestic routes across 11 time zones.

Following the break-up of the Soviet Union, the company which now carries the greatest number of passengers is Delta Air Lines, with 89,053,640 in 1994. The airline with the longest route network is the German airline Lufthansa, which covers 879,303 km *546,373 miles*.

Oldest airline Aircraft Transport & Travel was founded in 1916 and began regular scheduled flights from London to Paris on 25 Aug 1919, although it was swallowed up with several other airlines in 1924 to form Imperial Airways, the forerunner of British Overseas Airways Corporation, which with British European Airways later became British Airways. Of current airlines, the oldest is Koninklijke-Luchtvaart-Maatschappij NV (KLM), the national airline of the Netherlands. It was established in October 1919 and opened its first scheduled service (Amsterdam-London) on 17 May 1920.

Delag (Deutsche Luftschiffahrt AG) was founded at Frankfurt am Main, Germany on 16 Nov 1909 and started a scheduled airship service on 17 Jun 1910.

Personal Aviation Records

Oldest and youngest passengers Airborne births are reported every year.

The oldest person to fly has been Mrs Jessica S. Swift (b. Anna Stewart, 17 Sep 1871), aged 110 years 3 months, from Vermont to Florida, USA in Dec 1981.

The oldest Briton to fly is Charlotte Hughes of Redcar, Cleveland (1877–1993). She was given a flight on Concorde from London to New York as a 110th birthday present on 4 Aug 1987, returning four days later. In February 1992 she became the oldest Briton of all-time (⇨ Longevity).

Pilots *Oldest* Stanley Wood (1896–1994) of Shoreham-by-Sea, W Sussex, was still taking the controls of aircraft at the age of 96, the last occasion being when he flew a Piper Cherokee Warrior on 7 Jun 1993. His first solo flight had been an unofficial one during World War I, which means that his flying career spanned more than 80 per cent of the history of aviation.

Hilda Wallace (b. 26 Nov 1908) of West Vancouver, British Columbia, Canada is the oldest person to qualify as a pilot, obtaining her licence on 15 Mar 1989 at the age of 80 years 109 days.

Longest serving military pilot Squadron Leader Norman E. Rose, AFC and bar, AMN (RAF Retd) (b. 30 May 1924) flew military aircraft without a break in service for 47 years from 1942 to 1989 achieving 11,539 hours of flying in 54 different categories of aircraft. He learnt to fly in a de Havilland Tiger Moth in Southern Rhodesia, and then flew Hawker Hurricanes in World War II.

Most flying hours *Pilot* John Edward Long (b. 10 Nov 1915) (USA) has logged a total of 60,269 hr of flying as a pilot between May 1933 and April 1995 — cumulatively nearly 7 years airborne.

Most transatlantic flights
Between March 1948 and his retirement on 1 Sep 1984 Charles M. Schimpf, a flight service manager with Trans World Airlines, logged a total of 2880 Atlantic crossings — a rate of 6.4 per month.

Passenger The record as a supersonic passenger is held by Fred Finn, who has made 707 Atlantic crossings on Concorde. He commutes regularly between London and New Jersey, USA and had flown a total distance of 17,739,800 km *11,023,000 miles* by the end of March 1995.

Up to her retirement in 1988 Maisie Muir of Orkney, Scotland flew over 8400 times with Loganair in connection with business duties for the Royal Bank of Scotland.

Most aeroplanes flown James B. Taylor, Jr (1897–1942) flew 461 different types of powered aircraft during his 25 years as an active experimental test and demonstration pilot for the US Navy and a number of American aircraft manufacturing companies. He was one of the few pilots of the 1920s and 1930s qualified to perform terminal-velocity dives.

Human-powered flight Kanellos Kanellopoulos (b. 25 Apr 1957) averaged 30.3 km/h *18.8 mph* in his 34.1 m *112 ft* wing span machine flying from Crete to the island of Santorini on 23 Apr 1988, covering 119 km *74 miles* in 3 hr 56 min.

Helicopters

Earliest helicopters Leonardo da Vinci (1452–1519) proposed the idea of a helicopter-type craft, although the Chinese had built helicopter-like toys as early as the 4th century BC.

Fastest helicopter Under FAI rules, the world's speed record for helicopters was set by John Trevor Eggington with co-pilot Derek J. Clews, who averaged 400.87 km/h *249.09 mph* over Glastonbury, Somerset on 11 Aug 1986 in a Westland Lynx demonstrator.

◀◀ ◀◀ **Airports**

130

■ Fred Finn, Rolls Royce and Concorde. An appropriate photograph for the man who has flown a record 707 times on Concorde. He is a frequent spokesman for the air traveller and has appeared on a number of television programmes on both sides of the Atlantic, discussing various aspects of executive travel.

47. The Guinness Book of Records. All the proof I need that I am the world's most travelled man

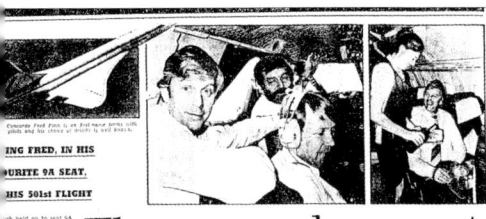

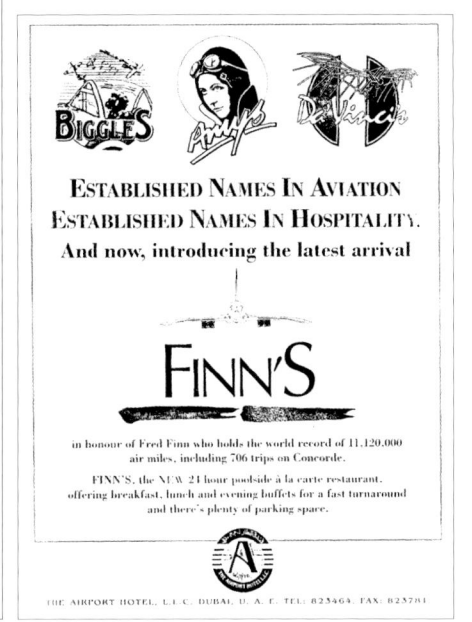

Sonic Boom

48. Press cutting of my travelling adventure.

Sonic Boom

49. My good friend Alain St Ange, former Seychelles Minster of Ports Tourism and Aviations.

50. One of the oldest surviving traditional ceremonies still in existence today, being presented with the Freedom of the City of London.

Sonic Boom

51. Playing Cricket for Virgin Celebrity with Mickey Dolan of the Monkeys in Santa Monica California.

52. International Cricket Crusaders 1968. I'm third behind Basil D'Oliveira.

139

Sonic Boom

53. One of the rangers protecting the rhino from poachers at the Ol Pejeta Conservancy, Kenya.

54. Catching Amberjack in Miami.

55. I was elated to be reunited with the greatest cricketing legend of all time - Sir Garry Sobers - at his home in Barbados in January 2024. We played together with the International Cavaliers in 1968.

3. Crazy airports

Arriving in the Seychelles was always an adventure. We would land on a runway that was a pontoon built into the ocean - the fire trucks were fire boats. On one of their islands you land on the football field, that island is that small. It was always worthwhile to risk this unconventional landing because the Seychelles is paradise on earth. Plus, it was a pleasure to see my friend Alain St Ange when I visited. He's one of the leading lights of African tourism (Seychelles is officially part of Africa) and was Seychelles Minister Tourism, Civil Aviation, Ports and Marine.

I would often fly into South Africa and meet senior South African business people on the way. One such man asked me to come and speak to his colleagues on a corporate retreat called Mala Mala in the Kruger National Park. So he arranged for me to fly in on a private jet, but we missed the curfew time and landed at 7.32 in the evening – which was illegal. We were both arrested, but since my friend was well known and a friend of a South African Minister in the government, he was there to see us quickly released to enjoy this beautiful retreat.

Nairobi is one of my favourite airports, because as soon as I land there, I know I'll soon be in the fantastic Kenyan countryside, where I'm the happiest. Even so, it can be a terrifying place to land or take off. When it rains, the frogs come out. And when the frogs come out, the birds arrive en masse to eat them. One time on a BA flight from Nairobi to Johannesburg in South Africa, we had two bird strikes right after take-off and had to abort, quite an experience in its own right in a 747. It cost the airline $1 million in damages to the plane. I was transferred to KLM which had waited for the runway to dry out.

In Nigeria, the normal rules of aviation didn't apply. You'd go to the bathroom whilst waiting for boarding to complete to wash and cool off from the high humidity in Lagos only to find that someone else had the same boarding pass and seat number as yours. They had taken your seat by the time you came back. On one particular flight I gave up my seat and decided to drive. The pilot ran out of fuel on the flight and landed in a field four miles short of the runway. Forty-seven people died. Lucky me again. You'd hear stories like this, with dozens of people dying when they couldn't find anywhere to land.

4. Lightning strike

These days, lightning strikes are a routine part of international aviation. They happen thousands of times a year, with no ill effects, because aircraft are designed to conduct electricity and keep everyone safe inside.

Back in 1963, just after I began flying, a lightning strike on a Pan Am 707 flying from Baltimore to Philadelphia ignited fuel in its tanks and caused it to crash in Elkton, Maryland, with the loss of all 81 people on board.

Aircraft manufacturers worked hard to rectify this vulnerability and since then, there have been virtually no other recorded examples of lightning strikes causing crashes, with one exception: a Lockheed Electra turboprop aircraft crashed in Peru in 1971 after the crew, under pressure to meet holiday schedules, deliberately ignored advice and flew through extremely poor weather, where the plane was struck by lightning.

The most amazing part of this story was that one passenger, 17-year-old Juliane Koepcke, survived the crash while still strapped to her seat, falling into dense jungle. She trekked for 10 days with a broken collar bone and other injuries before local fishermen rescued her and took her back to civilization.

My own lightning strike was dramatic, but not that dramatic. It was on my 500th Concorde flight and the weather Gods made the celebrations go with an extra bang. No harm done.

Chapter 8
Airlines: the Good, the Bad and the Ugly

In a lifetime of travel, I've been a passenger on literally thousands of planes. Over the years, I've compiled a mental map of the different airlines I've flown on. What kind of welcome they provide, the state of their aircraft and the level of service. Each has its own idiosyncrasies and character, along with a long and generally dramatic history. Each of them has suffered major accidents at some time, which I think can tell you a lot about the character of the airline – how did the flight crew respond to a crisis? What did the airline do in the aftermath? If you read their official histories, some of them don't even mention their crashes. So it's important to remember: flying can be a dangerous business.

Here are some reflections on what I've found in more than six decades of flying.

Pan Am

My relationship with Pan Am dates right back to the late 1950s. Along with British Airways, it's probably the airline with whom I spent most of my 15 million-plus miles in the air.

I was on the second flight of its Boeing 707 out of Paris to New York, which must have been around 1959. Then I was on one of the first scheduled Boeing 747 flights from Heathrow to New York. Back in those days I wasn't necessarily flying first class or business but even so the standard was exemplary. Pan Am unintentionally pioneered the very first "lie flat seats": you could detach the armrests across all four seats on a quiet flight, meaning you could lie right across and get a great night's sleep. I vividly recall waking up ready for breakfast around an hour before arriving into Heathrow from New York to the awful smell of microwaved croissants.

My first experience of flying first class with Pan Am came in around 1973. There was no business class in those days, the first airline to offer this was Qantas in 1979. In fact business class only became mainstream in the mid-eighties with Virgin Atlantic. I was flying Pan Am so often between New York and London, Tehran, Lahore etc that I was invited to sample first class.

I remember the first time I turned left upon boarding and settled into seat

5J. Just as on Concorde 9a, I had a regular allocated seat with Pan Am. On one occasion I found my seat occupied (but not allocated) by someone who described himself as a Swedish Lord. I think he was a lawyer or something. I went up to him and said: "Excuse me, I think you are sitting in my seat, here's my boarding pass." He replied: "What difference does it make?" So, I said: "If it makes no difference, get in your own seat."

Anyway, he proceeded to kick the back of my seat for the duration of the flight until I got up mid-flight and threatened to smack him one! (He did apologise when we disembarked).

There was another occasion where Christopher Lee – the best actor ever to play Dracula in my opinion - was in the seat behind me. "Will it be safe for me to go to sleep with you behind me?" I asked him. What a charming man, a real gent.

Morning croissants apart, Pan Am used to offer a daily special dish which was never advertised on the menu. I remember talking with the Pan Am London Airport Manager Ron McBride, who always used to come and see me off whenever I flew. He advised me of this special service, so I ordered a beautiful lobster dish with Ron which was then passed onto the crew. When I was on the flight the crew proceeded to inform me that my lobster had been given to an eight-year-old child!

I must have caused a bit of a scene as the captain came down and demanded to see my ticket. I told him straight that he had no right to see my ticket. As a result of this, the crew reported me to Pan Am as they were under the illusion that I was a crew or staff member and didn't have the right to make such demands.

A few days later I received a phone call from the president of the airline, Dan Colussy, asking me what I was doing tomorrow as he wanted to invite me to the Pan Am building in Manhattan (now crazily called the MetLife building; it should never have been re-named as it was built by the airline, for the airline and as far as I'm concerned it is part of the history of New York) for breakfast to discuss my experience on the flight. I accepted, caught the train in from my home and had breakfast with the president, where he explained to me that they were holding a conference for all the Pan Am flight crews which he wanted me to attend and sit next to him at the top table and be introduced so that everyone within the airline would know who I was and thus ensuring I wouldn't have this experience again.

I am quite sure that the "First Class silver service" offered upstairs on Pan Am's 747s was the greatest meal experience offered by any airline at the time and probably in history. The crew were trained at the Savoy Hotel in London on how to prepare and serve silver service. Everything was fantastic, from the menus which were so tastefully designed they really were quite something. All the roasts were freshly cooked fresh on board, not pre-heated, and it really was the best of the best with an exclusive wine list - rivalled only by Concorde, which had its own wine cellar. They would take your order while you were sitting downstairs in your First Class seat then come and call you: "Mr Finn your table is ready", upon which you would climb the spiral staircase where two tables of two and two of four were prepared and waiting. You could have roast beef, roast lamb, fresh salmon, whatever you wanted. Then they'd carve it at your table just like in an upmarket restaurant. So on an eight hour flight, you might spend four hours up there, having starters, main course, dessert, cheese, wines and cognac. You could even have a cigar after dinner if you wanted. It was like being on a private jet because there were only 12 people up there. Truly wonderful.

There was a period of ten years or so, from the mid-1960s to the mid-1970s, when Pan Am was pretty much the world's greatest airline. By the end of the 1960s it carried 11 million passengers a year and had 150 jets flying to 86 countries on every continent except Antarctica. It ran a helicopter shuttle between JFK, LaGuardia and Newark airports to downtown Manhattan, owned the Intercontinental hotel chain and in 1960 built one of the great terminal buildings – Worldport at JFK – with its vast 16,000 square metre roof suspended by steel posts and cables.

You really felt that you were being well treated on Pan Am: most of the cabin crew even had nursing qualifications!

Over the years I would estimate I must have flown in excess of 4 million miles with Pan Am, they really were a wonderful airline and their demise was something that should never have happened. The thing that caused the end of this great airline was mainly deregulation within the United States, which allowed all airlines to fly anywhere in the world. Pan Am did not operate any domestic flights as they were the United States' national flag carrier, in the same way that British Airways is with the United Kingdom. Suddenly they were faced with having to acquire domestic routes within the US in order to survive, which resulted in them buying the airline National, based in Florida, where all the crew wore bright orange uniforms and chewed gum, which went against everything Pan Am stood for. Their own crew had to have a degree and speak several languages. This naturally pissed off a lot of original crew with the airline.

All these other domestic US airlines like United, Eastern or Braniff (which served the best breakfast on any airline between Dallas and Chicago) also started flying to international destinations, which created very stiff competition for Pan Am. This competition intensified when Pan Am bought National Airlines, which was owned by Maytag Washing Machines, at an inflated price and acquired its ageing aircraft - which included DC10s which were not part of the Pan Am fleet, thus causing engineering and support issues as well as additional costs.

I flew on one of the Pan Am re-branded DC10s from New York to Rome. On this aircraft the kitchen was located downstairs in the forward cargo hold and the meals were transferred by a small lift. Anyway, on this flight I couldn't locate any of the first-class crew, so I proceeded to go down in the lift myself and found them in the "kitchen" celebrating someone's birthday, having a right old party. I thought if you can't beat them, join them, and I did!

Approximately six months after Pan Am bought National, de-regulation was introduced into the United States and Pan Am were now lumbered with competition, which resulted in them having to sell many of their routes to other US carriers.

The Lockerbie bombing in December 1988 made everything worse for Pan Am. An investigation found that a suitcase had made it into the forward cargo hold of the Boeing 747 from Frankfurt to Heathrow, without its owner on board. This then blew up over Scotland killing all 259 passengers and crew, along with 11 people on the ground. Pam Am argued that it couldn't have prepared for this act of terrorism, but the public mood turned against the airline. Then, when oil prices jumped during the Gulf War in 1990, it left Pan Am in deep trouble. Inevitably it filed for bankruptcy in 1991, where the two main benefactors were United and Delta, with the latter getting the bulk of the airline's assets.

One memory that has always stuck with me about Pan Am was the fact that I was on the very first 747 flight from New York to Nairobi via Dakar and Lagos (the flight was nearly 24 hours with all the stops) and the guy who opened the door for me was the same guy who closed the door on the final flight out of Nairobi, Tony Lewis, and I remember he gave me his 30-year Pan Am service badge. In 1977 they were the only airline to fly around the world, pole to pole. They also held a world speed record on a 747SP (this variant was shorter and faster than the regular aircraft). A truly wonderful airline and in my opinion the very best that there was.

British Airways

In the 1950s, when I first flew with British Overseas Airways Corporation (BOAC) – which later became British Airways – it had a definite air of superiority. It was almost as though you had to be accepted by them, rather than that they offered customers a service.

In its very first original form, the company was called Aircraft Transport and Travel Limited (AT&T) and operated the world's first daily international route, from Hounslow Heath – near present-day Heathrow – to Paris. It had a legacy stretching back to the earliest days of air travel, so you could understand how the company considered itself a cut above the rest.

First it turned into Imperial Airways from 1924, flying from Croydon to European cities and launching routes to Africa, the Middle East and India. This had even more of a superior feel to it: British gentry flying out to inspect the colonies.

Then in 1935 came the first mention of British Airways, when four private airlines merged, going back to BOAC in 1940 during the Second World War, under the Air Ministry. The company expanding quickly after the war ended, with its De Havilland Comet jets flying across the Atlantic to the United States from 1952. This really was the dawn of the jet age.

At this time, the UK government owned not only BOAC but also British European Airways and British South American Airways, as British aviation spread around the world. Then, after the first wide-bodied aircraft joined its fleet in 1974, BOAC merged with British European Airways to form British Airways again. The name has stuck ever since.

I remember when Sir Roy Watts was chief executive of British Airways, having come from British European Airways. He was a very well-liked manager who turned BA around from the mid-1970s, when it was one of the worst-performing airlines in Europe, to the early 1980s, when it could justifiably claim to be 'the world's favourite airline', with tremendous customer service and very high standards in the cabins.

When you talk to people who worked at BA at the time, they credit Roy, rather than Lord King, with the revitalisation of the airline, making it ready for privatisation in 1987. He slimmed down the workforce from 52,000 to 39,000, but somehow managed to keep people on side by making deals with the unions and making sure that customers' needs were at the centre of everything.

What I remember is that the old BOAC snobbism came to the surface: other executives smothered him and didn't treat him well – he wasn't considered 'BOAC material', meaning that he wasn't upper class enough. In the end, he drowned after throwing himself in the Thames at the age of 67, although that could be more to do with his health – he'd just been diagnosed with Parkinson's disease.

Sir Roy once sent me a letter saying: "This is to introduce Fred Finn. He has flown with British Concorde over 300 times. Please give him any assistance that he may require."

This was a very generous thing to do. I didn't want to abuse the privilege, but occasionally I needed to use it. For example, one time I had an appointment with Colin Marshall, BA chief executive and the BA flight I was on was running late, so I asked the BA check-in person if he could send a message to Marshall. He said: "Do it yourself!" I was determined not to be late, so I took a Gulf Air flight instead that would get me to London on time. I told Colin Marshall this story and that his check-in person needed a wake-up call! Marshall actually re-wrote the letter that Sir Colin Marshall gave to me at the 100th birthday of the Savoy Hotel in August 1989, which was kind of him.

Marshall was hired as BA's chief executive in 1983, with the instructions from the chairman Lord King to get it ready for privatisation. And King himself had been appointed by Prime Minister Margaret Thatcher, as part of her drive to privatise large sections of British industry and reduce the power of the unions, which she felt were restricting the country's growth prospects.

As a passenger, I liked the fact that British Airways put more emphasis on customer service. There used to be a time when the Cabin Service Director would come and find me in the airport lounge and say: "Right, Mr Fred, we're ready to board," and take my case. That level of service disappeared long ago, but you still felt with BA at its best that you were well-treated. There were expectations of passengers, that they should be well-behaved and treat the cabin crew with respect, but the same applied in reverse. It was about civility and standards.

On the flip side, the mess that BA got itself into with the dirty tricks campaign against Sir Richard Branson and Virgin Atlantic was just self-inflicted. They hacked into Virgin's passenger files and tried to poach their transatlantic customers, while smearing them in the papers. In my view, BA became complacent and allowed Virgin to become a rival, because it took customers for granted a little bit, while Virgin made them feel special and gave the impression that they'd have more fun on a Virgin flight. That was a criticism you could make of BA in the 1990s – it was more buttoned-up and formal than it needed to be (still some remnants of the old snobbism, perhaps).

Since I flew so often with BA, the airline came to me for advice on its flights, on airport services, on crew issues…all kinds of things. They had a commercial director called Howard Phelps who I got on with very well. He took me to see Terminal 4 at Heathrow ahead of the opening and asked what I thought. I told him the carousels were too small. So, they changed them.

Another time, I flew with BA to Cairo, which is a five-and-a-half-hour flight, and the cabin crew in First Class didn't really know what they were doing, because they'd only been trained to work on short haul flights. Here again, BA took my views seriously. I was asked by Terry Lakin, the fleet training captain, to fly to Cairo with him. Terry confirmed my fears and changes were made, which was good to see. And on a lighter note, when the ladies of the cabin crew earned their wings, Howard Phelps Commercial Director would ask me to pin them onto their uniforms at Cranebank where they were trained. which was a nice role to be asked to perform and I still see some of the them now when I fly

Under Colin Marshall, people felt good about BA. It was never really the world's best carrier but the service, the soft colours inside the cabin, it was like an old slipper, it felt comfortable. I knew when I got on to a BA plane, I'd see a friendly face. The food was OK, the crew were well-trained and safe, so it all meant, for me, that I liked to fly with them.

After Colin Marshall, Bob Ayling took over as BA chief executive in 1993. Like Roy Watts, Ayling tried to reduce costs and succeeded in shaving off £750 million, while setting up the budget airline Go in 1998, but it didn't do the trick: BA suffered a drop of 84 per cent in its profits and Ayling will always be remembered for his multi coloured tails on the BA fleet. Lady Thatcher famously draped a handkerchief over a model plane with the world colours logo, declaring it "awful". Bob Ayling was toast – sacked in March 2000 and replaced by Sir Rod Eddington.

Eddington was a cheerful Ozzie and had a witty turn of phrase. "I've had a lot of luck at BA," he said in 2005, as he left the airline. "All of it bad."

I write about his experiences with Concorde in another chapter, but from a BA point of view, one thing after another went wrong. A plan to merge with KLM fell through in September 2000. British Asia Airways, formed in 1993 to fly passengers between London and Taipei, collapsed in 2001. Go was sold to its management and an investment firm in the same year (it was then sold to EasyJet in 2002 and effectively disappeared). The September 2001 attacks on the World Trade Center in New York were devastating for international air travel and meant BA had to lay off hundreds of staff. And in a final piece of bad luck, Eddington oversaw BA selling its stake in Australian airline Qantas in 2004. He retreated back to Australia and handed over to an Irishman, Willie Walsh.

Things had been on a downward slide under Eddington, whether from bad luck or poor judgement. But in my opinion, when Willie Walsh took over in 2005, he didn't seem to care about the passengers or the crew, only about profit and shareholders. He came from the Irish national carrier Aer Lingus and was a former pilot and union delegate. The 44-year-old Dubliner has since played down that outburst as the youthful hyperbole of a pilot at Aer Lingus in the early 1980s. But his achievements, after a rapid ascent up the management ranks at Ireland's national carrier, ensured that the hard-headed label stuck with him at BA. His plan was to merge BA with other international carriers and form as big a group as possible, on the grounds of 'the bigger the better', certainly from a stock market perspective.

Spanish businessman Alex Cruz took the reins at BA in 2016 and immediately sacked 700 BA computer staff, outsourcing the jobs to India in a renewed attempt to save money. Sure enough, in May 2017, a computer glitch meant that hundreds of BA flights were cancelled affecting more than 75,000 people. Cruz turned BA into a kind of budget hybrid airline where you buy Marks & Spencer sandwiches instead of being served airline food, where the cabin crew regularly go on strike because they're treated so poorly. But if the shareholders are happy, then I suppose it's alright.

British Airways Flight 476 in 1976

A BA flight from Heathrow to Istanbul hit a regional plane above Yugoslavia on 10 September 1976 killing all 63 people on board. It was blamed on the local air traffic control which had failed to spot the colliding planes.

For decades, BA has been mercifully free of fatal crashes, making it one of the world's safest airlines. Changes to ATC regulations came in following the disaster.

Virgin Atlantic

One day I flew into New York on Concorde and caught the helicopter shuttle over to Newark. A guy came up to me at the terminal in Newark and said: "You're Fred Finn." So I said: "Yes I am". He said that Richard Branson would like to have lunch with me. I told him I'd be back in London in three or four days' time, but he said: "It's tomorrow." "When did you know about this?" I asked. He said: "We knew this morning that you'd be coming here this evening," so I said: "Well I was in London four hours ago, I just came on Concorde, and if you had told me whilst I was still in London, I would have stayed there." He said: "Well, we've got this flight, we've got a seat on it for you," so instead of going home, I got on another flight and flew back to London. I met Richard in London on a little boat in the river with his own chef. We had a great lunch together, on his houseboat in Pimlico. I spent three hours with him talking about what he wanted to do with Virgin Atlantic and what I could do to help him. So I helped him with ideas about providing a limousine for passengers and for Upper Class seats. At that time, companies were cutting back on First Class travel. Instead, Upper Class would give passengers a lot more than many First-Class seats did, like the limousine service for each guest, a masseuse onboard, a bar onboard. It was a fun way to fly.

Once it launched, passengers loved Upper Class and the bean counters loved it as well because they were paying for Business Class rather than First Class seats. Everybody was happy.

I did many things with Richard. I arranged for him to fly with the Red Arrows – the Royal Air Force Aerobatic Team. We drove up to their base at Scampton in Lincolnshire, which is 150 miles from London and took hours to get to. Since we were staying with the pilots at their homes, Richard was late due to him winning some music award in the New York. I remember he was on my car phone most of the trip to RAF Scampton arriving there close to midnight. It's a rare honour to fly with the Red Arrows and Richard, as a famous daredevil and adventurer, was thrilled to get the opportunity. The pilot took him on a hair-raising series of spins and loops, which made us all absolutely breathless on the ground, never mind what it must have felt like in mid-air. They perform manoeuvres which exert as much as 8G – meaning eight times the force of gravity – which can be enough to make people black out. And that was only the testing sortie. He did the full Red Arrows flight after lunch which I have always felt easier with because you have something to focus on. Richard did very well.

Richard stumbled out of the Hawk T1 aircraft looking distinctly green around the gills after that, but he absolutely loved it. It was one of the most memorable days, being so close to these astonishing pilots, really the best of the best of the Royal Air Force.

To mark my 10 millionth mile in the air, Richard Branson and Virgin laid on a fantastic party in London followed by a weekend trip to Los Angeles in April 1991. Richard hosted a champagne reception in a roof garden in Kensington, with ten air stewards and stewardesses in uniform, where there was a special presentation. Next there was a seafood dinner at Solomon's restaurant close to Gatwick, a night in Prestige Hotel South Lodge, a 'champagne astronaut breakfast' in the morning (though I'm not sure astronauts drink champagne, at breakfast or any other time!)

Around 30 of us flew out from Gatwick including the actress Gemma Craven and her husband David and Cathy Podewell, editors and columnists from the Times, the Daily Mail and the Mirror, various travel magazine writers and a bunch of TV camera crews. It was like a mini film festival! In Virgin Atlantic Upper Class, we had a celebration cake, leather gifts, a beauty therapist and special menus, followed by a welcome party in Los Angeles with a ribbon cutting ceremony and banner celebrating the 10 million miles.

We had two days of partying in the city of stars with celebrities like Cathy Podewell, who played Cally Harper Ewing in Dallas; we lunched at Gladstone's restaurant on the beach, went on a VIP tour of MCA-Universal Studios and danced the night away at Roxbury on Sunset Boulevard.

It was very generous of Richard to arrange all this for me. I guess it's a bit like celebrating your 100th birthday, these events spring up and people love to celebrate them.

Richard and I worked together for quite a few years. I wasn't a Virgin employee, but I was retained as a consultant, to advise him on travel and hospitality. When I represented Cellnet, I made sure they gave one of their phones to Richard, because they wanted famous people and celebrities to have them. But then every week his assistant would call me and say he'd lost his phone and could he have another one. When he did manage to find it, Richard would try to call me and dial the Cellnet chairman, because our numbers were similar to each other. "Not again!" the chairman would say.

I travelled pretty widely with Richard. I took him and his family on safari to Kenya, then played cricket with him in Santa Monica, watched by Pamela Anderson and some of the Los Angeles Lakers basketball team. More recently I flew with Richard on Virgin Atlantic's inaugural Dreamliner flight from London to Atlanta, where in typical Richard style there were two live bands on board – drum and bass group Rudimental and synth pop band Gorgon City. Their sets were streamed on live video from 35,000 feet to thousands of viewers back on the ground. It was a pretty hectic flight, with everyone dancing in the aisles and these bands rampaging around, playing trumpets and banging their drums. Sometimes it's an advantage to be a little bit deaf!

When you compare this nightclub atmosphere on board to the formality of British Airways, or the humdrum routine of most American airlines, you have to hand it to Richard. He really knows how to add sparkle to a brand, how to attract customers by giving them a sense of freshness, youth and adventure. One of the members of Rudimental, who played their number one hit "Feel the Love" on board the flight, said: "What a buzz. Having all the band together, playing to thousands of people around the world from a bar on a plane, you can't put a price on that. It's an experience we will never forget."

For Virgin Atlantic, you can't put a price on it either. Whatever Richard offered this band, he would have earned back many times in flight bookings and free publicity from people who knew there wouldn't be any live bands on their planes, but liked the idea that it just might happen.

Despite spending so many days of my life flying on Concorde, which of course was only available with British Airways and Air France, I always enjoyed the Virgin experience. From the very beginning, it was friendly, fun and different from the legacy carriers. Even the way that you could buy tickets in Virgin record stores was different and gave it an edge of youth and glamour.

Richard famously once asked a journalist if they knew how to become a millionaire. The answer, he said, was to start off as a billionaire and start a new airline. Even though Virgin Atlantic has had its financial ups and downs, selling shares to Singapore Airlines who then sold their stake to Delta, and even filing for bankruptcy protection in 2020, it's pretty amazing that Richard has managed to keep it up in the air for so long, celebrating it's 40th anniversary in June this year.

I think the British Airways libel case, which Virgin won after it discovered all the dirty tricks BA was playing, leading to an award of £500,000 damages to Richard, £110,000 to the airline and a legal bill of £3 million, changed a lot of people's minds about the business. It was not just a party airline, with sexy stewardesses and a casual attitude. It was a genuine contender to replace BA as the most important British carrier. Certainly, that was Richard's ambition and for many travellers, he succeeded.

Richard's many death-defying adventures whether it be hot air ballooning crossing the Atlantic, abseiling down skyscrapers or building rocket ships, meant I arranged for Cellnet to sponsor these endeavours. "The more he got in the news for his adventures, the more Virgin Atlantic became renowned as the airline you flew if you wanted an adventure," as Virgin itself puts it. "Screw it, let's do it," was Richard's philosophy.

I like to think that Richard saw something of himself in me. We share a restlessness, a love of sport, and adventurous personalities. We both left school at 16 and embarked on a lifetime of enterprise and new experiences, centred around travel and hospitality. If you ignore the several billion pounds that he's worth, we're almost identical.

Lufthansa

Lufthansa has a massive fleet of more than 700 planes – the second largest in Europe in terms of passengers carried behind budget carrier Ryanair. It also owns various other companies including Austrian Airlines, Swiss International Air Lines, Brussels Airlines and has its own budget airline EuroWings, as well as the repair business Lufthansa Technik and catering group LSG Sky Chefs.

I had a great experience with Lufthansa once. I was flying Pan Am to Kenya and the flight was over-booked. We had to go to Frankfurt and we missed the connection. The Lufthansa manager came over and said: "Here's two first class seats compliments of Lufthansa." So that made quite a good impression.

Its roots go back to 1926 and the formation of Deutsche Luft Hansa ('German Air Company') in Berlin. The business closed after World War II but then started again in 1953 under new management, flying both domestic and international routes on Super Constellation aircraft to New York, Canada, South American airports and Tehran. In the 1960s it went yet further afield, flying to Bangkok, Hong Kong, Lagos and Johannesburg.

Like so many other airlines, Lufthansa was seriously tempted by supersonic flight in the 1960s and set up a special committee to examine the prospects. It was chaired by Professor Ernst Simon of the airline's engineering division and looked closely at both Concorde and its American competitor the Boeing 2707. After careful consideration, he decided that the American option would be too costly to operate and Concorde's payload of 100 passengers was too low. "None of these designs could have been operated by Lufthansa at a profit," he declared.

Part of the problem was that, since the airline's main hub was in Frankfurt, which is around 350km away from the nearest coastline in the Netherlands, a supersonic plane would have to fly subsonic for a good distance before it could accelerate up to supersonic speeds. Even then, the distance between Frankfurt and New York was beyond Concorde's expected range, so it would need a refuelling stop in Shannon, Ireland, part of the way across the Atlantic. A Lufthansa manager once joked: "Tell me how many Concorde I should buy and I'll tell you when I have to declare bankruptcy." Although Lufthansa took out options in three Concorde's in 1967, it cancelled these along with most other airlines in April 1973.

Meanwhile in the 1970s, Lufthansa was plagued by reliability problems and was probably the most-often hijacked airline in the world – and there was plenty of competition. Its worst accident in those years came in November 1974 when a Boeing 747 crashed shortly after take-off from Nairobi, killing 59 out of the 157 people on board. The airline suffered four hijackings in 1972 alone, including one on a Boeing 747 with 172 passengers and 15 crew, which was diverted to Aden in the Middle East. The passengers were freed in return for a $5 million ransom payment paid by the German government. There were several more hijackings later in the 1970s until a group of international airlines got together and brought in better security arrangements.

I myself was caught up in a hijacking drama in Hamburg in 1977. I was on a British Airways flight, so I think the fashion for hijacking by German terrorists and freedom fighters had spread from Lufthansa to other airlines by then. I tell the full story of this episode in my chapter on Narrow Escapes.

One of the strangest aviation stories I've heard happened on a Lufthansa flight in January 1984. An unclaimed suitcase was spotted on a carousel in Los Angeles airport after coming off a Lufthansa flight from Germany. Upon opening it, airport staff found a dead Iranian woman who had been denied a United States visa in Germany and decided she would travel to the US in her own luggage. How she managed to get through customs and onto the plane is a mystery worthy of Agatha Christie (or Houdini).

My experience of flying on Lufthansa is that, hijackings aside, it is a reliable, efficient airline with clean, modern aircraft, great punctuality and some of the best airport facilities in the world. The First Class lounge in Frankfurt is absolutely world-beating, with its own spa, Michelin-starred chefs and a selection of 130 whiskies. Just as I used to experience with British Airways decades ago, Lufthansa's First Class passengers get their own personal assistant escorting them down through passport control and out to a waiting limousine, which drives them to their plane.

Germanwings flight 9525

The worst thing that's ever happened to Lufthansa was on 24 March 2015 when pilot Andreas Lubitz locked his co-pilot out of the flight deck and crashed Germanwings flight 9525 – an Airbus A320 – into the French Alps, killing himself and 149 others on their way from Barcelona to Düsseldorf. This terrible incident happened partly because airlines had made the cabin doors more secure, to protect the flight crew from terrorists in the wake of the 9/11 hijackings. It also turned out that Lubitz had a history of depression and had been hospitalised for mental health reasons in 2008 during a Lufthansa pilot training scheme. His doctor diagnosed suicidal tendencies and declared him unfit to work.

Following the tragedy, European regulators insisted that there should always be two pilots on the flight deck at all times.

After a break for COVID, during which the German government gave Lufthansa a €9 billion bailout in return for a 20 per cent stake in the company, and the airline announcing its plans to retire its entire fleet of A340s and A380s, in the summer of 2022 it decided that things weren't so bad really. In 2023 it decided to bring all of its A380s back into service and bought a 41 per cent stake in Italian airline ITA Airways. So I think we can say that it's back to prime health again.

KLM

From 1919 until its merger with Air France in 2004, KLM (originally Koninklijke Luchvaartmaatschappij or 'Royal Airline') was the longest continuously operating airline in the world. Beginning in Amsterdam, its first route was across the Channel to London on a de Havilland DH-16, followed quickly by routes to Copenhagen, Hamburg and Brussels. A sister airline started flights to the Dutch East Indies (now Indonesia) on a Fokker F.VII, which in the 1930s were the longest scheduled air routes available.

Planes in those days weren't always reliable and KLM suffered an unusually terrible week in July 1935 when three planes crashed one after another, leaving it with a shortage of both planes and pilots. During World War II, it lost many further planes, but built up a thriving Caribbean service. Then after the War, KLM pioneered routes across the Atlantic, becoming the first European airline to fly to New York in 1946, with other routes to South America launching in the same year.

As with other post-War airlines, KLM was part-nationalised in the 1950s to save it from economic collapse, but it kept on innovating new routes, including a transpolar flight from Amsterdam to Tokyo via Anchorage in Alaska where the crew were equipped with a winter survival kit and AR-10 carbine guns to shoot polar bears in case they had to make an emergency landing on ice.

In the 1980s and 1990s KLM agreed a series of partnerships: with Northwest Airlines in the United States (buying a 20 per cent share in the airline), with Kenya Airways (another percentage acquisition) and it began joint operations with Malaysian Airlines. It also merged two of its smaller subsidiaries, Cityhopper and Neterlines, into KLM Cityhopper. Despite fierce competition from budget carriers Ryanair and easyjet, KLM Cityhopper has done really well in recent years, flying its fleet of 61 Brazilian Embraer jets all over Europe.

I've always enjoyed flying with KLM. I used to take their flights down from Amsterdam to Lagos. They were definitely preferable to Nigeria Airways, which did everything wrong, as far as I can remember. They would have two passengers booked onto the same seat, they were forever taking bribes and passengers would bring their entire possessions on board with them. It was really chaotic.

On KLM's intercontinental First Class flights they give you little Delft porcelain models of those tall, narrow Amsterdam townhouses, filled with Dutch gin. These have become collectors' items – there are now 103 of them, one for every year of the airline's history – and I'm sure they attract passengers back to add to their collections. In 2021, to celebrate its 102nd birthday, the airline launched a new Delft Blue house based on the Tuschinki Theatre in Amsterdam. KLM President Pieter Elbers said of the new model: "Tuschinki's philosophy of creating a warm sense of home and giving customers a memorable experience is what KLM stands for too." That's what I've found with KLM, it's a welcoming and friendly airline.

KLM's main airport hub is of course Amsterdam Schiphol, one of the most relaxing places to depart from or arrive into. I like the way its gates are all designed in a wide arc, which gives you a kind of reassurance that you're not far from your destination, rather than the endless long straight corridors you have to trek along in most modern airports.

Once it had merged with Air France in 2004, the joint group was among the biggest airlines in Europe, helping it to weather the economic storms of COVID-19 and successive downturns in passenger numbers. I hope it can maintain its friendly ethos as part of such a big group.

KLM's Tenerife crash in 1977

The biggest blot on KLM's copybook came on 27 March 1977 when a Boeing 747 flight full of holidaymakers tried to take off from Tenerife's Los Rodeos Airport in the Canary Islands and smashed into another 747 operated by Pan Am with hundreds more tourists that was parked on the runway.

This incident was – and still is – the single worst air crash in history, causing 583 fatalities (unless you count the 11 September 2001 attacks on the World Trade Center). It led to multiple changes in aviation regulations and protocols, because there were so many things that could have been handled differently, which would have avoided the tragedy.

The trouble started with a bomb going off at Gran Canaria Airport, the neighbouring island to which both of the Boeing 747s were heading. That injured eight people and caused the airport to be shut down. All incoming flights to Gran Canaria were re-routed to Tenerife, causing congestion on the taxiways and runways.

In the middle of all this congestion, KLM flight 4805 piloted by veteran captain Jacob van Zanten decided to refuel in Tenerife, to save time later. Pan Am flight 1736, piloted by Victor Grubbs, wanted to take off but had to dodge around the KLM flight to get onto the runway. He was told to taxi down to exit three and turn off, but he disobeyed that order and sat on the runway, waiting for permission to take off.

Van Zanten, meanwhile, was in a hurry to leave because he was close to the limit of his duty time. Also, the weather was deteriorating and thick fog was settling on the runway. There followed a garbled conversation between van Zanten, Grubbs and the Air Traffic Control tower, with the KLM crew saying they were "at takeoff", the ATC telling them to "stand by for takeoff" and asking the Pan Am crew whether they were clear. Pan Am replied: "OK, will report when clear." This worried KLM's flight engineer, who asked van Zanten if he was sure the Pan Am flight was clear of the runway. "Oh yes," replied the captain as he pushed forward the throttle and set off down the runway.

"Goddam, that son-of-a-bitch is coming!" shouted Captain Grubbs on the Pan Am, when he saw the KLM plane's lights coming out of the fog. He threw down the throttle and tried to taxi onto the grass to avoid a collision. Captain van Zanten on the KLM flight, meanwhile, had spotted the Pan Am and suddenly rotated the aircraft nose in an attempt to fly above it. Too late. Even though the cockpit and front landing gear cleared the Pan Am, its engines, main landing gear and lower fuselage hit the right side of the other plane, tearing it to bits. The KLM plane was briefly airborne but, with damaged engines and wings, it stalled, rolled sharply and slid 1,000m down the runway in a huge fireball that burned for hours. All 248 passengers and crew died, along with 335 passengers and crew on the Pan Am plane.

After initially claiming that the ATC was to blame (they had possibly been listening to a soccer game on the radio) and that there had been a 'mutual misunderstanding', KLM eventually admitted responsibility and paid a $110 million settlement for property and damages, worth somewhere over $1 million per victim in today's money.

The incident led to changes in the way flight crews communicate with ATCs, to the way captains and their co-pilots make decisions and to more widespread use of ground radar at airports. KLM now has among the best safety record of any airline in the world. I had seven friends on the PanAm flight as flight attendants from Nashville where I lived. I actually thought that my wife Susan was also on that flight.

Air France

Air France is very much the French equivalent of British Airways. Created out of a group of French air companies, as BA was from British equivalents, it started off as a private enterprise, was nationalised after World War II and remained state owned until it returned to private hands in the 21st century (a bit later than BA's 1987) – then merged with its European rival KLM in 2004, a few years ahead of BA's merger with Iberia.

During the War, with Nazi Germany occupying its homeland, Air France operated from Casablanca in Morocco. This fact contributed to one of the greatest scenes in the history of cinema as Humphrey Bogart watched Ingrid

Bergman and Paul Henreid fly off through the fog in an Air France Lockheed Model 10 Electra, leaving him to his memories at the end of 'Casablanca'.

On many levels, Air France operates in a similar way to BA. It's a massive airline and always has been. Even in the late 1940s it had 130 aircraft, among the largest fleets in the world. Into the jet age, the airline had had more than 100 jets and 34,000 employees serving 150 destinations in 73 countries in 1983 making it the fourth largest passenger airline in the world. Like BA, it's a pioneer in aviation. It was a launch customer for the A320 fly-by-wire aircraft in 1988, and of course operated Concorde alongside BA between 1976 and 2003.

Whereas in the mid-1980s the French government deliberately tried to encourage competition in the air industry, by giving Air France's rival Union des Transports Aériens (UTA) some of its routes, by the 1990s, the decision was reversed in the face of growing competition as European markets were thrown open. Air France was allowed to acquire UTA in 1990 and in 1999 it formed a partnership with US carrier Delta Air Lines, which then turned into the airline alliance SkyTeam.

Despite its corporate merger with KLM, both airlines have kept their separate hubs, flights, logos and identities, which makes you wonder what the point of joining together was. Presumably there were various economies of scale and manpower reductions that saved them both money.

Air France's Mid-Atlantic crash in 2009
On 1 June 2009 an Air France A330 with 228 people on board fell out of the sky and into the Atlantic Ocean mid-way through a flight from Rio de Janeiro to Paris. This was one of the most difficult crashes to figure out, partly because the wreckage lay at the bottom of the Atlantic and it took almost two years for rescue teams to bring it back to the surface. When accident examiners listened to the voice recordings, they uncovered a terrifying period of three and a half minutes during which all three flight crew battled to control the aircraft, seemingly unable to understand what had happened to it. The aircraft had encountered severe turbulence and icy conditions. This caused the aircraft's sensors to give inaccurate readings, leading the flight crew to try to pull the aircraft up, but this only made it stall. Before long, with its speed down to 60kmph, flight AF447

started to descend, and yet the pilots still attempted to raise its nose into the air, when they should have pushed it down to regain control.

Despite the lessons of the KLM crash in 1977, which laid out how pilots should collaborate with one another, on Air France flight 447 it was every man for himself. One would be pulling a level back, another would be pushing it forward, cancelling each other out. An alarm sounded, telling them that the plane was stalling, but they appear to have ignored it.

What could have led to this calamitous lack of control at 2am over the mid-Atlantic? Although you could point to the inaccurate speed readings from the sensors, there were plenty of established protocols to deal with this. The most likely explanation for the pilots' confusion is that they panicked and couldn't compute what was going on. And why did they panic? The voice recording showed that the aircraft captain, Marc Dubois, had only had an hour's sleep the night before and the co-pilots had spent the previous three nights in Rio de Janeiro. "The BEA [the Bureau d'Enquêtes et d'Analyses – which examines French air crashes] was unable to retrieve data regarding their rest and could not determine their activities during the stopover," reported the press.

Air France and Airbus were both sued by the families of the victims, but were both acquitted of corporate manslaughter, with the courts deciding that it was most likely pilot error.

Once again, new lessons were circulated to other airlines and mistakes publicised to spare future passengers from the same terrible fate.

Qantas
More than 100 years old, Qantas was founded in 1920 making it the second oldest continuously operating airline in the world after KLM and before Russia's Aeroflot in 1923.

It is famous for never having had a fatal crash and Qantas has made its safety record a major selling point and proudly points to its status as 'the world's safest airline' according to AirlineRatings, which it's achieved for 10 out of the last 12 years. This isn't only about crashes, it's about incidents of any kind, the age of the fleet, how good the pilot training is and about its health and safety.

One downside of Qantas' big focus on safety is that the airline is super strict on sticking to the rules. During COVID, passengers had to provide more certificates to show they were negative, for longer, than other airlines. So although Australia is a really laid back country once you're there, getting onto a plane – and getting through customs – can be a pain in the backside. For evidence, watch some of the 238 episodes of *Nothing to Declare Australia* (also known as *Border Security: Australia's Front Line*).

Qantas started out as Queensland and Northern Territory Aerial Services, nicknamed 'The Flying Kangaroo' and it still uses an image of a kangaroo on its tail fins. Its founder was Sir Hudson Fysh, a veteran of the Battle of Gallipoli in the First World War and one of the leading pioneers of air travel in Australia. In the late 1910s he waded through rivers and crossed deserts in search of suitable landing strips, then convinced fellow war veterans and businesspeople to fund the venture, to serve what he called "the sparsely populated and practically roadless areas of western and northern Queensland and North Australia."

Given that Australia is so far away from everywhere else, Qantas became the country's main physical connection with the world and flies to all seven continents, the only airline that can say this. Sightseers regularly take trips to Antarctica.

After the Second World War, in which it lost half of its aircraft to enemy action and accidents, Qantas was nationalised in 1947 and lost its domestic routes, flying internationally for the next 45 years until it was re-privatised in the 1990s and merged with Australia Airlines, which ran the domestic routes. Along the way, Qantas had a 13-year flirtation with Concorde, starting in 1960 when its General Manager Sir Cedric Turner wrote an article in the Sydney Morning Herald headlined 'Qantas will buy supersonics'. The huge distances between Australia and its main trading partners would be slashed, he promised, in an aircraft which didn't need windows because there wasn't much to see. "By the time the passenger boards the aircraft, settles back, has a meal, a rest and a cup of coffee, it will be time to land," he wrote. Sydney to London would take just 10 hours, Sydney to Singapore would take three and to Auckland – just 45 minutes. Qantas took out options on four Concorde's and six Boeing 2707 aircraft in 1960.

Both of Concorde's supersonic American competitors Boeing and Lockheed were confident that they would win the race to Qantas' custom. Hall Hibbard at Lockheed predicted that by 1970 the airline would fly supersonic on all of its long-haul routes. But once the US government withdrew funding from Boeing's 2707 project in 1971, Australian enthusiasm fell away for the whole supersonic idea. And once Boeing came out with its 747 jumbos, the Australian carrier quickly bought four, in 1967.

Concorde's sales team intensified its efforts to persuade Qantas to buy in 1972, as American airlines Pan Am and TWA backed away from their commitment to the aircraft. Concorde could make Qantas 'the world's supersonic round-the-world airline'. Concorde could become Qantas' all-First Class aircraft, leaving its Boeing 747s to carry economy fares, they proposed. Rather than booking a ticket based on cabin class, passengers could choose between different speeds.

The issue became hotly debated by the Australian public, with some making an environmental case, worried that Concorde would damage the ozone layer. Others were concerned about excessive noise at airports or about comfort. When Qantas CEO Bert Ritchie toured Concorde during its visit to Sydney, he was asked whether he planned to order any. "Not unless you fancy flying to Europe in something the size of a London tube train carriage," he replied bluntly.

In the end, economics had the final say. Australians were more interested in reaching Europe on economy fares than getting there fast, and by the early 1970s there were daily 747 flights to Europe. In June 1973, Qantas cancelled its Concorde options.

From 2000 onwards, Qantas had to compete with Richard Branson's Virgin Blue low-cost airline on domestic routes and with various major airlines including Virgin Atlantic, British Airways, Cathay Pacific, Air France and the Middle Eastern carriers on international routes. There was a brief idea in 2008 that British Airways and Qantas would merge, but that came to nothing.

Like several other carriers, Qantas had a financial crisis in the early 2010s, made worse by a row with its workers in 2011 which led to all its planes being grounded. It bounced back from that and in 2018 completed the first commercial non-stop flight between Australia and Europe, flying from Perth in Western Australia to London Heathrow.

With its new generation of Airbus A350-1000 aircraft, Qantas is now planning to schedule even more extra-long-haul destinations, flying Sydney to London from 2025 as well as competing with Air New Zealand on the

Auckland to New York route. Its 20-hour Sydney to New York route (via Auckland) is already operating with Dreamliners.

The Big Three US airlines

American Airlines

The world's largest airline by number of passengers carried, by fleet size and passenger-kilometres flown, American Airlines is the Big Daddy of the industry. This doesn't mean that it's always fun to fly with them, but it means there's lots of flights going wherever you want to go, at least within the United States, and you know what you're likely to get in terms of service.

American started off in the 1920s through the merger of several smaller airlines. These included Robertson Aircraft, which flew its first mail route in April 1926 between Chicago and St Louis, Missouri, with Charles Lindbergh as its pilot. From here, American expanded to taking passengers between New York and Chicago on its first flagship aircraft, the Douglas DC-3. In an early attempt to develop customer loyalty, American started the Admirals Club, with one base at New York's La Guardia airport.

In the 1950s, as the US economy boomed, American began flying longer distances and approached Douglas to build a new aircraft: the DC-7 emerged and was very popular with American's passengers, followed in 1959 by the Lockheed Electra. With the advent of jet engines in the 1960s, American began flying the Boeing 707 both domestically and internationally. It also introduced the world's first electronic booking system.

Continuing its drive to build its brand and get repeat custom, American started the first loyalty program in 1981, called AAdvantage. This promoted the rest of the airline industry to do the same. It also pioneered the 'hub and spoke' airport and flight system, setting up hubs at Dallas/Fort Worth in Texas, Chicago, San Jose, Raleigh-Durham and Nashville.

In the early 2000s, American swallowed up TWA, which had run into financial trouble. It also endured the Twin Towers attacks on 11 September 2001: the first plane to crash into the north tower of the World Trade Center was American Airlines flight 11 from Boston to Los Angeles. The global downturn in aviation following this incident hit American, as with the rest of the industry, but it bounced back in 2005 and expanded for the next few years, especially into the Far East.

In 2011, however, American's parent company AMR filed for bankruptcy and after a period of cost-cutting, the airline merged with US Airways in 2013, creating the world's biggest airline. Of course, the bigger you are, the more that can go wrong. And American has had its share of issues in recent years, including cabin crew strikes, passengers claiming they've been kidnapped by the airline and layoffs in the wake of the pandemic, as the amount of business travel has fallen.

Still, with almost a century of tradition behind it and huge resources, I'd expect American to stay at the top of the heap for decades to come.

American Airlines flight 191
Setting off from O'Hare Airport in Chicago on its way to Los Angeles Airport on May 25, 1979, there was little to worry the flight crew on American Airlines flight 191. Yet within seconds of take-off, its left engine flew up and over the wing, the aircraft lost control and banked steeply to the left and crashed less than a mile from the end of the runway killing all 258 passengers and 13 crew on board, together with two on the ground. It is still the deadliest aircraft incident to have happened in the United States outside of 9/11.

According to an eyewitness, the left engine was "bouncing up and down quite a bit," as the plane took off. Although most of the cockpit voice recording was lost, one brief piece was recovered. There was a loud thump, probably the sound of the engine detaching from the wing, followed by the first officer saying: "Damn!"

In the investigations that followed, experts pointed out that a plane should be able to fly on one engine. But when the left engine separated, it cut through the plane's hydraulic systems, so the flight crew couldn't tell whether the slats on the left wing were activated. Although the aircraft had backup power switches, the crew didn't use these, probably because they only had 31 seconds between the engine flying off and the crash into a ploughed field, also hitting a trailer park, an old aircraft hangar and several cars. With 21,000 gallons of fuel on board, the aircraft exploded into a fireball on impact.

The crash investigation centred on the maintenance of the left engine in the weeks leading up to the incident. It turned out that, at an American Airlines facility in Tulsa, Oklahoma, in March that year, the engine and the pylon which attached it to the wing had been removed for servicing. But instead of removing the engine from the pylon, then the pylon from the wing, as McDonnell-Douglas recommended, American had devised a short cut. They detached both pieces at once, saving themselves 200 working hours per aircraft and reducing the number of cables and fuel lines they had to disconnect.

During maintenance on this aircraft, the engine and pylon unit were disconnected using a forklift truck and crane. Half way through the process, the workers had a change of shift. Once the next set took over, the forklift truck's arms had dropped a little, due to reduced hydraulic pressure. This damaged the pylon and engine to a degree: not enough to cause immediate failure, but enough to result in fatigue cracking over the next eight weeks.

As a result of this accident, new procedures for both aircraft maintenance teams and for flight crews were introduced, to prevent any recurrence of the problem. It also underscored the importance of listening to manufacturers when they tell you how to maintain their aircraft.

Delta Air Lines
A fierce rival to American Airlines, Delta can boast that its turnover and profits sometimes exceed American's, even if it carries fewer passengers and has fewer aircraft. There are lots of similarities, but some important differences.
Delta started out as a crop-spraying airline, based in Macon, Georgia, in 1925, combatting the boll weevil infestation of cotton crops. It grew to be the world's biggest crop-spraying business, with 14 aircraft, before branching out into passenger services in 1929, flying from Dallas, Texas to Jackson, Mississippi.

Then in 1953 Delta began the first of a remarkable series of acquisitions. It bought Chicago and Southern Air Lines, then over the next 56 years bought US-based airlines with virtually every point in the compass in their names. In 1972 it bought Northeast Airlines and in 1987 it acquired Western Airlines. In 2008 it followed up with Northwest Airlines. In between, Delta bought the lion's share of Pan Am's trans-Atlantic routes and its Shuttle service.

Delta made its mark on American aviation through processing an ever-higher number of passengers. In 1979 it celebrated its 50th anniversary by boarding 1 million passengers in a single month, the first airline to reach this milestone.

Then in 1997, on the back of a massive expansion drive, it recorded 100 million passengers in a single year.

Along the way, Delta has innovated all kinds of technological advances, from check-in kiosks to virtual online systems, from in-seat video screens to mobile bag tracking. It has also signed a succession of deals with other international airlines, including Air France, Virgin Atlantic and Korean Air. It was a founding member of the SkyTeam airline alliance.

In September 2005 Delta filed for Chapter 11 bankruptcy and then, in November of that year, launched one of the biggest expansion programs in its history, setting up 124 new nonstop routes and 41 new destinations in the next year. This is one of the biggest differences between the US and Britain. When British firms go bust, that's it, they're finished. In the US it seems to give them wings. By 2010 Delta was ready to invest an extra $2 billion to improve customer experience, renovating its aircraft and airport lounges and in 2017 it announced pre-tax income of $6.1 billion. How's that for a post-bankruptcy bounce? In 2012 it bought a 49 per cent stake in Virgin Atlantic from Singapore Airlines for $360 million.

I've generally had a good experience with Delta. In fact, on some occasions it was brilliant. If they liked you, they'd tell you about a secret business class lounge, which had no markings on it. They'd just tell you to make your way to a certain door and go in. Once you got there, it had everything you could possibly need. Absolute luxury.

Delta Air Lines Flight 191
On 2 August 1985 a Lockheed L-1011 TriStar flying from Fort Lauderdale to Los Angeles was approaching Dallas/Fort Worth airport in Texas, where it was due to make a scheduled stop. All three-flight crew were highly-experienced, seasoned professionals. Ted Connors was known as a meticulous pilot who was especially cautious when it came to turbulent weather. Rudolph Price was described as an 'above average first officer' who knew the TriStar extremely well. And Nicholas Nassick was an 'observant, alert and professional' flight engineer. Both Price and Nassick had served with the US military in Vietnam.

When Dallas/Fort Worth's air traffic control told him that there was a chance of thunderstorms, Ted Connors proposed flying around the bad weather, but as they neared the airport, they flew directly into a rainstorm. At an altitude of

1,000 feet, they saw lightning coming out of a cloud in front of them and fierce rain pelted the cockpit. "You're gonna lose it all of a sudden," said Connors to Price, followed by "Push it up, push it way up," as they tried to gain height. "Hang on to the son of a bitch!" said Connors ten seconds later, as the plane kept descending, despite their best efforts. Even when the crew tried to abort the landing, the TriStar just carried on falling. After skidding along a field for a few hundred feet it smashed into a car on Highway 114, killing the driver instantly, then hit street lights, burst into flames and finally crashed into two water tanks on the edge of the airport.

Although 137 people died in the incident, the speedy response of the airport emergency services saved the lives of many survivors, who were in the rear section of the aircraft and somehow escaped the flames and impact of the 200mph crash. All three-flight crew died, along with five out of the eight cabin crew.

What the Delta Air Lines flight 191 taught investigators was that pilots needed a better understanding of low altitude 'wind shear', a phenomenon particularly associated with thunderstorms, where there is a sudden downdraft, or microburst, which can force an aircraft suddenly downwards, no matter what its pilots are trying to do. It resulted in new training for pilots, teaching them to detect wind shear and how to deal with it, along with new equipment for aircraft capable of spotting wind shear before it became a problem.

In a subsequent trial, which took place in 1988 and 1989 and took more than two years to prepare for, Delta was found responsible for the crash because of its pilots' negligence and had to pay millions of dollars in compensation to the families of the victims. I thought that the verdict against the flight crew was a bit harsh, given that nobody at the time was equipped to deal with this problem. Thankfully, it is exceptionally rare and nowadays pilots know what to do.

United Airlines

In contrast to Delta's rapid recovery from bankruptcy in 2005, United Airlines had a far tougher time when it went under in 2002, not long after the terror attacks of 11 September 2000 in which two United aircraft were involved: one into the South Tower and one headed for the Capitol Building, where the passengers fought back against the hijackers. (Two American Airlines planes were also involved in the attack: one flown into the World Trade Center's other tower and one crashing into the Pentagon.)

United started out with a great pedigree. It was founded by William Boeing along with some partners in 1928 to deliver mail, acquiring and merging with various other aviation companies including Pratt & Whitney and the first US scheduled airline Varney Air Lines. After more acquisitions, it was delivering mail from coast to coast, taking 27 hours to make the journey.

Following a scandal over airlines and mail services in 1930, United Aircraft and Transport Corporation was split into three: one manufacturer east of the Mississippi – United Aircraft – one to the west – Boeing Airplane Company – and United Airlines. This company soon expanded all across the country, flying passengers from its bases in Chicago, San Francisco, Denver and Washington D.C.

United claims to have been the first airline to introduce 'air stewardesses' when it hired the registered nurse Ellen Church in 1937. Later, it was the first to have flight simulators to train commercial pilots and the one US airline to operate 'men only' flights, between 1953 and 1970, between New York and Chicago. Women and children were barred from the flights, which operated as a 'club in the sky', with 'cocktails, steak dinner, and cigar and pipe smoking permitted.' This was just a little before my time flying around the US, but it sounds quite appealing!

Less appealing was United's record of mid-air collisions in the 1950s and 1960s, with three flights banging into other aircraft over the Grand Canyon, in southern Nevada and over New York City. As a result, airlines and regulators worked together to develop more advanced air traffic control systems, thank goodness.

Despite its roots with Boeing, United was an early customer of French manufacturer Sud Aviation, and was the only American airline to operate its Caravelle jetliner in a scheduled passenger service. Like other US airlines, however, it bought plenty of Douglas DC models, before Boeing brought out its great range of jets in the 1970s. In 1978 United ordered 30 Boeing 727-200s for a total cost of $1.2 billion, the industry's biggest order up to that date. Although Delta acquired the majority of Pan Am's assets after the Lockerbie crash of 1988, United also picked up a fair amount, including its Latin American and Caribbean business and its routes to London Heathrow.

In the 1980s United diversified into hotel and car rental ownership, buying Hertz (1985) and Hilton International (1987). Then it quickly sold them in late

1987, making people wonder if they knew what they were doing.

In 1994, the airline proposed a deal to its workers. If they agreed to a drop of between 15 and 25 per cent in their salaries, they would receive 55 per cent of the company stock. This seemed like a great deal to many of the pilots, baggage handlers and other employees, so they went for it. The cabin crew voted not to join in. Even though things seemed to go well for a few years, as the workers' unions were able to bargain for higher pay, it was a short-sighted bonus. When United went bankrupt in 2002 the workers' shares became worthless. They even lost their pension plan in 2005, the largest default in corporate American history.

United bumped along near the bottom of consumer satisfaction scores following its bankruptcy, while in 2009 the airline was rated 11th out of 19 US airlines for lost, damaged, delayed or stolen baggage. As with hotels and cars, United launched a budget airline called Ted in 2004, then closed it five years later. It needed a boost and decided that merging with another major airline could do the trick. Continental Airlines and United joined together in 2013, keeping the United name.

United's reputation for customer service wasn't helped by an incident in 2017 where the company offered compensation to any passengers who would give up their seats so that four staff members could take their places. Nobody volunteered, so United chose which passengers would have to leave the plane. One of these, Dr David Dao, put up an almighty struggle, so United called the cops and had him forcibly yanked out of the aircraft, giving him bloody injuries as they did so. Other passengers took videos of the scene and it gave United a very poor reputation for some time.

I guess because underneath all the poor corporate decisions and messiness, United still manages to fly millions of people from one place to another, the company is in pretty good shape. It recently made another huge order, this time for 270 narrow-body planes, split between Boeing and Airbus, so it must have plenty of money.

United was never my favourite when I lived in the States. Maybe because it was so big, and didn't seem to have a personal touch. Its planes weren't as nice as those on other airlines, either.

United Airlines flight 232

For the first hour of United Airlines flight 232 from Stapleton International Airport in Denver to O'Hare International Airport in Chicago on 19 July 1989, there were no reported problems. Then at 3:16pm, the passengers heard a loud bang and the McDonnell Douglas DC-10 began to roll to its right, while shuddering violently. Captain Alfred Hayes found that neither the autopilot nor the manual controls were working, so he closed off the left engine and increased power to the right, which helped to stabilise the aircraft.

From the cabin, out stepped Dennis Fitch, a DC-10 training instructor who happened to be among the passengers that day. He began to operate the thrusters that powered the remaining two engines, while Hayes struggled with the regular controls. Fitch managed to line the plane up with the runway at Sioux City, Iowa, and they attempted a landing. Without proper control, the DC-10 came down too fast and too steeply, leading to the right wing, then the tail section and the cockpit breaking away from the plane as it bounced along the ground in a ball of flames. Out of 296 passengers and crew on the flight, 110 passengers and one flight attendant died, mostly from injuries, with some suffering smoke inhalation. The flight crew all survived.

In response to the crash investigation, new rules came out for turbine manufacture and to aircraft control system design, to give pilots more chance of retaining control in such circumstances. A TV movie called Crash Landing: the Rescue of Flight 232 starring Charlton Heston and James Coburn came out in 1992.

Lesser-known airlines (and some that no longer exist)

Since I've been flying for more than 65 years, I've seen a lot of airlines come and go. Here are some of the ones I remember flying with:

British airlines:

Dan-Air
This off-shoot of ship-broking business Davies and Newman, whose initials gave the airline its name, started off in 1953 with a single aircraft flying out of Southend before moving to Gatwick in 1960. A decade later it was Britain's

56. One of England's finest opening batsmen ever, a fantastic friend since 1968 - Sir Geoffrey Boycott.

57. The British High Commissioner attending the opening of the Lords Taverner's Cricket Tour of Kenya 1993 arranged by Myself.

Sonic Boom

58. Presenting a charity cheque to President Daniel Arap Moi with the British High Commissioner and HRH Prince and Princess Michael of Kent.

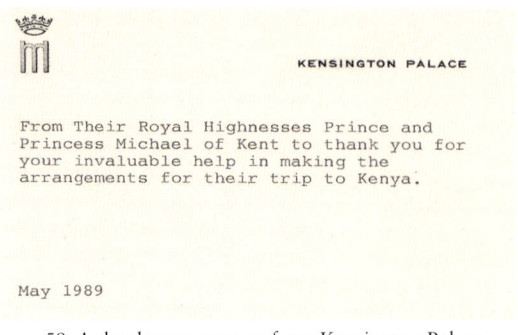

From Their Royal Highnesses Prince and Princess Michael of Kent to thank you for your invaluable help in making the arrangements for their trip to Kenya.

May 1989

59. A thank you message from Kensington Palace.

60. With great gratitude and deep respect from troops of 3rd Battalion of 30 Mechanised Brigade Ukraine.

174

61. It's been a very rewarding experience working with the orphanage at Nanyuki. (Alamy)

62. Diani Beach orphanage, Mombasa.

Sonic Boom

63. Sunset View Island Camp Lake Baringo in Kenya.

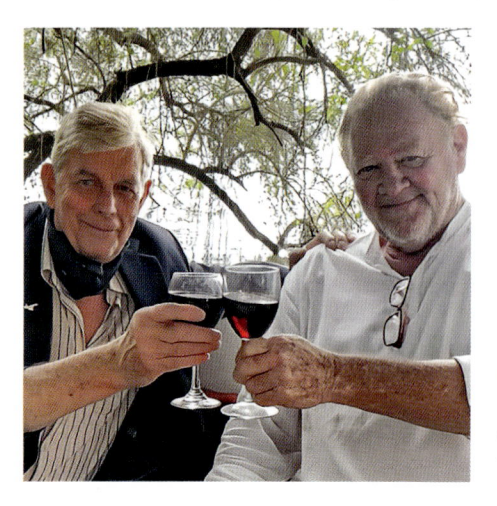

64. One of my dearest friends and supporters, Perrie Hennessey RIP. Former chairman of Lonrho Hotels Kenya, welcoming me to Island Camp.

Sonic Boom

65. Ron Dennis, David Gower and Myself at RAF Wattisham.

66. Saying goodbye to the F4 Phantom was a surprisingly emotional affair.

67. Dominic Riley at the end of our F4 Phantom Flight.

68. My other seat on Concorde. On the occasions they had sold my regular seat (9a), I flew here.

Sonic Boom

69. Captain Mike Bannister immediately after landing at London Heathrow from New York's JFK Airport on BA's last commercial Concorde flight on 24 October 2003.

70. With my darling wife, Alla, following her citizenship ceremony in April 2024.

largest independent airline with the biggest charter fleet and by the late 1980s it carried more than 6 million passengers a year.

Its demise was short and brutal. In the early 1990s it ran out of money and following unsuccessful attempts to merge with a competitor, British Airways snapped it up for a nominal sum of £1.

British Island Airways (BIA)

British Island Airways existed between 1970 and 1991 with a brief gap in 1980 when it merged with some other small airlines to form Air UK, before splitting off again in 1982. I would fly on BIA to Jersey, where I worked for a while, and it was a nice little airline with a fleet of Boeing 737s.

The recession of 1990 to 1991 did for BIA as it did for Dan-Air. In this case it simply went bust, nobody even paid a pound for it.

Aurigny Air Services

When I wasn't flying with BIA to Jersey, I'd get on an Aurigny flight, which was just as good and flew the Britten-Norman Trislander planes with three piston engines, one of the very few airlines to do so. Later it ran daily services between Stansted and Guernsey on a Saab 340 aircraft, which was pretty rare too. And one of the passenger seats was next to the pilot.

Aurigny had been around since the late 1960s when it started flying between the Channel Islands themselves. Then it spread across to Southern England and Northern France. The airline survived a succession of downturns before it was acquired by the State of Guernsey in 2003 and is still operating today, mostly bringing tourists to the Channel Island beaches.

British Caledonian

Of all the UK airlines I've flown on that aren't called British Airways, British Caledonian was the one that impressed me the most. For a few years, when British European Airways (BEA) and British Overseas Airways Corporation (BOAC) were state-owned monopolies, British Caledonian was a private, independent, more attractive alternative.

It launched in 1970 with the acquisition of British United Airways (what a lot of airlines called themselves British-something in those days). Despite being

Scottish in its name and logo, carrying a Scottish lion on its tail fin, British Caledonian based itself at Gatwick and flew all over the UK along with some European, African and South American routes. It then picked up slots at JFK in New York and LAX in California.

The writing was on the wall when British Airways was privatised in 1984. Two years later it hit the buffers, as it lost customers and money. Too small to compete with BA or the American airlines, Caledonian was too big to survive as a niche operator. It sold its assets to BA for £237 million in 1987 and was never seen again. Bcal was a terrific airline and lots of politics went on to get them out of the skies at the time.

International airlines
Aeroflot
Russia's national airline, and of the USSR before that, is a disgrace to aviation, quite frankly. How any airline can still be operating when it has suffered more than 700 incidents, killing more than 8,000 passengers over the course of its history, is a mystery. But then, Russia is famous for ignoring the rules to which most other countries agree and treating its own citizens with disdain.

Sometimes if you're flying in or out of Russia, you have little choice but to fly Aeroflot. I remember taking a flight from Moscow to Norway on the airline. The service was ok, the cabin crew were helpful. But it's the small details that you remember, like the wooden door between economy and business class. It wouldn't surprise me if the whole plane had been made out of plywood, they're such amateurs. Even the Russian space programme is a disaster: after its moon landing failed in August 2023, India's succeeded a couple of weeks later.

Fortunately for non-Russian passengers, most countries have banned Aeroflot from flying to them since the invasion of Ukraine.

Ethiopian Airlines
By sharp contrast with Aeroflot, Ethiopian is one of the safest airlines in the world, certainly in the African world, with an up-to-date fleet, high professional standards and a great service ethic. It's also a remarkably big airline, serving dozens of countries around Africa and elsewhere and 125 destinations. Since the 1960s, pilots and aircraft technicians have studied at Ethiopia's highly-

ranked colleges and the airline looks after the planes of many other companies. If you're given a choice of airlines when you're flying in or out of Africa, this is the one to pick.

I worked as the senior consultant to Captain Mohammed and I was extremely impressed with the safety and service standards. I was presenting the airlines of the year awards with Sir Charles Forte and I was saying that it's easy for the major airlines to fly in and out of Africa, however Ethiopians fly around sub-Saharan Africa every day in complete safety. And even when Ethiopia had a Russian-leaning dictator, Captain Mohammed insisted that if he was going to run the airline he wanted Boeing planes. As a result Captain Mohammed Ahmed was appointed CEO in 1980 and slashed the workforce by 10 per cent.

The airline continued the acquisition of Western, rather than Soviet aircraft, despite the links between the communist government and the Soviet Union, purchasing the Boeing 727 in 1979 and the Boeing 767 in 1984. The airline soon had the 767ER and was flying from Detroit to Addis Ababa non-stop with a full load of passengers. I do believe because of Ethiopian two-engine flights across the Atlantic two engine flights were allowed by the aviation authorities. It was due to this record of quality and safety that they built Boeing parts under licence in Addis Ababa at great savings in cost but retaining Boeing quality.

Ukraine International Airlines (UIA)

I love this airline, it's fantastic. For a few years I was an ambassador for UIA, as a part of me becoming a friend of the Euro 2012 football championship which Ukraine co-hosted with Poland. It's quite a young airline, only started in 1992 when the government decided it wanted an alternative to the Soviet-era Ukraine Airlines, which was controlled by Aeroflot until the USSR broke up.

They invited an Irish group called Avia International to run the airline and I became good friends with the Irish MD Richard William Creagh 'Dick' as he was known to everyone, as well as the Ukrainian head of the company. They invited me on the inaugural flight to New York and I took Tom Stuker on the return for JFK to Barispol Kyiv – the American frequent flyer who claims to have done more miles than me (but hasn't really). Besides Irish partners, UIA also made deals with Austrian and Swiss airlines.

The Russian invasion has knocked out quite a lot of UIA's operations of course. Let's hope that it can bounce back quickly once the war is over.

Aerolineas Argentinas
In the days when I was arranging licensing deals in South America, I'd fly into Buenos Aires with Aerolineas. It was the flag carrier of the country and did a great job, despite frequent changes of ownership and dipping in and out of state control. It was founded by Juan Perón, whose wife Eva became famous in Andrew Lloyd Webber's musical for singing *"Don't Cry for me Argentina"*. Another curious piece of history is that one of its first pilots was Antoine de Saint-Exupéry, who wrote the story of the Little Prince.

Nigerian Airways
My least favourite airline, even worse than Aeroflot. Everything that you could imagine going wrong on a flight seemed likely to go wrong. Flights were frequently overbooked more than usual due to a high level of no shows. There was even a time where upon using the washroom at the airport that someone else thought they would jump in my seat. I decided to then take the trip by road rather than fly. Just as well really as on that particular flight, it landed four miles short of the runway! The whole operation was plagued by bribery and corruption. People would come into the cabin with half of their worldly goods, including the kitchen sink, it felt like. Terrible safety record, terrible punctuality and service. I once rang for attention and a stewardess asked: "What's the emergency?" I asked for a beer, so she brought me a local Harp. After 45 minutes I asked for another. "You've already had it," she told me. They had one beer between all the passengers.

Nigerian ran between 1958 and 2003 when it finally collapsed, owing more than half a billion dollars and owning just one plane. They'd tried bringing in foreign airlines to manage things, including British Airways, KLM and South African Airways, but it never worked out.

And some more…
The Taiwan-based China Airways is very good, I liked the service they offered. And All Nippon Airways, which I flew from Tokyo to Okinawa one time. In

the 21st century a lot of us travel with Middle Eastern airlines: I've flown with Emirates which is very good, they're very nice people. You have to wonder how Emirates can afford to have such a massive fleet of A380s. Presumably there are state subsidies, because the level of luxury is unbelievable. Even the economy seats almost turn into flatbeds.

Chapter 9
The World's Most Travelled Man

I never set out to cross aviation boundaries, it just happened. When things like the Virgin Atlantic party for my 10 million miles happen, it's nice, you feel part of something, there's a funny sense of achievement (even though I've just sat on my backside for thousands of hours). According to the newspapers, who have looked at all the records and logbooks and tax returns, I'm the world's most travelled man. I'm in the Guinness Book of Records for the most trips on Concorde, which of course is a record that will never be beaten. As for the 'most travelled' record which I've held since 1983, Guinness stopped listing that one in the printed books, although the last time I looked there is still a Guinness web page saying that in 2003 I had flown 13,900,000 miles, the furthest as a passenger (as well as mentioning my Concorde record). Here's the link: www.guinnessworldrecords.com/world-records/most-air-miles-flown-by-a-passenger. I'm now up to more than 15 million miles (without counting the bonus miles accumulated as some others do).

What's crazy is how upset some people get about this record. I get hate mail and people threatening me. There's an American called Tom Stuker who claims to have flown further than me, but this seems quite spurious since a few million of his miles were supposedly flown during the pandemic, when barely any planes were flying. I've met Tom and we got along fine, we did some publicity shoots and were on NBC television. He's linked with United Airlines and I guess they would like to see an American have the record. My friend Ben Lord (Chairman of Save Concorde Group) thinks Stuker is like Donald Trump, boasting about his exploits, when anyone who does the maths can see he's not flown the miles he claims. That's why Guinness dismissed his claim for the record. He continues to embellish his record without having his flight log published or independently verified.

The fact is that someone, one day, will doubtless overtake my record - except my Concorde record which can never be broken - especially if new hypersonic aircraft start flying to Singapore and Sydney in three hours. But the chances are that I'll be long gone by that time. For now, I'm enjoying the little bit of limelight that shines on a very seasoned traveller, who has seen the inside of more planes than most people have had hot dinners.

Sonic Boom

My travel has created interest for people, especially as a speaker. It's always a pleasure to go to dinners, conferences, parties and meetings and tell audiences about a lifetime of travel, how the business has changed out of all recognition, how I started flying across the Atlantic in a piston engine plane, commuting from New York to London for four years. One week it will be a company in the Middle East, like Advantage Travel in Dubai: I went out there with the tennis legend Martina Navratilova. The next week it could be a travel industry event like the Crystal Cabin Awards in Hamburg, where they were intrigued by the idea of an 84-year old man who still loves travelling and has so many stories to tell.

I have been invited to do a talk at Cranfield where one of my friends, Professor Sir Iain Gray, is professor of aerospace studies. He wants to invite me because, he says, the students get plenty of time to look at the scientific and technical side of aviation, all the stresses and strains on materials, but not so much on the social side. He would bring me in to talk about what makes a good experience, how aviation has evolved over the decades, my recollections of what you could call a 'golden age' of flying.

I can see his point. Engineers love to build things which perform amazing tasks, or go faster, higher or deeper than ever before. But with aviation, as with all transport engineering, you have to think of the passengers above all. The passenger's point of view might be quite different to the engineers.

I feel a bit let down by today's airlines. It's all very well talking about innovation and engineering and business models. When you take a step back, airlines today are mostly low-cost hybrids. They've lost much of the attraction that they had. The seats are narrow, and the pitch is cramped. It's all for profit and they too often forget the people. When you go back to earlier times, passengers used to sit in a big armchair. Now, it's become so commercialised and so uncomfortable. They pack people in.

There was a time when I thought about trying to break the round-the-world record, but then my friend David Springbett set a new record of 44 hours and six minutes in 1981 and I thought – good for you! He was a fellow aviation fan and flew very frequently on Concorde. He also set a new record for travelling from the City of London to Wall Street in New York, in three hours 59 minutes and 44 seconds in the early 1980s. Sadly, David passed away in December 2022, leaving behind an enormous collection of Concorde and aviation memorabilia along with one of the world's great stamp collections (he was a former chairman of Stanley Gibbons, one of the world's greatest stamp companies).

As for me, people realise that I've done something that they'll never do, or something that they aspire to. I often meet young people such as my friend Ben Lord who came up to his half million flight in August 2023 on a BA 787 Dreamliner flying with his parents to Singapore for the start of a holiday to Australia where they were able to fly First Class cheaper than Business Class. And there's others who are just starting on their lifetime of travel and they're looking for advice and encouragement. I tell them: off you go! Take the initiative and see where it leads you. You'll not regret it.

Jet lag

Maybe it's a controversial opinion, but I don't believe that jet lag exists. I think people get de-hydrated, stressed and tired, and then feel pretty run down. But there are some simple measures you can take to counter these effects.

First you have to factor in all the time costs around air travel. Even before you fly, you're spending time packing, worrying about documents, taking the dog to your friend's house… If you're flying from, say, London to San Francisco, the flight itself will be around 11 hours. But you have to get to the airport, spend time checking in and going through customs and security, then waiting to board. During the flight, you're inside a steel and aluminium tube and – on most flights – the air is coming through the engine, so it's dry, which dehydrates you. At your destination, you have to go through more checks and delays for luggage and customs, before finding your hotel or getting home. The whole of a journey like this can easily be 18 or 20 hours. That is a really long day, by any measure.

When I used to fly on Concorde, we would travel through the same time zones as passengers flying across the Atlantic on regular planes, except we'd do it in three and a half hours instead of seven or eight. And on Concorde, nobody suffered jet lag. Sometimes I'd even fly across the Atlantic twice in a day and still have no jet lag.

My tips are to take a water spray to hydrate your face every so often, to counteract the dry air from the engines. And close your eyes for a few minutes every half an hour, to give them some time to moisturise.

Another tip is to fly on an airline which uses the Boeing Dreamliner, because this aircraft gets its cabin air directly from outside, rather than through the engines, and it makes a huge difference to the humidity. Your skin doesn't dry out, your eyes aren't so sore. It's a beautiful airplane, the cabin pressure is lower and Boeing has researched the ideal lighting to make passengers feel relaxed. I really recommend it. I believe that the Airbus A350 now has this attribute as well.

Once I get onto a plane, I always set my watch to the local time at my destination and start to live on that time. Once I arrive, I go to bed at local time and always find that I wake up fine in the morning. I know some people advise not to drink alcohol on flights, but I find that a glass or two of red wine suits me fine. What affects me more is champagne, which just goes straight to my head, but then it does the same thing down on the ground. It's more a question of how you pace yourself.

Maybe I have a genetic resistance to jet lag, but all I can say is that I've flown more than 2,000 times across the Atlantic and never had it in my life. Or use my famous exercises from your seat. Aerial Isometrics.

Tips to get upgraded

These days, upgrades are thin on the ground, but there's always a small possibility that you'll be offered one. So if you're keen to fly Business Class on an economy fare, here are some tips:

• Dress smartly. This is the first and most important tip. No airline is going to upgrade someone in shorts and tee shirt or a baggy tracksuit. Personally, I always dress in a jacket, with smart shoes and trousers out of respect for the cabin crew. (When I first flew with Pan Am, it was like an upmarket dining club: they wouldn't take passengers unless they were wearing a tie!)

• Rather than asking straight out for an upgrade, I'd suggest saying: "If you're looking for an upgrade candidate, can I volunteer?" This makes it sound as if you're trying to do them a favour, like when they're asking for volunteers for off-loads. Some airlines, especially in the States, will offer money to offload passengers. You can even bargain with them: "$200?" "I won't get off for that." "$500?" "OK."

- Fly at times of the year when business travellers are less likely to book, such as bank holidays. There will be fewer Business Class seats taken and you stand a better chance of an upgrade.
- Be polite and smile. Upgrades are at the discretion of the booking staff: they're most unlikely to respond to pushiness or someone shouting "Do you know who I am?"
- Join loyalty programmes. Even at the lowest level, loyalty programmes put you at the front of the queue for upgrade consideration.
- Turn up extra early for your flight. This strategy isn't foolproof, but sometimes works. If the flight has Business or First Class seats free, they may be offered to the first passengers who arrive at check-in.

Fear of flying

If you have a fear of flying, it's definitely not a smart idea to get drunk beforehand, that will only make you feel worse and, at an extreme, could mean the airline refuses to let you on the plane – I've seen that happen several times. My advice for nervous fliers is to speak to someone who flies a lot, who can talk them through it and reassure them. I've flown 15 million miles and I'm still here to tell the tale, so it can't be that dangerous!

I used to do 'fear of flying' courses for Pan Am and similar courses are offered by many of the big airlines these days. They're 98 per cent successful. I think a fear of flying comes mainly because you can't see where you're going and you can hear all sorts of funny bumps and rumbles going on with the wheels and the flaps coming down. It's a very strange environment compared with most things on dry land.

Here's a quick list of suggestions to help with a fear of flying:
- Study the figures. If you fly from London to New York, the chance of crashing is one in about 5.3 million. You'd have to fly every day for 14,700 years before you died on that route. That's even more than I've done! So people always like to fly with me since it's going to be thousands of years before I have another incident.
- Distract yourself. Prepare in advance - take a book or some puzzles, download a TV show onto your iPad or laptop, watch the inflight movies, listen to music, eat and sleep. I find that doing a mix of these things helps the time to pass quickly and I'm never bothered about how long or dangerous the flight could be.

- Book an aisle seat. This has the disadvantage that you may be nudged during the flight by people walking up and down, but it means you're not trapped by other passengers if you want to get up during the flight. Many people feel safer in an aisle seat, because it gives them a greater sense of control.
- Read up about how safe aircraft are these days. The chances of both engines failing are extremely slim. And even when that does happen, as in New York in 2009 when pilot Chesley Sullenberger's Airbus A320 suffered a double bird strike, an aircraft can glide down, even landing on water. All 155 passengers and crew survived. You could watch the movie *Sully*, starring Tom Hanks as the pilot, and replay it in your head to remind yourself that even some mid-air disasters have happy endings.
- Download a relaxation or meditation app, then during the flight get up, walk around and stretch. There are also useful exercises you can do while seated, by using my famous Aerial Isometrics.
- The cabin crew are trained to help anxious passengers, so speak to them if you're becoming stressed. They've doubtless been on far more scary flights than the one you're on, so they'll reassure and calm you.

Cabin dramas

In the course of 15-plus million miles, I've seen pretty much everything that it's possible to see in an aircraft. So here are a few choice episodes that stick in my mind:

One-hit wonders on the rampage

I've seen a few of these scenes, where lesser-known rock bands end up in First Class and slowly but surely begin to mis-behave. It starts with too much alcohol, as the cabin crew run back and forth filling their glasses. Then as the champagne takes effect, their voices get louder and louder and they grow bolder.

It's almost like watching an old movie for the fourth time. In scene two, the singer tries to fix the drummer up with the air hostess, the drummer gets embarrassed and throws some food at the singer, the guitarist then joins in and throws some ice cream at his manager, but misses and hits the wife of a travelling chief executive, who complains to the captain and threatens to sue everyone. Pandemonium.

Kiss of life

One night on a flight from JFK to London there was an old chap sitting by himself towards the back of the cabin, minding his own business. We settled down to a meal and then a movie (this was before screens in the back of seats – everyone watched the same film). Shortly afterwards there was some kind of commotion and two stewardesses and a steward rushed to look after the old chap. He was behind me, so I couldn't see what was going on, but everything soon calmed down because when I looked again, he seemed to be fast asleep with a blanket over his head.

Meanwhile, a retired paint salesman from Milwaukee began entertaining the cabin with takes of his terrible son-in-law, how his wife was run over by a truck, the chemical qualities of paint, all the while fuelling himself with non-stop drinks and growing ever drunker and louder. One passenger after another would make an excuse to sit elsewhere as he moved through the cabin seeking a receptive audience.

Finally, when the lights came up at the end of the movie, we saw him in the far corner, having lifted the blanket from the old man's face, and appeared to be kissing him! A hostess rushed over and hissed: "What on earth do you think you're doing?"

He lifted up the old man's arm and offered it to her. "He's dead! Feel his pulse!" said the drunken paint salesman, before he reached over and blew into the old man's mouth. "I'm giving him the kiss of life!"

The stewardess was calmness personified. "Well I hope you're good at it, because he's been dead for at least two hours," she said.

The Mile High club

I've seen every variation of this thrill-seeking behaviour, from couples under the blankets to others screaming and banging away in the bathroom, up to the point where other passengers have thought an attack was going on and rushed to help.

I was on the NBC *Today* show in New York and although we discussed what we were going to talk about the evening before, during the show the presenters started to giggle a little and I knew what was coming so they started hinting about a certain club. I said the executive club? No, not that one, the one that has something to do with miles. I replied if you're talking about the Mile-High

Club then you had better ask my friend Richard Branson about that. Joining the Club on Concorde had its own cachet and it certainly happened during flights I was on. It's what I call a supersonic bang! You may wonder if I joined that club but I am allowed to keep that anonymous!

And the British actor Ralph Fiennes had sex with a Qantas flight attendant while flying from Sydney to Mumbai in 2007. They apparently carried on in a hotel later that day. She was sacked by the airline, but said she didn't regret it.

You might think that this was a rare event, but a survey of American airline passengers in 2010 found that 17 per cent of them had had sex in an airplane bathroom, 5 per cent with a stranger on a plane and 3 per cent with a crew member. This appeared in The Boston Globe newspaper, so it was a reputable survey. Given that around 40 per cent of Americans (130 million people) fly at least once a year, it means almost 4 million Americans have had sex with a cabin crew member.

Hard to believe, but with Americans, you never know.

Countries I've visited

In the course of my travelling career, I've visited more than 150 countries. Here are a few of my favourite places:

Kenya

I lived in Kenya for a while, and it's one of the most unique countries on Earth. I belong to a club called the Mount Kenya Safari Club, which has nothing to do with safari but was founded by the film star William Holden and his girlfriend Stefanie Powers, who starred in Hart to Hart. Their home was 6,000 feet up, and it was warm during the day, cool at night, and there's no mosquitoes or anything like that. You can drive by the starlight; you don't need lights just its show its possible

There's a mountain called Mount Kenya, and it's 17,500 feet high sitting on the equator. There's snow on it, and it's one of the most amazing sights. Forty minutes from there, you're at Nakuru. Now, Lake Nakuru, when you fly around it, looks like it's got pink sludge in it. In fact, it's pink flamingos, millions of them. Another 40 minutes from there is the Maasai Mara National Reserve, which joins the Serengeti as the largest free-range safari region in the world. I drove across the Maasai Mara and Serengeti, and it took six days. They have the migration of the wildebeest, which you can see from the moon. From space, you can see there's these two million animals moving for months to graze.

Seychelles

Another place I like is the Seychelles, a group of islands in the Indian Ocean. Each one is different, but they have the best beaches on God's earth. The islands are granitic, so you've got all these granitic shapes, and one of the islands, Praslin, has the 'coco de mer', the biggest coconut in the world. The seeds can weigh up to 10 kilos. They've also got the Seychelles tree frog, which is green. And there's amazing culture, with dancing and singing on the beaches in their multi-coloured dress. Basically, these islands have taken the best of Asia, Europe and Africa and mixed it up into a beautiful stew.

Ukraine

Ukraine is a very diverse country. It's the biggest country in Europe. It makes fantastic wine, and it's got the most beautiful women on Earth. Ukraine's background is very much different from that of Russia, which makes it all the more painful that Putin is trying to obliterate its culture and force it to become Russian. It was part of the Ottoman Empire, the Austro-Hungarian Empire, and was on the Silk Road from China to Europe. It's very beautiful there, and that's why Ukrainian women are so beautiful.

I've lived in Ukraine for years and am married to a Ukrainian woman, who still has many of her family over there. We live in Surrey and go back there when we can.

Georgia

And then, of course, there's the little country of Georgia. It's got the highest mountain in Europe and is the oldest wine making country in the world. They've been making wine there for four or five thousand years, and they're still making it in these big clay pots and seal them with beeswax. Then, bury it into the earth to make the wine. The grapes there are called Superavi - these are black the whole way through, and when you get this wine, it's actually almost black. And the flavour… you've never tasted anything like it.

The food is renowned, and using the leftover grapes, they make a distilled drink called chacha - it's very potent. The people are very friendly, the culture is very good, the dancing is a thing to behold, and then you can drive down to Batumi, which is like Monaco. It's on the Black Sea, absolutely splendid, and it's got all the international hotel chains there. It's an amazing place.

Chapter 10
A Passion for Cricket

August 21st, 1948, a day that I'll always remember.

The greatest cricket team in the history of the sport, starring the finest player ever to take the field, came to my hometown of Canterbury.

Of course, as an eight-year-old, I had little idea of the enormous historical importance of this moment. I knew that I loved cricket and people were talking about the Australian touring side and about their captain Sir Don Bradman. How it was his final Test series and how he'd set out to stay unbeaten for the entire trip. But this was no preparation for the occasion.

When I reached the ground, the atmosphere was electric. Thousands of people turned out to welcome this phenomenon of sport. Just like at Lord's, Old Trafford and Headingley, where record crowds of up to 158,000 watched the matches, the St Lawrence Ground in Canterbury was packed and buzzing. I thought at the time how magic this was.

The Australians won the toss and batted first, with Bill Brown scoring a stylish century, followed by Arthur Morris's 43 and Don Bradman's 65 – each boundary cheered raucously by the throng. They closed on 361 all out.

Then Kent strode out against the fearsome Australian fast bowling attack. They barely had time to peer down the wicket before Ray Lindwall, Sam Loxton, Bill Johnston and Colin McCool had skittled them for 51 runs, including six ducks! What skill, what drama, what a way to entertain the crowd!

At this point, I decided my future lay as a fast bowler. Now that I'd seen these legends of the game in action, I wouldn't rest until I could strike the same fear into opposition batsmen charging in and firing down the ball like Lindwall in his pomp.

This match also gave me a first taste of media coverage. I was standing near the radio broadcast position and a commentator called Peter West said: "We've been watching you all day. Would you like to be interviewed on the radio and give us your thoughts on the game?" So, at eight years old I made my debut as a broadcaster on BBC Sport.

After that, I wrote to Peter and he kindly offered to take me along to matches where he was commentating. On these trips, I'd find myself sharing a car with England internationals like Fred Trueman and Brian Close, and Alan Davidson who everyone called Daddy Davidson, which was a real privilege and thrill.

Much later on, after staying in touch with Peter for years, he recommended me to play for the MCC – the pinnacle of the English game – so I played about a dozen trial games for them and became a full member in the late 1960s. And the players that I met as a kid, like Trueman, Close and Kent's fantastic captain Colin Cowdrey, became friends and colleagues over the course of my decades in the sport, with professional games, overseas and English tours, charity matches and an amazing community of fellow cricket enthusiasts.

So the seed of that 1948 match germinated into a lifelong passion which I'm extremely grateful for. It shows how people respond positively when you show a genuine interest, how they enjoy nurturing your passion and inviting you to share in the game they love. Looking back, I can say that cricket was the catalyst that introduced me to things that would become staples of my life: hospitality, travel, aviation, even Concorde.

In those early childhood days, I would do anything to play or watch cricket. I'd hang a ball from the ceiling in my bedroom and smash it with a bat for hours on end. In the summer I used to stay with a great aunt at Greatstone above her bakery shop. Her home opened up to the sand dunes, so I would get anyone to hold a bat on the firm damp sands at Greatstone, near Dungeness, and bowl at them all afternoon.

In those early years, my father encouraged my cricket career. But then our relationship went off the rails and by the time we moved to Exmouth, when I was in my early teens, he became positively unhelpful. He was on the selection committee and was one of the umpires. He'd tell the local club that I wasn't available when they called to see if I could play, even though he was involved in cricket through his school and coaching the Devonshire colts.

At the age of 22, working in the merchant navy, I set sail for Australia from Southampton on a 28-day voyage that took up through the Suez Canal, the Red Sea, the Indian Ocean, through Bombay and Singapore before we arrived in Perth. This gave me a chance to play with some local teams and visit some relatives in Fremantle (a suburb of Perth). On another sea journey, with the Union Castle Line, I sailed on the Pendennis Castle as Quartermaster and played cricket in South Africa, including Cape Town – one of the world's most scenic places to play the game. In the summer, if I wasn't sailing anywhere, I'd play for all kinds of teams, including the International Crusaders, alongside Basil D'Oliveira and Sir Geoffrey Boycott. We are still the best of friends.

One night, towards the end of the International Crusaders tour, we'd been playing at Plymouth and Geoffrey didn't have a place to stay, so I invited him back to my place. I remember my daughter Becky, who would have been six or seven at the time, being a bit surprised to be turfed out of bed so that Geoffrey could sleep there. Another time, I was visiting Geoffrey in his village of Woolley, halfway between Sheffield and Leeds in Yorkshire. I remember it distinctly, because there was no pub! So instead, we took a walk around a pond in a neighbouring village, which was teeming with beautiful ducks. They were donated because Geoffrey didn't want a duck killed when he got a duck so they sent the live ones instead. "You've never had so many ducks, have you Geoffrey?" I said, which brought out a gruff Yorkshire reply. Actually, he was given a duck every time he scored one, at the time by a duck farm, I suppose because of the irony that he barely ever scored a duck in any form of cricket.

At a party to celebrate my 600th Concorde flight at Simpsons of Piccadilly, which British Airways, Rolls Royce and Cellnet generously sponsored, Geoffrey came along and then joined us afterwards at Stringfellows nightclub in Covent Garden. He remembers going but – a bit like me playing cricket with legends – wondered how on earth he ended up there!

Like many things in my life, finding myself playing cricket alongside Sir Geoffrey Boycott, Fred Trueman, Tom Graveney and Basil D'Oliveira was pretty mind-blowing. I definitely wondered what I was doing there.

In some ways, this is the beauty of cricket. Just as there's an unspoken code – the spirit of cricket – that players abide by, which is about fairness and making the game competitive, about giving the other side respect and appreciating good play, there's also a sense of inclusion. Basically, cricketers love to play. They recognise that it takes up a lot of time, that the fielding team will spend hours jogging into bushes to retrieve balls, that the ground staff have spent weeks making the wicket playable, that a whole retinue of supporters will umpire, score, make the tea and wash the kit. Players like me are the lucky ones who get to perform on the stage, often in the most beautiful spots. We generally realise how fortunate we are and welcome fellow enthusiasts, without caring too much about their actual cricketing abilities.

That's why people like the Australian Keith Miller, one of the greatest all-rounders the game has ever seen, was happy to be acquainted with me, a very minor player in comparison. Known for his love of the sport and of competitive cricket, rather than winning at all costs, Keith promised me one of his jackets from the Invincibles Tour of 1948, though sadly he died before he could give it to me.

Keith was great mates with Denis Compton, another absolute genius of the game. Like Miller, who played Aussie rules football as well as cricket, Compton was a professional footballer alongside his cricket career – he played 60 games for Arsenal and won the league in 1948. They also both served in the war – Miller as a pilot and Compton as a gunner.

Miller and Compton exemplified the spirit of cricket, in my view. They would go to watch the horse racing, then have some fun in the evening, then play first class cricket the next day. In fact, in 2005 the English Cricket Board and Cricket Australia named an award for the Player of the Series in Ashes tests the 'Miller-Compton medal'. It was a great pleasure to be around both of these guys. Many years after our playing days, we all ended up on the high table at Lord's for a charity dinner, sitting next to former Prime Minister Sir John Major.

Comparing cricket in those days, back in the 1960s and 1970s, with today, it's a different world. It was only in 1963, after all, that the 'gentlemen' and 'players' distinction was dropped between those who played for money and the – by inference – socially superior amateurs. Even though the MCC ended the division, cricket maintained a sense of raffish irreverence for many years. How many footballers have flown a Tiger Moth over a ground, as David Gower did in Australia in 1991? Or capsized a pedalo the night after a World Cup match in St Lucia, like Freddie Flintoff?

In the 40s and 50s, players touring Australia would have to spend a month on a boat to get there, practising their batting and bowling on the deck. No chance to cry off because you felt homesick or to see your family. It was more like being in the armed forces: you stick to the task. Today, players get paid a fortune and play on perfect, manicured, covered wickets, tended to by physiotherapists, psychotherapists and nutritionists. They're spoilt rotten and don't even have to play for the counties that nurtured them any more. County cricket is the nursery for Test cricket in my opinion.

The peak of my playing career, from a purely sporting point of view, came at the end of the 1960s when I played a handful of professional games for a mixed Somerset and Gloucestershire second XI team. But quite honestly, I had much more fun, more memorable times and more camaraderie on the many tours I've been on, whether as a player or an organiser-cum-travel agent and fixer.

The friendliness that exists within the cricketing world is exceptional. One time I sat at the head table with British Prime Minister Sir John Major at a Lord's Taverners dinner. Then a year later, we were both at another Taverners dinner, again I was at his table and said: "Hello Fred," the minute he saw me without any one with him to remind him who I was. For a country boy from deepest Kent, this was definitely a surprise and honour!

In the 1990s I helped arrange a Lord's Taverners tour to Kenya, which was one of the highlights of my life, never mind my cricketing life. We had former England players David Gower, Brian Close, Derek Pringle and Fred Rumsey, then celebrities including lyricist Sir Tim Rice, best known for his musical collaborations with Lord Andrew Lloyd Webber and the editor of the Daily Mail Brian Vine, who loved cricket almost as much as he loved champagne and free press trips. He looked on in amusement through his monocle and guaranteed us plenty of positive coverage in his paper.

We started off in Nairobi at the Nairobi Club with marquees all around the ground - it reminded me of Canterbury Cricket Week. The British High Commissioner bowled the first over, the wives and girlfriends sat around drinking gin cocktails and then we had a barbeque after the game. It was extremely civilised, partly thanks to the sponsorship I'd arranged with Guinness, KLM and Lonrho Hotels which meant all players had free flights and their partners had the best deal in the world: a two-week safari with cricket and cabaret for around £400 at the time. It took a year to put together. Brian Close wrote to me and said it was better than any England tour he had been on.

Next we drove up to Nanyuki, on the foothills of Mount Kenya, to play at an old polo ground with a pavilion, which probably hadn't seen a cricket match for 50 years. It was chilly up at altitude, so all the guests got hot water bottles, we had tables set across a little creek and had another delightful match, with the vast peak of Mount Kenya rising 5,200 metres behind the ground.

Once cricket was done, we all decamped to Ol Pejeta, a game conservancy 20km west of Nanyuki. I was driving along just having passed a pride of lions when I saw this strange green figure which turned out to be John, an ex-SAS soldier brought to Kenya to stop poaching who was now managing the ranch, walking towards us. He got into our Mitsubishi Pajero and we went to rescue the other passenger in the other vehicle that John was driving. They all managed to get into my vehicle with John standing on the back platform holding on to the roof. We again passed the pride of lions and John's wife remarked: "Is this meals on wheels?"

Ol Pejeta is one of the finest safari spots in Kenya with the rarest game animals, including black and white rhino, dozens of prides of lions and the only chimpanzees in Kenya. Quite a treat for visitors.

Over the years, quite a few of the decisions I've made came down to cricket. I moved to Jersey to play cricket and ended up running a hotel there. In New York I would play cricket out on Staten Island. It had a ground at Walker Park, with a thatched roof pavilion. It was apparently the first-place tennis was played in America, or so they said. I played with West Indian guys who worked at JFK Airport and brought along soul food to eat at tea.

Even now I love to watch the local teams where I live in Surrey, or turn up for friends who are playing and do a spot of umpiring. Recently I was asked to umpire at a friendly match in a most quintessential English setting at Ixworth Abbey near Bury St. Edmunds in Suffolk. It's a lovely game.

Some of the great cricketers I watched and played with:

Sir Colin Cowdrey
Colin Cowdrey was a legendary Kent and England cricketer, widely regarded as one of the finest batsmen of his era. Known for his elegant style, impeccable technique, and sportsmanship, Cowdrey's impact on the game extended beyond his impressive statistics. He remains one of the most beloved figures in the history of English cricket. As a child, I loved watching him play for Kent and followed his career from then on.

He made his debut for Kent in 1950 at the age of 17 and soon displayed his prodigious talent with the bat.

Cowdrey's classical batting style, characterised by his graceful stroke play and impeccable timing, made him a joy to watch. He possessed a wide range of shots and a keen understanding of the game, which allowed him to adapt to various conditions and situations. His ability to play both pace and spin with equal ease made him a highly versatile batsman.

In 1954, at the age of 21, Cowdrey made his debut for the England national cricket team against Australia. He quickly established himself as a key figure in the team's batting line-up. Known for his composure and determination, Cowdrey played several memorable innings against some of the most formidable bowling attacks of his time.

One of Cowdrey's most significant achievements came in 1962 when he became the first cricketer to reach 100 Test matches, a milestone that was a testament to his longevity and consistency. Throughout his career, he amassed more than 7,600 Test runs, including 22 centuries, at an average of over 44. His exceptional batting skills and leadership qualities led to him captaining the England team in various matches and series.

Cowdrey's impact on the game extended beyond his playing abilities. He was admired for his sportsmanship and fair play, earning him immense respect from opponents and fans alike. His calm and dignified demeanour on the field earned him the nickname "The Gentleman Cricketer."

Off the field, Cowdrey was highly regarded for his contributions to the development and promotion of cricket. He served as the President of the Marylebone Cricket Club (MCC) from 1986 to 1987 and later became an influential administrator in the sport. Cowdrey's efforts to expand cricket's reach globally helped popularise the game in non-traditional cricket-playing nations.

After retiring from international cricket in 1975, Cowdrey remained involved in the sport as a cricket commentator and broadcaster. He shared his deep insights and knowledge of the game with millions of fans, further solidifying his place as a respected voice in cricket.

In recognition of his outstanding contributions to cricket, Cowdrey was knighted in 1992, becoming Sir Colin Cowdrey. His impact on the sport has been immortalised in various ways, including the naming of the Cowdrey Stand at Lord's Cricket Ground in his honour.

Cowdrey passed away on December 4, 2000, leaving behind a lasting legacy in the world of cricket. His exceptional batting skills, sportsmanship, and dedication to the game have inspired generations of cricketers.

David Gower

Renowned for his graceful stroke play and artistic flair, David Gower's career spanned over a decade and left an indelible mark on the game.

Born in Tunbridge Wells, not far from where I grew up, Gower displayed an early affinity for cricket. He made his debut for Leicestershire in 1975 at the age of 18, quickly establishing himself as a promising young talent. Gower's batting style stood out from the crowd, characterised by his fluid footwork, impeccable timing, and ability to effortlessly score runs all around the wicket.

In 1978, Gower made his international debut for the England national cricket team, and it was clear from the start that he possessed a rare gift. His elegant stroke play and natural talent captured the imagination of cricket enthusiasts worldwide. Gower's ability to dominate bowling attacks with his stylish batting made him a delight to watch.

One of the defining moments of Gower's career came during the 1985 Ashes series against Australia. He played a pivotal role in England's triumph, scoring vital runs and showcasing his sublime stroke play. Gower's contributions earned him the Man of the Series award and solidified his reputation as one of England's greatest batsmen.

Off the field, Gower's laid-back and charismatic personality made him a beloved figure among fans and teammates. He exuded a sense of calmness and nonchalance, which sometimes drew criticism from pundits who believed he did not take the game seriously enough. However, Gower's carefree demeanour belied his dedication and love for the sport.

In 1992, Gower retired from international cricket, leaving behind a legacy of stylish and entertaining cricket. After retiring, he pursued a successful career as a cricket commentator and broadcaster, bringing his insights and charm to television audiences around the world. Gower's engaging and articulate commentary further endeared him to cricket fans, who appreciated his deep understanding of the game.

Beyond cricket, Gower has also pursued other interests, including golf and media engagements. He has authored books and appeared in various television programs, showcasing his versatility and passion for storytelling.

After his professional career was over, Gower and I would play for the Lord's Taverners. One day he mentioned that he was getting married and – knowing that he lived in East Africa as a boy – I offered him a honeymoon in Kenya. He drove over to my home and we put the trip together.

I attended his wedding to Thorunn at Winchester Cathedral alongside cricketers Alan Lamb, Bob Willis and Sir Ian Botham, who was best man. Then the happy couple set off to Kenya where they were treated like royalty by Perrie Hennessey (RIP) at Island Camp. Gower wrote an enthusiastic review of the trip in the London Evening Standard, saying "It was all down to Uncle Fred"!

Sir Geoffrey Boycott
Geoffrey was born in the same year as me – 1940 – and became one of the finest opening batsmen of his generation. He was known for his resilience, technical prowess, and unwavering focus at the crease.

Born and raised in West Yorkshire, Boycott demonstrated an early aptitude for cricket. He made his debut for Yorkshire County Cricket Club in 1962 and quickly showed a meticulous technique, compact defensive stroke play, and ability to occupy the crease for extended periods that set him apart from his peers.

Boycott's international career began in 1964 when he made his Test debut for England against Australia. He soon became an England mainstay, renowned for his patience, concentration and ability to grind out runs. Boycott's batting style, characterised by his defensive solidity and calculated stroke selection, made him a challenging opponent for any bowling attack.

Throughout his career, Boycott amassed over 8,000 Test runs at an average of more than 47, including 22 centuries. He displayed exceptional consistency, regularly providing a solid foundation for the English team. Boycott's ability to weather difficult situations and frustrate bowlers earned him the reputation of being an immovable object at the crease. These days, it's one of the funniest sights on television to see his reaction when an English batter swipes wildly at the ball and gets caught – something he would never have done!

One of Boycott's defining performances came during the 1977 Ashes series against Australia. In the fifth Test at Headingley, he played a monumental innings of 191 runs, which helped England achieve a remarkable victory.

The other thing to remember about Geoffrey is that he played in an era when the West Indies were rampant, with four extremely quick bowlers firing down at you. He was very brave to face that time and again.

Off the field, Boycott's outspoken nature and strong personality often courted controversy. His intense dedication to his craft and desire for personal success sometimes clashed with team dynamics and management. Despite these challenges, Boycott's impact on the game and his contributions to English cricket cannot be understated. He retired from international cricket in 1982, ending his illustrious career as one of the leading run-scorers in Test cricket. He transitioned into a successful career as a cricket commentator, analyst, and journalist, where his sharp insights and strong opinions continued to captivate audiences.

I've very much enjoyed spending time with Geoffrey over the years, whether playing alongside him in charity matches or socialising around the country.

Fred Trueman
Another Yorkshireman, Fred Trueman was born in 1931 only about 15 miles away from where Geoffrey Boycott started out. But rather than batting, Trueman became one of the greatest fast bowlers in the history of the sport. He had a fiery temperament, aggressive bowling style, and exceptional skill. After joining Yorkshire at the age of 18, his natural ability to generate immense pace and swing quickly caught the attention of selectors, earning him a place in the England national cricket team.

In 1952, Trueman made his Test debut for England against India, marking the beginning of a remarkable international career. He became the first cricketer to take 300 Test wickets, achieving the milestone in 1964. Trueman's aggressive approach and intimidating presence on the field made him a feared opponent, as batsmen struggled with his thunderbolts.

Trueman's fiery temperament often fuelled his performances. He had an unwavering self-belief and a competitive spirit that drove him to succeed. His aggressive on-field persona and willingness to challenge batsmen made him a crowd favourite, and his battles with rival players became legendary.

Over the course of his career, Trueman represented England in 67 Test matches, taking an impressive 307 wickets at an average of 21.57. His finest performance came in the 1956 Ashes series against Australia, where he claimed 29 wickets in just five matches, propelling England to a series victory.

Off the field, Trueman was known for his colourful personality and blunt wit. He was unafraid to express his opinions, often attracting controversy with his candid remarks, making him a popular figure in the cricketing world and beyond. He used to smoke the most gigantic cigars and would party hard when we were on tour. One night, Fred and I sat in a bar in the West Country with Lance Gibbs, Chris Lloyd and Roland Kanhai drinking and laughing. I got a right earful from the manager the next morning, who blamed me for keeping them out late.

Trueman retired from international cricket in 1965 but continued to play domestic cricket for Yorkshire until 1968. After retirement, he became a cricket commentator and broadcaster, providing insightful analysis and sharing his wealth of experience with audiences around the world. Trueman's witty and distinctive commentary style made him a beloved figure in cricket broadcasting. As he once said, discussing his bowling with someone who remarked that the TV pictures were in black and white: "I'd have been even faster in colour." When he passed away in 2006, I felt a bit sad that there wasn't much coverage in the press, for someone who had done so much for his sport and for the country.

Sir Garry Sobers
In a world where the word legend is used incredibly often, it is truly applicable to Garry Sobers. In my opinion, he is, without a doubt, probably the greatest all-rounder that the game has ever seen. He became the first batsman to score six sixes on 31 August 1968 where he was captain of Nottinghamshire playing against Glamorgan at St Helen's in Swansea. In that same year, I had the enormous privilege to play with Garry and the International Cavaliers where he was every inch a gentlemen of with the most incredible zest for the spirit of sportsmanship. Out of only 11 occasions the award has been bestowed upon Barbadians, he is one of only two living National Heroes of his homeland - Barbados. In January 2024, I was invited to Barbados by Hadley Bourne, CEO of Grantley Adams International Airport to visit British Airways Concorde G-BOAE 'Alpha Echo' and from the moment I began planning the itinerary for this trip, I had hoped I might have the chance to be reunited with Garry and I was overjoyed when that became a reality. We spent a morning reminiscing fond memories of our dear mutual friend, Sir Geoffrey Boycott and our time spent playing all together. His zest for the spirit of cricket and sportsmanship, even all these years later, couldn't have been more apparent when he humbly said "All I wanted to do was entertain those who came to watch us play." I am so proud to know Garry and consider him a cherished friend and one of my all-time cricketing heroes.

Chapter 11
Giving Back

Being able to travel all over the world, as I have done, is a great privilege. Many people never leave their own town or village, never mind their country or continent. It's also been my privilege to meet hundreds of well-known people from the worlds of business, sport and entertainment.

What I discovered many years ago is that I have a talent for putting people together and persuading them to work with each other for a common goal. At first, I used this talent for business: I had to bring politicians, businesspeople, manufacturers and administrators together to agree licensing deals. There were always plenty of obstacles, but I found ways to resolve the problems and get everyone going in the same direction.

Later, it turned out that these same skills could apply to charitable work. To raise funds for a good cause, you might have to engage entertainers, hire a venue, book the catering, invite a thousand guests (preferably ones with money to spend), drum up some prizes for the auction and make sure there would be press coverage.

One of the key things I could contribute was valuable prizes. After spending so long in Kenya, bringing dozens of people on safari to the Masai Mara, to some of the great hotels of the country and to its beach resorts in Diani, I had built up excellent relations with many of the leading hoteliers and tourism companies over there. They were extremely grateful for the publicity that I'd achieved for them, together with financial support I'd provided through commercial sponsorship. In return, they were happy to give my guests a couple of free nights' lodging, or a free safari.

I used to work with OK magazine and run competitions for safaris to Kenya. They would get 60 or 70,000 phone calls on a premium line and they'd offer me half of the revenue, so I'd give that to the Kenyan businesses and get them massive publicity. In exchange for a couple of days complimentary stay, the Kenya hotels would get tremendous publicity in the UK which was worth a great deal to them.

The same applied to my relationship with Richard Branson and Virgin Atlantic. Since I'd collaborated closely with Richard for years, advising him on the formation of the airline and working as a sort of ambassador for the brand, I was able to offer Virgin tickets as prizes in charity auctions. Equally, my close relationships with hoteliers and travel people in the Seychelles meant I could offer holidays there too.

In each of these cases, there was no financial benefit to me, just to the charity concerned, but it meant that all kinds of charities were keen to have me on board, since a world-class safari trip to Kenya or a week in the Seychelles is just the kind of prize that people will pay top dollar for.

My relationship with Kenya, as a business traveller, tourist, charity donor and sometime travel agent goes back decades. At least 40 years ago I first visited Nanyuki, on the slopes of Mount Kenya and came across its orphanage, where children slept on the floor, or several to a bed. It was a desperately poor community and there was very little help from the state.

Since that time, I've arranged for many of the parties I send out to Kenya to visit the orphanage at Nanyuki, including Sir Richard Branson, Sir Tim Rice, Noel Edmonds and many others. They either donate financially to help the children or else take out boxes of clothes and equipment to help with their schooling.

These days, each child has its own bed and many of them have been funded through schooling, giving them a chance to better themselves. It's been a very rewarding experience working with the orphanage. Quite a few other British groups now support the children and gather donations of money and clothes, so the difference from when I first visited in the 1970s is amazing.

Elsewhere in Kenya I've supported other orphanages, some of them with dozens of children needing help. In between Mombasa and Nairobi there are eight such places, some of them in the Taita Hills. In the 1990s I organised trips where British people would collect second-hand children's clothes and box them up to take out. One time, in 1997, we had 24 packing cases full of clothes! I persuaded an airline to transport them free of charge to Mombasa, then arranged for a safari company owned by my friend the rally driving champion Mike Kirkland to transport the clothes and some of our visitors to the orphanages.

The biggest orphanage was in the town of Wema, where there lived 65 girls, who stood in perfect lines and sang in harmony for us when we arrived. They lived in dormitories, 22 girls together, with barely any room to themselves. They were absolutely overjoyed to wear their new tee shirts and dresses. Some of the girls had escaped childhood prostitution and being forced to beg on the streets.

Another orphanage, this time for boys, was nearby. Here, we met Emmanuel, who had arrived at the home as a young child, but was already taking drugs. He was now dedicated to his schoolwork and determined to become an airline pilot when he grew up. A third orphanage up in the mountains in Wharuba had several children with learning disabilities. This is a particular issue in Kenya, where disability is seen as a stigma and as a curse on the family, so children are often ostracised. In this orphanage, as in Nanyuki, the administrators make a big effort to nurture disabled children and give them a bright future.

On one trip I arranged, HRH Prince and Princess Michael of Kent came along and we had a ceremonial handover of a cheque from them for £13,900 to President Daniel Moi to support the Nanyuki orphanage, after I'd persuaded Pan Am and Mount Kenya Safari Club to donate tickets and holidays to the cause. President Moi turned to the Princess and said: "When you're with Fred, you're in good hands," which was nice of him to say.

In 1993 I arranged a Lord's Taverners cricket tour of Kenya, which I write about in my chapter on cricket. Once again, I made sure that we contributed to the Nanyuki orphanage. This made sense, given that the Taverners is a charitable foundation and all its members get involved because they want to give something back.

For this trip, I raised more than £100,000 in sponsorship from companies like the Kenya Breweries, which is part of Guinness. It took a hell of a lot of effort to put the whole thing together, but it raised hundreds of thousands of pounds for charities including the Nanyuki orphanage, Gertrude's Garden Children's Hospital (which was founded in Nairobi in 1947 by an English colonel in memory of his wife) and the Jaipur Foot Project (which provides prosthetic limbs and has helped thousands of Kenyans to walk again).

When I raised funds for these kinds of charities through the Taverners, I'd promote them on TV or in the press. One time we were on Good Morning TV show for several mornings in a row, which is the kind of publicity that you just can't buy. Another time we set up a fashion shoot with Mount Kenya as a backdrop and it appeared in glossy magazines.

Keeping up good relations with the hoteliers was key for this trip. I was fortunate that I could call on Lonhro Hotels for help – they had a wonderful place in Nairobi, the Norfolk Hotel, and the Mount Kenya Safari Club up in the mountains, which were perfect for what we needed. In the event, rather than us being grateful, Lonhro Hotels wrote a lovely note to the Taverners saying how grateful they were that I'd put the tour together and chosen them as hosts, since it was such an accolade for Kenya. This is what I mean by the value of publicity and famous names. Having some of the great crickets of the age, like Brian Close and David Gower, gave everyone a lot of excitement. The Taverners' patron HRH Prince Edward couldn't join us, but he sent a nice message thanking me for organising the tour and wishing us well.

The Lord's Taverners was a fantastic charity for many years, supported by HRH The Duke of Edinburgh, by many of the great cricketers of the 20th century and some world-class sportspeople and entertainers. If you look through the line-ups for some of the matches, you'll see players like my Somerset teammate Fred Rumsey, Farokh Engineer (who played 46 tests for India), Derek Pringle (who took dozens of wickets for England and was actually born in Nairobi) and Alan Lamb, South African-born but played for England and scored 14 centuries.

Playing in the same teams as these guys was, again, an amazing privilege and having them give up their time and energy to support charities that I recommended was hugely rewarding. I'm so grateful to them. I used to put up safaris to Kenya, trips to the Seychelles, dinners at Mosimann's restaurant or club, tours of the Houses of Parliament with lunch thrown in… I probably raised £200,000 for them all in all.

By the time that I set up the 1993 trip to Kenya, the Lord's Taverners was already 43 years old and going strong. It started in 1950 at the Tavern at Lord's Cricket Ground in St John's Wood in London (hence the name), when a group of cricket fans sat around thinking how lucky they were to watch their favourite game in such a fantastic location. How about doing something to help those less fortunate? That's how it started and the philosophy of helping others while having fun yourself carried on ever since. They've funded more than a thousand minibuses to help disabled and under-privileged children get access to sport and give them more opportunities; they've funded playing fields, wheelchair versions of sports like basketball and rugby; and helped many girls get into cricket through the Lady Taverners, which ran between 1980 and 2021, when it folded into the main organisation.

Along the way, they've welcomed everyone from John Mills, Brian Johnston, Laurence Olivier, Richard Attenborough, Trevor Howard, Eric Morecambe, Margaret Thatcher, Judith Chalmers and Angela Rippon to play or support the charity, which has given it tremendous appeal to the public and transformed the lives of many children with disabilities.

My one reservation about the Taverners is that, at least in the 1990s, they would spend a lot on administration. They had an office in Queen Anne's Gate, around the corner from Buckingham Palace, which I felt was an extravagance, and were run for a time by an ex-military man called Patrick Shervington who annoyed people unnecessarily. Now that David Gower is president, I'm sure things are much better-managed.

The Variety Club of Great Britain does a fantastic job for young people with disabilities, along similar lines to the Taverners. I was involved in the London branch of the Club, but they were active all over the country and indeed the world. Variety started in Pittsburgh in the United States, in 1927 when a month-old baby girl was left in the Sheridan Film Theatre with a note asking 'show business people' to look after Catherine because her parents were too poor, and already had eight other children. A group of 11 men banded together to form the Variety Club to take care of this poor baby's living and education expenses, the story became national news and the Club has raised hundreds of millions of dollars ever since, with annual fundraising balls.

Variety launched in Britain in 1949, just ahead of the Lord's Taverners. Its annual Awards are one of the highlights of the show business calendar, giving out prizes to the biggest stars and helping to raise millions for the charity. I went to a Variety Club Ball once and the star attraction was David Bowie. He didn't show up until very late in the evening and all he sang was the Lord's Prayer, which wasn't quite what people were expecting.

My own contributions have been Kenyan safaris and airline tickets, along with a guest appearance at one of their dinners by the Chuka drummers from Mukuuni in Mount Kenya national park. In Variety's own magazine, they kindly thanked me for negotiating the "sensational Chuka dancers and drummers" at the annual dinner. "Our Mr Finn is a most interesting man," they continued. "He is a star feature in the Guinness Book of Records as the world's most travelled man... Thank you Mr Finn and long may you support Variety and enjoy your travels."

The drummers themselves were also very grateful for the chance to perform in London to a huge crowd of VIPs and stars assembled by Variety. They wrote me a charming letter explaining how they wanted to present me with a traditional headdress made from the skin of a colobus monkey, together with its tail. They explained that they use this animal's skin "due to its great proudness." They also offered me a traditional African drum, "another very prestigious instrument used by Chuka drummers." They were very keen to demonstrate their respect for me and to name me as "a traditional elder". This was all very nice and I was delighted with the letter.

Offering safaris, airline tickets and other goodies meant that I was invited to all manner of fancy dinners and receptions. There were parties for Sparks, a charity supporting medical research for children, such as the one hosted by Lord Cheshire attended by HRH Princess Michael of Kent (again), who was their patron. Sparks did great work in medical research into children's diseases for many years, then was eventually swallowed up by Great Ormond Street Hospital in 2021 when it ran out of money during the pandemic.

A similar charity was Action Research for the Crippled Child, which started out in 1952 looking for cures for polio, then broadened into a general charity for childhood diseases in the 1960s and dropped its un-politically correct name in 1990. Now it's simply known as Action Medical Research. I did a lot of work for them in the 1980s and 1990s, mainly at black tie events in London such as the Volkswagen Annual Ball at the Intercontinental Hotel, where TV stars like Bernard Cribbins and Michael Aspel would rub shoulders with sports people like footballer Trevor Brooking, tennis player Annabel Croft, swimmer Duncan Goodhew and athlete Roger Black.

These were medium-sized charities, whereas Save the Children was enormous, one the world's largest. It was founded in 1919 by two sisters to help children left in poverty by the First World War and has grown ever since to help millions of children worldwide. Originally, I was introduced to them through Cellnet, which employed me as a consultant in the 1980s and 1990s. I went to Silverstone and drove in a warm-up event before the Grand Prix and they were one of the charities involved. They invited me to Simpsons Piccadilly's 50th anniversary where I donated a couple of big prizes and was introduced to HRH Princess Anne, while Sir Michael Parkinson (RIP) was the compere. I think HRH The Princess Royal has done a fantastic job in so many ways. Such a hard working and smart woman.

I helped Save the Children raise tens of thousands of pounds through arranging prizes at their Gala evenings and at a Charity Dinner and Ball during the World Travel Market, where I was honoured to sit next to WTM's head Tom Nutley. Auction prizes included a weekend for two in New York courtesy of Virgin Atlantic, which I arranged. Of course Save the Children has big overheads, because it employs more than 100,000 people, but it has big ambitions – it wants to prevent any child dying from unavoidable causes under the age of five, make sure that they get enough to eat, medicine when they need it and receive a solid education. Can't argue with that.

Some events I attended were memorable more for the drama surrounding them than the fundraising. In 1990 I went to a lunch hosted by the International Congress for the Family, a right-wing American group that opposes same-sex relationships and abortion. Somehow, they'd persuaded Diana, Princess of Wales to make a speech, which was odd, given how sympathetic she was to gay people in general. During the event, a group of lesbians marched onto the stage holding banners saying: 'Lesbian Mothers Aren't Pretending'. They were bundled off the stage and out of the building, where they joined a crowd of their supporters. Fairly odd to hold the event in Brighton in the first place, unless the organisers were deliberately trying to stir up trouble.

One year, I helped to organise a Burns Night – the traditional celebration of all things Scottish, normally held around the UK on 25 January every year. On this particular year, I arranged for this to be held in Kyiv in March, since it was more convenient for the Ukrainian guests. This was a great success, partly thanks to my friend Robert McNeil, who owns one of the biggest marketing companies over there, along with hotels and nightclubs. We had entertainers fly over from Scotland including claymore fighters and bagpipe players. And we raised thousands for Lions Club Ukraine, the Kyiv branch of the US-based charity started in 1917 in Chicago that encourages businesspeople to assist their local communities. It's now active in 200 countries and set up in Ukraine in 1993.

Kyiv's Burns Night raised more than $400,000 for the Lion's Club, which mainly went towards equipment for children's hospitals, like incubators and dialysis machines. I donated a week's holiday in the Seychelles among other prizes. Robert O'Neil remembers that we had 650 people coming to Burns Night, all dressed in black tie, and that my prizes were always the highlight of the evening, raising tens of thousands of dollars each.

Alongside Robert, I'd support other big events in Kyiv each year, such as the Ukrainian-themed Kozak Night and the Ambassador's Ball. All in all, he would raise upwards of $300,000 a year for good causes, helping thousands of children, orphans and elderly Ukrainians.

"We are very fortunate to have known you for more than 20 years and to have had the opportunity to work with you, on both PR and corporate events," Robert wrote to me recently. "It has been a huge privilege to work with you. You always light up the room, wherever you go. Fred is a walking talking Encyclopaedia of Life of Travel of course everything to do with aircraft and surely the finest storyteller/dinner companion ever. I would say the same of him. He's a man of great integrity and generosity and I'm grateful to have him as a friend."

Robert's company Pulse has helped so many people in Ukraine over the years. Never more so than since Russia's invasion in February 2022. Today I fundraise to help get medical supplies such as tourniquets, pressure bandages and flak jackets directly to people like my sister-in-law and brother-in-law who can deliver them to people on the front line. And teach the troops how to use them. I also help arrange places for refugees fleeing to safety in France and the UK.

Back home in London, I went to a Burns Night another year and it wasn't much to write home about. I told the organisers that I was sure I could put on a better show. So they commissioned me to do my best. Instead of £34,000, we raised over £93,000 at the next event, with a fantastic array of acts including the Red-Hot Chilli Pipers and fierce bidding for the many great auction prizes.

One of the charities we funded was Make Some Noise, which itself distributes money to around 100 small charities helping young (and some old) people deal with mental health challenges, gain independence and tackle poverty. It supports everything from food banks to domestic violence helplines. Make Some Noise was founded by media conglomerate Global which owns Classic FM, Capital Radio, LBC, Heart and Smooth radio stations.

Make Some Noise wrote to me afterwards saying how incredibly grateful they were "for helping us create a truly successful and wonderful Burns Night fundraising event this year. Your generous contributions on the evening and efforts in curating an unforgettable auction are deeply appreciated!" Always nice when people like what you do – and when you triple their fundraising efforts.

The Nordoff Robbins charity makes some noise, with a deeply therapeutic purpose. It employs music therapists who work with severely disabled people, some with learning difficulties, who benefit from the way that music can "unlock feelings and memories and bring us together," as the charity puts it. Disabled people are given the opportunity to participate in making and performing music, "unlocking their creativity and capacity for connection."

It actually dates back to 1959 when Paul Nordoff and Clive Robbins began working together, on the basis that anyone, no matter how ill or disabled by conditions such as dementia, can respond to music in a life-enhancing way. This is a great philosophy to have, and it appealed to a group of professional rugby players called Legends of Rugby, who began running fundraising events for Nordoff Robbins in 1995.

Over the past three decades, musicians including Sir Paul McCartney, Eric Clapton, Sir Elton John and Robert Plant have played benefits for the charity and the Legends of Rugby dinners have booked acts like Madness, Stereophonics and Keane. I've been to their annual dinners, with ex-international rugby player Martin Bayfield as host. He's an enormous unit! I'm well over six feet high and I barely come up to his shoulder. Victor Ubogu, another England player, who was born in Nigeria, runs the club and does fantastic work for them. We went over to Kenya and found out that rugby was big in the Nairobi prisons. Apparently once the prisoners get into the sport they're transformed: once they leave, they don't reoffend. We held a couple of dinners to raise funds for them and Victor went into the prisons to talk with the guys and even played a bit with them. I love to see that kind of connection taking shape, it's so positive.

In a change from my fundraising efforts connected with travel and sport, I found myself helping out the Royal Air Force Benevolent Fund. This was more of an aviation connection. A lot of the Concorde pilots were former RAF pilots. As with the other charities I've supported, I'd offer holidays and tickets at their fundraisers and started to get noticed. The Red Arrows leaders invited me to fly with them and on one occasion I invited the whole team back to my home in Guildford after a flight.

When the Phantom jets were finally retired from RAF service in 1990 after 21 years, the Commanding officer invited me to the farewell dinner, one of only four civilians present that evening. That was a special honour. I would help the Red Arrows find their after dinner speakers, like Barry Cryer and Bernard Breslaw, which always went down well. The only thing you had to beware of was drinking too much beer before dinner, because they were very strict about everyone staying in their seats while the speeches went on. Sometimes that was a tight squeeze.

As with my connection with Save the Children, I met people from Tommy's Team – a charity raising funds for St Thomas's Hospital in London – through driving with Cellnet. Once again we were at Silverstone doing a Grand Prix warm up, with celebrities and sportspeople. There was Jeremy Clarkson and an Olympic runner who crashed his car and decided to line up to run instead of drive. We raised £120,000 in 20 minutes.

Ron Dennis – founder and former CEO, chairman and owner of McLaren – and I were already friends. He'd asked me to get a picture of me with a McLaren F1 car in front of Concorde, so I got it and it was plastered all over the media. Great publicity for everyone. Then at this event at Silverstone I asked Ron if he fancied coming to RAF Wattisham, near Ipswich, for the Phantom farewell. He said: "Sure, I'll fly the McLaren private jet over there." I warned him that it wasn't so easy just to expect an RAF base to welcome someone in their own plane, but I'd see what I could do. I pulled some strings with Group Captain Allcott and Ron was cleared for landing.

It was a surprisingly emotional affair, saying goodbye to the Phantom. Not quite on a par with the farewell to Concorde, but getting on that way. Some of us were keen to keep the aircraft on in a heritage capacity, but the Americans insisted that we take the reheats off the engine, which would have made it impossible to fly.

One other RAF Benevolent Fund event I enjoyed was the Battle of Britain 50th Anniversary Appeal in 1990, held at the Guildhall in the City of London, with HRH Duke of Kent and Sir John Major, who was Chancellor of the Exchequer at the time, shortly to become Prime Minister. As a Battle of Britain baby, born just weeks before it started, I felt an emotional connection with this appeal.

Those buggers didn't get me then and they've never got me yet.

Conclusion

Now that I've finished writing these memoires, there are a few things that stand out for me.

One is the importance of being grateful for what we have. In the days when we were flying on Concorde, we knew it wouldn't last forever – the planes had a limited lifespan, like any aircraft – but we thought the service would surely go on into the 2010s. A momentary disaster in Paris and the whole supersonic passenger plane phenomenon disappeared, never to reappear (so far). It was the monopoly actions of Air France in league with Airbus in a coup that stopped the supersonic experience because reportedly, Air France never made any money from Concorde and Airbus was more intent on the A380. BA could have taken on the Air France maintenance costs and continued flying - that was the strategy of BA until Airbus doubled the maintenance costs. BA could have instigated legal action against Airbus for this but capitulated and that's what stopped BA from continuing service in the recently renovated aircraft.

Another is how tough it can be, in the 2020s, to form connections. Working from home, meeting on video links, communicating purely on emails – sometimes with robots rather than human beings… It feels like people are losing the ability to relate to each other.

In a lifetime of travel, it is the human connections that have been most important to me. I met someone in London who casually suggested I should visit him in Canada, so I did. One thing led to another and before long I was driving right around the United States on an expense account, meeting hundreds of crazy, lovely, beautiful people wherever I went.

In Africa I met businessmen, politicians, orphans, gamekeepers. Those relationships have lasted a lifetime and still bring great financial and social benefits to people in Kenya, for example, through my efforts to publicise their resorts and children's homes. It's hard to believe that this depth of relationship would have developed if we'd only chatted on Zoom, or I'd made a virtual tour of Mount Kenya.

The game of cricket is a distillation of human contact and relationships. You're part of a team, yet in other ways it's an intensely personal game: a lone bowler against a lone batsman. How you communicate with and support each other is vital to the outcome. And off the field, cricket is the most social of all sports, as I've been privileged to discover.

Will the next generation value this time spent outdoors, on green fields, learning a pretty technical game of skill and judgement? Or will it retreat into dark living rooms and bedrooms to play video games and worsen the obesity epidemic? the next generation value this time spent outdoors, on green fields, learning a pretty technical game of skill and judgement? Or will it retreat into dark living rooms and bedrooms to play video games and worsen the obesity epidemic?

You don't get to become the world's most travelled person by sitting around. And I worry about a future world where travel is frowned upon, whether for environmental reasons, because of cost or because people simply can't be bothered.

Travel doesn't just broaden the mind, it invigorates the body, it keeps the world's economies turning, it introduces people and cultures to one another, which helps everyone get along better, and it makes us appreciate the wonders of the world – natural and man-made – for ourselves.

So, if I could leave you with one message, it would be: get out there. Travel the world. See new places, meet new people. Take to the skies.

Fred Finn, July 2024

Acknowledgements

There are a great deal of people who have been extremely kind to me at various stages of my life - whether it be through my career, through travelling or for their direct involvement with this book.

Firstly, I would like to thank my wife, Alla for her love and support in the rather mammoth effort compiling my life story into this book. I would also like to thank David Nicholson, author and journalist; Adrian Meredith, who I have known for almost fifty years during his tenure as the Official Photographer for British Airways and in particular, Concorde, for the use of some of his stunning images in my book. Stewart Peter, for his loyal friendship to me in recent years, David Scowsill, former President and CEO of World Travel and Tourism Council for his unwavering support in providing wise counsel at various stages of creating this book. Djois Franklin – my Co-Founder of Quicket and SeatMaps.com for your unsurpassed efforts in creating an unrivalled app that I am so proud to be associated with. Graeme and Cheryl Lomax have been so kind with their hospitality and friendship in a time of need – you were such stars! Mike Kirkland, Southern Cross Safari's, Martin Dunfold, owner of Carnivor and Tamarind Group (Kenya), Chris Modigell, Master Hotelier, Perrie Hennessey (RIP) whose friendship with me began from his time in Zimbabwe through to Island Camp, Lake Baringo in Kenya for his endless support on all my charitable endeavours for various causes across Kenya.

I am beyond grateful to Sir Richard Branson for a friendship spanning for well over forty years where his team at Virgin continue to recognise and support me. I have had a long association with Marriott Hotels staying in over 7,000 of their hotel rooms during my years of travel and I am particularly grateful to David Bartlett, Area Director - Europe for his continued recognition of my support to Marriott. The legendary cricketer and my dear friend Sir Geoffrey Boycott; my old friends Elaine Bagnall and George Buchanan, my colleague from our days working with Empire Pencils Co; Robert McNeil, CEO Pulse International in Kyiv; and Paul Evans for his assistance in compiling the first manuscript iterations of my book. To Snappy Snaps in Surbiton who constantly support my charitable endeavours printing various items for me. Jean-Yves Darcel, owner of Le Beaujolais – a little bit of Provence in central London and Judith Blincow, owner of Mermaid Inn in Rye, East Sussex for your magnificent contributions in the support I've co-ordinated for Ukraine.

Sonic Boom

71. Alla my wife, Katya my daughter and me with Concorde G-BOAF 'Alpha Foxtrot' at Aerospace Bristol.

72. My dear friend, Ben Lord and I, onboard the USS Intrepid overlooking G-BOAD in New York during our VIP visit there in May 2024. I am so pleased to be able to share some of my platform and what I do with Ben given his zest for Concorde's legacy and my part in that.

v

I am immeasurably indebted to a most terrific friend, Ben Lord, Chairman of Save Concorde Group whose tireless, tenacious efforts with anything we collaborate on but in particular this book alongside knowledge and kindness delivered so selflessly can never be surpassed which has made a particularly indelible impact on my life in recent years.

Alla and I have both seen how strong Ukraine has been since the unprovoked invasion by Russia. Despite this, our daughter Katya, has overcome adversity and done so well with her studies, languages and business degrees, we are truly proud of her.

I pay tribute to my family in Ukraine, Ihor my brother-in-law and his talented wife Svetlana, our nephews Sasha and Fred, who lived for a while with us in the UK, away from the atrocities of war and for our family's collective help in supporting the armed forces of Ukraine.

I would also like to record my special appreciation to my British Airways Concorde family, including Captain John Hutchinson and Norman Britton, flight crew, Gilly Mayes-Pratt, whose daughter I was proud to walk down the aisle in 2022. I adore seeing Julie Reynolds, Cabin Manager and Wilma Boyd, a wonderful companion for my series of lectures on the QE2. Every BA crew, be it Concorde or otherwise, have always been fantastic whenever I have flown.

And to those that I should have thanked but didn't include here. You know who you are and will always be very much in my thoughts. Please accept my apologies for any omissions.

INDEX

A
Addis Ababa, *183*
Aden, *156*
Advanced Research Projects Agency, *84*
Aerial Isometrics, *132, 189*
Aeroflot, *183–84*
Aerolineas Argentinas, *184*
Aerospace Bristol, *55, 180*
Africa, *44, 47, 108, 118, 126, 141, 147, 183, 194, 198, 217*
Ahmed, Mohammed, *183*
Airbus, *46, 52, 69–71, 162, 165, 172, 217*
    A300, *47*
    A320, *157*
    A330, *69*
    A350, *189*
    A380, *69*
Air France, *31, 33, 37, 39–40, 47–48, 50–52, 66–67, 69, 154, 157, 159–62, 165, 168, 217*
    Concorde, *10, 45, 48, 52*
    Concorde F-BCFA, *68*
Airline Alliance SkyTeam, *161*
Airlines, Kenya, *158, 183*
Air New Zealand, *165*
Ali, Muhammad, *19, 101, 106*
Alpert, Herb, *126*
American Airlines, *8, 30, 37, 96, 154, 165–67, 170–71, 182*
Amsterdam, *75, 157–158*

Anderson, John, *38*
Anderson, Pamela, *153*
Andress, Ursula, *92*
Andrew, Prince, *45*
Anka, Paul, *89*
Apollo Space Programme, *13*
Argentina, *34, 116, 128, 184*
Armstrong, Neil, *13, 107*
ARPA, *84*
Asia, *40, 194*
Aspel, Michael, *212*
Athens, *34, 123*
Atlanta, *153*
Atlantic City, *94*
AT&T, *147*
Aubusson Carpets, *10*
Auckland, *164–65*
Aurigny Air Services, *181*
Australia, *iii, 9, 40, 89, 117, 150, 163–65, 197, 199, 202–5*
Ayatollah, *119–20, 122*
Ayling, Bob, *150*

B
BAE Systems, *71*
Bagnall, Elaine, *v*
Bahrain, *9, 34, 39–41, 45*
Ball, Clifford, *76*
Baltimore, *142*
Bangkok, *34, 155*
Bangor, *16, 88*
Bannister, Mike, *12–13, 16, 43, 60, 179*

Bannister, Roger, 79
Barbados, 68, 70, 206
Barcelona, 157
Barispol Kyiv, 184
Battle of Britain, 71, 73, 216
Baxter, Raymond, 25
BBC Sport, 196
BEA (British European Airways), 51, 147–48, 162, 182
Beckham, Victoria, 44
Belgium, 75
Bell Inn, 6–7
Bell X-1, 25, 85–86
Below, Tim, 10
Benn, Tony, 31
Bennett, Tony, 99
Bentley Arnage, 12
Berlin, 155
BIA, 181
Biden, 106
The Blade, Charlie, 92
Blair, Tony, 43
Blériot, Louis, 11
BOAC (British Overseas Airways Corporation), 16, 33, 37, 60, 65, 80–81, 100, 147, 182
BOAC
    Argonaut plane, 118
    Comet, 81
    Service, 80
Bob Ayling, 150
Boeing, 25–26, 30, 32, 34–35, 37, 68–69, 71, 143, 155–56, 159, 164, 166, 171–72, 181, 183

B-29, 86
Dreamliner, 188
Museum of Flight in Seattle, 68
Stratocruisers, 80
Boot, Florence, 91
Boot, Jesse, 91
Boston, 3, 39, 166
Botham, Ian, 204
Bourne, Hadley, 206
Bowie, David, 211
Boycott, Geoffrey, 205
Boycott, Sir Geoffrey, 198, 204
Boycott Kt OBE, Sir Geoffrey, iii
Boyd, Wilma, v
Bradman, Don, 196
Braniff, 32, 37, 146
Braniff Airlines, 43
Branson, Sir Richard, 22, 46, 149, 151–52, 192–93, 207
Brazil, 34, 39, 75
Breslaw, Bernard, 215
Bristol, 15, 26–28, 31–32, 46, 66, 70, 87
Bristol Aeroplane Company, 65
British Airways, 1, 7–8, 14, 16–17, 19, 36–37, 39–43, 46, 48, 51–52, 146–48, 154, 156, 160–61, 181–82, 206
    Concorde, 10, 14, 206
British Caledonian, 17, 96, 182
British European Airways. *See* BEA
British High Commissioner, 173–74, 200
British Overseas Airways Corporation. *See* BOAC

viii

British South American Airways, *147*
British United Airways, *182*
Britton, Norman, *8, v*
Bruno, Angelo, *92, 94*
Brussels, *157*
Brussels Airlines, *155*
Buchanan, George, *101, v*
Buckingham Palace, *16, 211*
Buenos Aires, *128, 184*
Bugatti, *10*
Burns, Robbie, *45*
Bush, George W, *43, 106*

C

CAA, *66*
Cabbage Patch Kids, *113*
Cabin Crew, *3, 5, 40, 145, 149, 151, 169, 171, 182, 189, 191*
Cahill, Graham, *65*
Cairo, *123, 149*
Calcutta, *81*
Calvert, Brian, *2, 4, 6–7, 13, 57*
Canada, *19, 46, 68, 89, 96, 116, 155, 217*
Canary Islands, *159*
Cannon Noel, *73*
Canterbury, *72–74, 78–79, 101, 196*
    Cathedral, *73*
    Cricket, *200*
Cape Town, *69, 89–90, 198*
Carter, Jimmy, *106, 108, 120*
Casablanca, *161*
Cash, Johnny, *21–22, 78*
Cathay Pacific, *165*

Cellini, Dino, *92*
Chairman Mao, *107*
Chalmers, Judith, *210*
Channel Islands, *87, 181–82*
Charities, *208–12, 214–15*
Charles, King, *45*
Chicago, *101, 146, 165–66, 170, 172, 213*
Chile, *116*
China, *107, 109, 194*
Chirac, Jacques, *51*
Chuka Dancers and Drummers, *211–12*
Civil Aviation Safety, *51*
Clark, F.G., *28, 31, 39*
Clapton, Eric, *44, 215*
Clarkson, Jeremy, *70, 216*
Clements, Darren, *59*
Collins, Phil, *22, 44*
Comet, *79–81*
    IVs, *7*
Compton, Denis, *199*
Concorde, *i–ii, 1–11, 13–52, 56–58, 60, 65–71, 144–45, 150–51, 154–56, 163–64, 178, 180, 186–88, 216–17, v*
    Alpha Foxtrot, *42*
    Cabin, *42*
    Class, *1*
    F-BTSC, *11*
    F-BTSD, *67*
    F-BVFB, *68*
    F-BVFC, *67*
    F-BVFF, *67*
    F-WTSS, *67*

G-AXDN, *65*
G-BFKX, *43*
G-BOAA, *45, 66*
G-BOAB, *66*
G-BOAC, *47, 65–66*
G-BOAD, *68*
G-BOAE, *68, 206*
G-BOAF, *42–43, 47, 66*
G-BOAG, *68*
G-BSST, *65*
Lounge, *1, 22*
Nose Cone, *61*
Prototype, *65*
Concorde Flights
 first commercial, *45*
 last passenger, *47*
Connors, Ted, *169*
Continental Airlines, *30, 50*
Cook, John, *7, 46*
Cooper, D.B., *122–23*
Copenhagen, *157*
Cowdrey, Sir Colin, *201–2*
Crashes, *16, 25, 35, 50–52, 69, 80, 82, 142–43, 162–63, 166–67, 169*
Craven, Gemma, *153*
Crash Landing, *127, 172*
Cricket, *ii–iii, 6, 62, 77, 87, 91, 196–204, 209–10, 217*
Cruz, *151*
Cryer, Barry, *215*
Cuba, *122*
Cutlass, Oldsmobile, *99, 129*

D

Dallas, *43, 98–99, 146, 153, 168*
Dan-Air, *181*
Davidson, Alan, *197*
De Gaulle, Charles, *27*
Delta, *146, 154, 167–71*
Delta Airlines, *100, 167, 169*
Dennis, Ron, *177, 216*
Denver, *98, 170, 172*
 John, *23*
Designers, *28–29, 83*
d'Estaing, Valery Giscard, *14, 34*
Detroit, *98, 183*
Dix, John, *92*
Dolan, Mickey, *139*
D'Oliveira, Basil, *139, 198*
Dorchester, *93*
Dubai, *187*
Dubois, Marc, *162*
Duffey, Peter, *17*
Dunlevy, John, *65*
Duxford, *65*

E

Eames, John, *46*
Easyjet, *150, 158*
Eddington, Rod, *150*
Edmonds, Noel, *129, 208*
Edwards, Sir George, *38*
Egypt, *103, 107*
Egypt Air, *123*
Eisenhower, President Dwight, *84*
Elizabeth, *79, 117*

x

Queen, *118*
Elizabeth II, *79*
Emirates, *185*
Empire Pencil Co, *112, 120, v*
Empire Pencil Company, *111*
Engineer, Farokh, *210*
Ethiopian Airlines, *124, 183*
EuroWings, *155*
Evans, Paul, *9, v*

F

F-85 Jetfire, *99*
F-86 Sabre, *99*
Ferguson, Bob, *119*
Ferrari, *18, 31*
Filton Air Base, *70*
Filton Airfield, *44*
Finn, Fred, *iii, 7–11, 57, 96, 116, 148, 151, 218*
Fitzgerald, Ella, *99*
Fitzgerald, Scott, *103*
Flintoff, Freddie, *199*
Florida, *91, 99–100, 121–22, 146*
Forte, Sir Charles, *183*
France, *10, 26–28, 30, 39, 47, 65–67, 73–74, 214*
Frankfurt, *146, 155–156*
Fred, Doris, *64*
Frost, David, *5, 12*
Fysh, Sir Hudson, *163*

G

Gagarin, Yuri *85, 88*
Gatwick, *152–53, 181–82*
Genair, *17*

General Motors, *99, 102*
Germany, *68, 72, 83, 109, 124, 156*
Gibbons, Stanley, *188*
Gibbs, Lance, *iii, 206*
Goodwood Flying School, *17*
Gorbachev, Mikhail, *23, 61*
Gorgon City, *153*
Gower, David, *177, 199–200, 203, 210–11*
Graveney, Tom, *iii, 198*
Gray, Sir Iain, *24, 187*
Grubbs, Victor, *159*
Guccione, Bob, *66, 94–95*
Guinness Book of Records, *ii, 136, 186, 211*
Gulf Air, *148*

H

Hamburg, *116, 124, 156–57, 187*
Harmer, Barbara, *17*
Hasbro, *100–101, 103, 111–14, 116*
Hassenfeld, Harold, *100–102, 112–13*
Hassenfeld, Henry, *111–12*
Hassenfeld, Herman, *111*
Hassenfeld, Stephen, *113*
Havilland, Comet, *18, 25, 81, 147*
Havilland, DH, *81*
Havilland, DH-16, *157*
Hawker Siddeley, *26*
Hawk T1, *152*
Hayes, Alfred, *172*
Headingley, *196, 204*
Heathrow, *3–4, 6–8, 13, 16, 41–43, 45–47, 66, 80, 100, 143, 146–47, 149, 151*

Hennessy, Perrie, 176, *204*
Hemingway, Ernest, *103*
Herchoff, Steve, *94, 96–97*
Heseltine, Michael, *14*
Hijack, *122, 124*
Hodge, Patricia, *129*
Holden, William, *44, 193*
Holland, *75*
Holly, Buddy, *82*
Holz, Robert, *34*
Hong Kong, *40, 42, 128, 155*
Hostages, *119, 121–25*
Hotelissimo, *49*
Howard, Trevor, *210*
Hutchinson, John, *8–11, 128, v*

I
Iceland, *88*
Indonesia, *41, 157*
Iran, *116, 119–22*
Ireland, *87–88, 116, 150, 156*
Irons, Jeremy, *23*
Island Camp, *176, 204*
Israel, *103, 107, 112*
Ixworth Abbey, *201*

J
Jardinaud, Gilles, *49*
Jersey, *61, 90–92, 96, 181, 201*
Jet Lag, *4, 13, 188–89*
JFK, *3, 7, 16–17, 22, 43, 45, 106, 124–25, 127, 145, 184, 191*
John, Elton, *21, 215*
Johnson, Boris, *106*
Johnson, Lyndon, *106*

Johnston, Bill, *196*

K
Kanhai Roland, *206*
Keniston, Laurence, *10–11*
Kennedy, John, *85*
Kent, *73, 75, 77, 87, 101, 174, 201, 209, 212, 216*
Kenya, *76, 79, 115–18, 131, 153, 155, 173, 176, 193, 200–201, 203–4, 207–10, 215, 217*
Kilvington, Steve, *10*
KLM, *141, 150, 157–58, 160–61, 163*
KLM's Tenerife crash, *159*
Korean Air, *168*
Korolev, Sergei, *84*
Koslov, Mikhail, *35*
Kruger National Park, *141*
Küchemann, Dietrich, *25*
Kyiv, *v*

L
Lagos, *141, 147, 155, 158*
Lake Nakuru, *193*
Lakin, Terry, *149*
Lamb, Alan, *204, 210*
Las Vegas, *92–93, 99, 130*
Leney, David, *5, 21, 46*
Lewis, Tony, *147*
Licensing, *94, 111, 113–14, 121–22, 184, 207*
Lightning Strike, *141–42*
Lilongwe, *127–28*
Lindbergh, Charles, *165*
Lindwall, Ray, *196*
Lions Club Ukraine, *213*

Lloyd, Chris, *206*
Lloyd Webber, Andrew, *184, 200*
Lockerbie Crash, *171*
Lockheed, *164*
Lockheed
    Electra, *142, 166*
    L-1011 TriStar, *169*
Lodge, Matthew, *10*
London, *1, 3–4, 22, 39–45, 69–70, 80–81, 88, 92–94, 100–101, 150–53, 164–65, 187–88, 190–91, 210–12, 216–17*
    Airport, *41*
    Eye, *16, 60*
    Flying School, *76*
Long Island, *3, 88*
Lord, Ben, *24, 32, 68, 186, 188, v*
Lord Cheshire, *212*
Lord King, *148*
Lord's Cricket Ground, *202, 210*
Lord's Taverners Cricket Tour, *173*
Los Angeles, *69, 98–99, 152–53, 156, 166, 169, 193*
Loxton, Sam, *196*
Lubitz, Andreas, *157*
Lufthansa, *32, 37, 155–57*
Lympne Airfield, *63, 74–7598, 201, 207–9*
Lowe, Jock, *18–19*
Lubitz, Andreas, *157*
Lufthansa, *32, 37, 155–57*
Lympne Airfield, *75*

M

Maasai Mara, *194*
Major, John, *23, 200, 216*
Malawi, *128*
Malaysia, *41–42, 46*
Malaysian Airlines, *158*
Manhattan, *3, 21, 111, 144*
Marcot, Jean, *49*
Marshall, Colin, *148–50*
Marshall, Sir Colin, *148*
Marty, Christian, *47, 49*
Marylebone Cricket Club (MCC), *197, 199, 202*
Mayes Pratt, Gilly, *19, v*
McBride, Ron, *144*
McCord, Antony, *10*
McDonnell Douglas,
    DC-7, *165*
    DC-8, *25*
    DC-10, *17, 50, 146, 172*
Mckenna, Dame Virginia, *61*
McLaren, *216*
McLaren F1, *2, 216*
McLean, Don, *82*
McNeil, Robert, *v*
Menneveux, Nicole *10*
Meredith, Adrian, *46, 53, 56–58, 60, 134–35, v*
Mermaid Inn, *73*
Merrill, *112–13*
Mexico, *122, 125–26*
Mile High Club, *192*

xiii

Miller, Tim, *21*
Moi, Daniel Arap, *174, 209*
Mombasa, *118, 175, 208*
Morgan, Piers, *70*
Morgan, Sir Morien, *70–71*
Moscow, *61, 182*
Mosquito, *72*
Mount Kenya, *117, 193, 200, 208–9, 211, 217*
Mount Kenya Safari Club, *44, 126, 129, 193, 209*
Murfreesboro, *101, 103, 105*

N
Nairobi, *117, 141, 147, 156, 200, 208–10*
Nairobi Club, *200*
Nakuru, *193*
Nanyuki, *126, 200–201, 208–9*
Nanyuki orphanage, *175, 209*
Napa, *97, 100*
Nashville, *1, 21–22, 98, 160, 166*
National Airlines, *146, 182*
Newark, *125, 151*
New Jersey, *7, 21, 88, 100, 103–4*
New Orleans, *98, 104*
New York, *17, 21–23, 33–34, 39–40, 43–45, 66–70, 80, 96–97, 100–103, 143–44, 146–47, 150–52, 155–56, 187, 190–92*
New York Helicopters, *22, 44, 125*
Nigeria, *116, 141, 215*
Nigeria Airways, *158*
Nippon Airways, *185*

Nixon, Richard, *106–7*
Nordoff Robbins Charity, *214*
Nordoff, Paul, *215*
North American F-86 Sabre, *99*
Northeast Airlines, *168*
Northwest Airlines, *158, 168*

O
Obama, Barack, *106*
Oil, *72, 104, 121*
Oldsmobile Cutlass, *99*
Ol Pejeta Conservancy, *131, 200–201*
Olympus, *9–11, 28*
Oman Air, *185*
OPEC, *38, 103*
Oregon, *122–23*
Orphanage, *117, 175, 208–9*
Owen, Kenneth, *27*

P
Pair of Shoes, *92–94*
Palestinian Liberation Organisation (PLO), *122*
Pan Am, *30, 33, 37–38, 80, 100, 125, 142–47, 159–60, 168, 171, 189–90*
Paris, *11–12, 17, 23, 39, 47, 50, 52, 65, 67, 69, 143, 147*
    Crash, *9, 43, 51, 66–67*
Parton, Dolly, *22*
Pencils, *100, 112, 115–16, 130*
Penthouse Club, *94–95, 100*
Pevsner, Donald, *52*
Phantom, *177, 216*
    F4, *6, 177–78*

xiv

Farewell, *216*
Flight, *178*
Phelps, Howard, *149*
Pinlet, Frédéric, *9–10*
PLO (Palestinian Liberation Organisation), *122*
Poland, *111, 184*
Powers, Stefanie, *193*
Presley, Elvis, *89, 99, 100, 130*
Princess, Anne, *212*
Princess, Diana, *45*
Princess, Elizabeth, *118*
Princess, Margaret, *42*
Princess, Michael, *174, 209, 212*
Pringle, Derek, *200, 210*

Q
Qantas, *31, 37, 143, 162–65*
QE2 Liner, *21*
Queen Elizabeth II, *16, 42*

R
RAE, *See Royal Aircraft Establishment*
RAF, *See Royal Air Force*
Ramon, Jacky, *10*
Rampling, Charlotte, *92*
Reagan, Ronald, *106, 108–10, 121, 130*
Red Arrows, *6, 16, 21, 59–60, 152, 215*
   Hawk T1, *133*
Red Lion Inn, *73*
Regency Hotel, *100*
Reynolds, Julie, *20, v*

Reza Shah Pahlavi, *119*
Rhode Island, *111*
Rice, Sir Tim, *208*
Rice, Tim, *200*
Riley, Dominic, *178*
Ritchie, Bert, *164*
Robbins, Clive, *215*
Robertson Aircraft, *165*
Roitsch, Paul, *38*
Rolls Royce, *10, 33, 71, 198*
   Coupé, *12*
   Olympus, *2, 8, 14*
   Silver Spur *II, 12*
Ross, Diana, *44*
Royal Aircraft Establishment (RAE), *25*
Royal Air Force (RAF), *10, 15, 18, 152*
Rudimental, *154*
Rumsey, Fred, *200*
Russia, *25, 83, 107, 119, 182, 194, v*
Russia's Aeroflot, *163*
Ryanair, *155, 158*

S
San Francisco, *98, 170, 188*
Sagana Lodge, *117*
Saudi Arabia, *9, 46*
Savalas, Telly, *92*
Save Concorde Group, *24, 186, v*
Savoy Hotel, *145, 148*
Schott, Bill, *7–8*
Scotland, *28, 33, 43, 66, 88, 213*
Scott, Leslie, *45*

Senegal, *47*
Seoul, *42*
Serengeti, *117, 194*
Seychelles, *128, 141, 161, 194, 207–8, 210, 213*
Shah, Mohammad Reza, *119*
Shelbyville, *101, 104, 111–12*
Sinatra, Frank, *89, 92*
Singapore, *5, 8, 34, 40–42, 75, 81, 128, 164, 186, 197*
Singapore Airlines (SAI), *9, 40–42, 168*
SkyTeam airline alliance, *168*
Snow, John, *91*
Sobers, Sir Garry, *206*
South Africa, *81, 89, 92, 127, 141*
South America, *34, 158, 184*
Soviet Union, *83, 108–9, 121–22, 183*
Space, *i, 2–3, 5, 15, 29, 53, 65, 82–85, 117, 194*
Spitfire, *11*
Springbett, David, *12, 187*
Springsteen, Bruce, *5, 22*
Sputnik, *82–84*
SR71 Blackbird, *5*
STAC *see Supersonic Transport Aircraft Committee*
St Ange, Alain, *138, 141*
Stansted, *181*
Steiner, Eric, *93*
Stewart, Rod, *21, 44*
St Martins, *73, 78*
Streep, Meryl, *21*
Stuker, Tom, *184, 186*
Sud Aviation, *27*

Suggs, *44*
Sullenberger, Chesley, *191*
Supersonic Transport Aircraft Committee, *26–27*
Swiss airlines, *184*
Swiss International Air Lines, *155*
Sydney, *34, 163–65, 186, 193*
Sykes, Mark, *93–94*

T

Talbot, Ted, *29*
Taylor, Elizabeth, *82, 103, 123*
Tehran, *34, 119–22, 143, 155*
    Hostage Crisis, *108*
Tenerife, *159*
Tennessee, *101–5, 111–12*
Thatcher, Margaret, *9, 42, 108, 148, 210*
Tokyo, *34, 40, 42, 69, 158, 185*
Tonka Toys, *113*
Tornado, *46*
Trans World Airlines, *30 33, 37–38, 164, 166*
Treetops Hotel, *117*
TriStar, *169*
Triumph
    TR4, *9*
    TR4A, *12*
Trubshaw, Brian, *15-16, 18, 32*
Trueman, Fred, *197–98, 205*
Trump, Donald, *103, 106–7, 109, 186*
Tupolev
    Tu-104, *34*
    Tu-144, *13, 34–35, 68*

xvi

TWA, *See Trans World Airlines*
Tye, John, *14, 20*
Tyson, Mike, *45*

U
Ubogu, Victor, *215*
Uganda, *115, 123*
Ugle, Peter, *9, 11, 65*
UIA, *see Ukraine International Airlines*
UK, *9, 11, 65–67, 71, 73, 108, 113, 116, 207, 213–14, v*
Ukraine, *85, 109–10, 183–84, 194, 213–14, v*
Ukraine International Airlines, *183*
UNESCO, *10*
UNESCO Heritage Site, *73*
Union des Transports Aériens (UTA), *161*
United Airlines, *170, 172, 186*
United Kingdom, *146*
United States of America, *4, 26, 39, 44, 46, 82–83, 84–85, 88, 97–98, 104, 109, 112–14, 119, 121–22, 145, 147, 156, 158, 165–66, 168, 170*
US *See United States of America*,
USSR, *82–85, 182, 184*
Ustinov, Dimitri, *84*

V
Van Zanten, Jacob, *159–60*
Variety Club, *211–12*
Venezuela, *39, 88, 115*
Vialle, Beatrice, *17*
Vickers, *15*

VC10, *7, 15, 100, 119*
Vietnam, *105–8, 169*
Vine, Brian, *200*
Virgin Atlantic, *143, 151, 153–54, 165, 168, 207, 213*
Vladimir Putin, *109*

W
Walker, Murray, *129*
Walpole, Brian, *6, 13–14, 18, 39, 46*
Walsh, Willie, *150*
Watergate Scandal, *107, 130*
Watts, Sir Roy, *148*
Weber, Johanna, *25*
West, Peter, *196*
Westray, Richard, *18*
White House, *106*
Wickets, *196, 198, 203, 205, 210*
Williams, Bryn, *129*
Windsor, Barbara, *92*
Wine, *21, 80, 194*
Wogan, Terry, *44, 129*
Woodman, Eva, *46*
World Trade Center, *50, 125, 150, 159, 166, 170*

Y
Yeager, Chuck, *64, 85, 86, 88*